Envisioning Critical Race Praxis in Higher Education Through Counter-Storytelling

A volume in
Educational Leadership for Social Justice
Jeffrey S. Brooks, *Series Editor*

Envisioning Critical Race Praxis in Higher Education Through Counter-Storytelling

edited by

Natasha N. Croom
Iowa State University

Tyson E. J. Marsh
University of New Mexico

INFORMATION AGE PUBLISHING, INC.
Charlotte, NC • www.infoagepub.com

Library of Congress Cataloging-in-Publication Data

A CIP record for this book is available from the Library of Congress
http://www.loc.gov

ISBN: 978-1-68123-405-2 (Paperback)
       978-1-68123-406-9 (Hardcover)
       978-1-68123-407-6 (ebook)

Printed in the United States of America

CONTENTS

ENVISIONING CRITICAL RACE PRAXIS IN HIGHER EDUCATION THROUGH COUNTER-STORYTELLING

Natasha N. Croom and Tyson Marsh

> *CRT is a theoretical treasure . . . that we as scholars*
> *are still parsing and moving toward new exegesis.*
> —Ladson-Billings, 2005, p. 119

Twenty years ago, Gloria Ladson-Billings and William Tate (1995) introduced critical race theory (CRT) into the educational research lexicon. Today, educators expand upon central concepts of CRT as "a new generation of scholars who see CRT as a valuable tool for making sense of persistent racial inequities in US schools" (Ladson-Billings, 2005, p. 115) continue to employ it across educational contexts. This edited book is an extension of a CRT in education project, and as such its purpose is to provide educators in post-secondary contexts with tangible narratives that demonstrate how racism and intersecting forms of oppression manifest in higher education and to provide concrete examples of how higher education constituents apply/employ critical race praxis. Praxis in CRT, or a racial and social

Envisioning Critical Race Praxis in Higher Education Through Counter-Storytelling, pages vii–xvii
Copyright © 2016 by Information Age Publishing

justice-oriented and critical race informed practice, remains an elusive and contested concept. Praxis is elusive in that many continue to question how to apply critical race theory in productive and justice-oriented ways, and it is a contested concept because not everyone agrees on the factors that constitute legitimate CRT praxis. Although it is contested and elusive, many who employ CRT praxis agree that the primary goal of such informed work is the elimination of racial oppression in society broadly (Stovall, 2004), and, for the purposes of this book, higher education specifically.

CRITICAL RACE THEORY IN EDUCATION

Critical race theory in education is a framework for analyzing and challenging the relationship between race, racism, and power across educational structures, policies, and practices (Ladson-Billings & Tate, 1995). According to Solórzano (1998), "a critical race theory in education challenges ahistoricism and the unidisciplinary focus of most analyses, and insists on analyzing race and racism in education by placing them in both a historical and contemporary context" (p. 123). While there is no canonical structure for CRT in education, there are unifying and interconnected tenets: racism as endemic, interest convergence, intersectionality, experiential knowledge, and social justice. Each is briefly described below.

- Racism as Endemic. Race is a product of social thought and interactions rather than simply a set of objective fixed characteristics. Founders of critical race theory posit that racism is normal, ordinary, and ingrained in American society, making it difficult, at times, to recognize due to its embeddedness in social structures, laws, and practices that shape our social worlds (Bell, 1992; Delgado & Stefancic, 2012; Ladson-Billings, 2000).
- Interest Convergence: Critical race scholars argue that there is little incentive to eradicate racism; therefore, the interests of people of color will only be met if those interests converge with elite-White people, and often only when there is a greater benefit to the dominant group. Further, in order to reveal the self-interests of benefiting dominant groups and the historic and contemporary ingrained systems of power and privilege, dominant ideologies of liberalism, race-neutrality, objectivity, colorblindness, and meritocracy must be unmasked and challenged (Calmore, 1992; Crenshaw, 1991; Harper & Patton, 2007; Solórzano, 1997; Sweeney, 2006).
- Intersectionality: Critical race feminist scholars pushed forward the notion that each person has many intersecting social identities that are experienced and perceived in a variety of ways depending

on the convergences of power, privilege, and oppression associated with each identity. Thus, Black working-class women may experience the social world in dramatically different ways than White working-class women or Black middle-class women and men. Additionally, while we could assume that there are marginalized and subordinated groups, there is no monolithic or essentialist experience. All Black middle-class women do not automatically have the same experiences simply because they identify with or are perceived to be a part of any particular identity groups.

- Experiential Knowledge: This tenet supposes that the voices of communities of color who experience racism are valuable, valid, and crucial to uncovering, addressing, and eliminating the persistence of racial inequity and inequality. Moreover, this knowledge is often provided through narrative and counter-storytelling and used to challenge majoritarian interpretations of ideologies, policies and practices, which lack more contextually and historically accurate analyses of race and racism as they are enacted upon people of color in the U.S. (Delgado-Bernal, 2002; Harper, Patton, & Wooden, 2009; Ladson-Billings, 2000; Solórzano & Yosso, 2001).

- Social Justice: CRT scholars agree that the broader goal of this work is to end racial oppression as a part of a larger agenda to end all forms of oppression (Tate, 1997, p. 234). If the larger goal is to be met, an interdisciplinary approach must be taken to address social oppression (Bell, 1987; Solórzano & Delgado-Bernal, 2001). Lastly, praxis, or an "iterative process by which the knowledge gained from theory, research, personal experiences, and practices inform one another" (Ford & Airhihenbuwa, 2010, p. S31), is necessary to bring the empowerment of people.

PRAXIS AND COUNTER-STORYTELLING

Education leads to enlightenment. Enlightenment opens the way to empathy. Empathy foreshadows reform.
—Derrick Bell

As faculty members at our respective institutions, we support students in their preparation as educators across K–12 and post-secondary contexts through teaching courses, conducting research, and doing service and outreach that emphasizes the need for more justice-oriented and equity-based educational experiences and systems for all. As faculty of color, with varying other social identities and who were introduced to critical theories at differing points in our own academic journeys, we take seriously the requirement for students to move their knowing, understanding, and thinking out of the classroom and into the multiple social spheres in which we all exist. While there are many questions we struggle through together, the most prominent for those studying critical social theories, such as CRT, is often, "so, what do we do now?" This reflection on what one does with knowledge is one step towards praxis.

For the purposes of this book, praxis can be understood as the reflections of critical theories of race in our actions (i.e., research, scholarship, activism, advocacy), or informed action, toward transforming oppressive systems. As aforementioned, one of the tenets of CRT is that of social justice; praxis is necessary to bring about the empowerment of people of color, and/or other marginalized social groups, and deconstruction of systems of social oppression. Praxis as a concept can be traced back to Aristotle, Marx, and Gramsci; however, it is the work of Freire, influenced by the latter two scholars, that most resonates with us. Freire submitted that, informed action is the process of acting within a particular theoretical framework informed by both theory and experience (Freire, 2000). For example, those employing critical race praxis would be ensuring that their practices and decisions (e.g., in classrooms, communities, campuses, etc.) were informed by critical race theory *and* their experiences—a balance of theory and practice. Further, this work is done to create new anti-oppressive knowledge and ways of being, not simply recreate oppression in other contexts. As Hughes and Giles (2010) stated, critical race praxis can be used to "analyze, reinterpret, deconstruct, and reform educational settings" (p. 41).

Our hope with this book is to provide examples of how educators and scholars alike are envisioning a critical race praxis in their social spheres. For some, learning about critical race theory can be overwhelming because they cannot, for many reasons, readily or immediately identify with it, while for others it is overwhelming because they identify with every word—new language describing their everyday lives. Despite these subtle differences between the two, both sometimes struggle to know what to do with CRT in their perspective worlds. As editors of this volume, we believe critical race theory, alongside other critical theoretical frameworks, is, as Lather (1986) shared, a "theory adequate of the task of changing the world...open-ended, nondogmatic, informing, and grounded in the circumstances of everyday life...premised on a deep respect for the intellectual and political capacities of the dispossessed" (p. 262). Moreover, we submit that one of the most effective ways to understand the racialized circumstances of everyday life and move toward the empathy that Bell claimed would lead to true reform is through storytelling.

Counterstorytelling is inarguably one of the most powerful tools of critical race theory. For oppressed communities, such as racially minoritized ones, storytelling (and counterstorytelling) is a rich tradition in which knowledge and wisdom is passed through generations as tools of survival and liberation (Delgado, 1989). Counterstories function to (1) build community among marginalized individuals and groups, (2) challenge knowledge and wisdom claims of dominant groups, (3) illuminate alternative realities of those at the margins of society, and (4) provide context in an effort to transform current systems of belief and value (DeCuir & Dixson, 2004; Delgado, 1989; Lawson, 1995; Solórzano & Delgado Bernal, 2001; Solórzano & Yosso, 2002). According to Solórzano and Yosso (2002), "The counter-story is also a tool for exposing, analyzing, and challenging the majoritarian stories of racial privilege" (p. 32). We chose counterstorytelling for this book in order to offer scholars space to push back on dominant racialized discourses within higher education and to name how critical theories of race, when integrated into our ways of being, knowing, and doing, can help us transform our particular contexts and circumstances.

Counterstories can be presented in multiple forms, and no matter the form, each story is situated within a critical sociopolitical, -historical, and -cultural analysis and critique. The more traditional types of counterstories are autobiographical, biographical, and composite narratives (Solórzano & Yosso, 2002). Autobiographical narratives are personal accounts of the authors' lived experiences with racism and other forms of oppression; biographical narratives, however, are third person authored stories told about other peoples' lives. Composite narratives are drawn from various sources, which could include both autobiographical and biographical stories, to share the racialized and marginalizing experiences of communities of color. The chapters in this volume draw on all three of these forms of counterstory and present, perhaps, a fourth variation. These chapters present themselves on the surface as traditional research papers, ones that we might find in scholarly journals; we argue, however, that if the overarching goal of the work is to "cast doubt on the validity of accepted premises or myths" (Delgado & Stefancic, 2001, p. 144) about communities of color in higher education—in favor of anti-oppressive experiences, practices, policies, and structures—then the work, in our eyes, is to be considered a counterstory.

Honoring the diverse storytelling traditions across racially minoritized cultural practices, we believe combining praxis and counterstorytelling is one way to reach a diverse audience of educators trying to understand how critical race theory can be and has been used to work toward transforming educational experiences and systems for racially marginalized groups. The next section introduces the scholars and chapters that appear in this book. To be clear, this book is not meant to be prescriptive, but rather an opportunity to read what others are doing to "utilize theory to make an active change in the situation and context[s]" in which they exist, operate, and have a locus of control (Brayboy, 2006, p. 440).

THE CHAPTERS

Do the best you can until you know better. Then when you know better, do better.

—Maya Angelou

Within this edited book, *Envisioning Critical Race Praxis in Higher Education through Counterstorytelling*, scholars provide a rich variety of counterstories that highlight how they each use critical race theory and its subsequent tenets and constructs in their own lives as students, administrators, and faculty. Collectively, their work can help to answer the elusive question of "now what?" and push the conversation further concerning what critical race praxis can be. The book comprises nine chapters, and the chapters are broken down into three sections. While each section represents different constituency groups in different experiential capacities (students, administrators, faculty), it is important to note that the sections are connected—meaning that there are elements of each area throughout the book. Student experiences are heavily connected to the work of faculty and administrators, while the decisions that administrators make affect students and faculty daily. Additionally, what also holds these sections and chapters together cohesively is the contributors' focus on using critical race knowledge in ways that push more justice-oriented agendas forward, regardless of their positionality in the institutions.

The first three chapters present varying types of counterstories related to student experiences in higher education. In Chapter 1, "The Importance of Racial Literacy and Racial Dialogues in Emerging Race Scholar Identity Development for Graduate Students of Color," Blanca Vega, Dianne Delima, and Kendall Williams focus their attention on the process by which masters-level graduate students of color construct a racial scholar identity. They put forth that race scholar identity development requires racial literacy and the normalization of educational space to discuss race and racism. They posit that racial dialogues informed by critical race theory are integral to the development of a race scholar identity framework/model. Vega, Delima, and Williams present two first-person counterstories that push back on the ways race conversations are erased from student affairs and higher education graduate preparation programs.

In Chapter 2, Lisette Torres shares a first-person counter-story in traditional Bell (1987) fashion about being a Puerto Rican woman in science doctoral education. In "Tigre del Mar: A Boricua's Testimonio of Surviving a Doctoral Science Education," Torres introduces Yemayá, Goddess of the Ocean, and Yucahú, a Celestial God of Taino peoples, who help her understand through use of critical race theory how racism and Whiteness manifest in the very nature of science and science graduate education. Torres illuminates how the process of being and becoming a woman scientist of color via doctoral education and socialization causes internal distress as she found herself continually questioning whether she belonged in her science field because of who she is rather that what she was capable of knowing and doing. At the end of the chapter, Torres offers several ideas towards a critical race praxis that disrupts racism in favor of creating an equitable system of graduate education that embraces reflection, being, and identity as critical factors in science.

In Chapter 3, "Being in the Black–White Binary: Admission Letter to an Asian American Graduate Student," Joyce Lui pens a reflective letter to her future self in hopes of illuminating the many ways the construct of the Black–White binary manifests in doctoral education. As an Asian American woman, Lui shares several stories of her many racialized experiences in graduate school, pushing against a dominant narrative that suggests that Asian Americans do not experience racism, consider themselves as racially minoritized beings, or participate in within and across race collectives toward racial justice. Lui offers several recommendations for faculty, staff, and administrators related to understanding systemic issues of racism embedded in institutional policies and practices of higher education.

The next three chapters focus on the leadership roles of higher education administrators and administrative work. Chapter 4 is titled "Leadership, Accountability, and Diversity in Higher Education: A Critical Race Counterstory." In it Eugene Fujimoto and Noemy Medina illustrate how the accountability movement in higher education contributes to continued race and class based social and educational inequity. Through a composite counterstory experienced through the lens of Henry, an associate vice president for diversity, Fujimoto and Medina articulate the many mission incongruent decisions that can be made by university leadership in the name of accountability and efficiency. Through familiar conversations about state funding cuts, student completion rates, and institutional recruitment efforts, the authors illuminate critical decision points and use critical race theory to make sense of how these decisions impact how institutions enact their missions and how university leadership can become complicit and complacent in an era of public accountability. Fujimoto and Medina argue that CRT can inform one's approach to leadership by interrupting institutional decisions that perpetuate inequity and inequality on campus.

Ignacio Hernández, Jr. authors Chapter 5, "La Comunidad es la Fuerza: Community Cultural Wealth of Latina/o Leaders in Community Colleges." Through a counterstory, Hernández introduces readers to five Latina/o composite characters. Through the narrative, Gerardo, Erica, Luis, Martín, and Analisa push back on several narratives about Latina/os in higher education and community colleges through use of Yosso's (2005) community cultural wealth model. Through their intertwined connections and set in the all-too-familiar annual conference colleague interaction, Hernández offers several ways praxis, via Yosso's work, can be used to advocate for the continued investment of resources to build upon the existing capital of Latino/a community college leaders.

In Chapter 6, "Voices from the Margins: Illuminating Experiences of African American Women Senior Administrators in Higher Education," Brenda Marina, Sabrina Ross, and Kimberly Robinson center the experiences of African American women who hold senior administrative positions in institutions of higher education. They present counterstories, albeit through a more traditional style of scholarly writing, that make visible the multilevel structures and practices in higher education institutions that may disadvantage African American women who seek senior positions. Uniquely, Marina, Ross, and Robinson also offer narratives about their own sense making, experiences, and aspirations in this chapter. Using critical race theory as a methodological, theoretical, and analytical tool, they offer critique of the policies and practices related to recruiting, hiring, and retaining African American women senior administrators.

The last three chapters focus on the multiple ways faculty employ critical race theory, from understanding their own existence and survival in the academy to informing pedagogy and practice. Vonzell Agosto, Zorka Karanxha, and Deirdre Cobb-Roberts author Chapter 7, "Critical Race Media Literacy and Critical Incidents of Retreating to Teachable Moments." Through this chapter, these scholars demonstrate how critical race theory can be used as a framework to provide professional development in one's department around culturally relevant pedagogy and multicultural education for their faculty colleagues. Combining CRT and critical media literacy to analyze media depicting racialized critical incidents in classrooms, Agosto, Karanxha, and Cobb-Roberts share how they understood and pushed back on their colleagues' responses to these occurrences. Lastly, they offer an opportunity for readers to engage with and challenge the concept of "the teachable moment," arguing that educators must understand not only where the student is but also their role in facilitating the learning in those moments using more critical perspectives.

In Chapter 8, "First-Generation Pre-Tenure Faculty of Color: Navigating the Language of Academia," Anjalé Welton, Montrischa Williams, Herb Caldwell, and Melissa Martinez examine the experiences of pre-tenure faculty of color who also identify as first-generation. Adding an intersectional perspective to the tenure-stream faculty of color literature base, they use Yosso's (2005) navigational capital to articulate how faculty of color who are first-generation college graduates and/or have first-generation citizenship status navigate racialized, classed, and citizenship-based experiences throughout their academic careers. Pushing back on dominant narratives such as "poor families of color do not support education," Welton, Williams, Caldwell, and Martinez offer several opportunities to critique ingrained

Eurocentric ideologies and institutional cultures in an effort to move toward more equitable higher education environments and opportunities.

Jessica Harris authors Chapter 9, "Liberatory Graduate Education: (Re) Building the Ivory Tower through Critical Race Pedagogy." Harris focuses on illustrating how hidden curriculum in higher education reproduces racial and gender inequity for women graduate students of color. She calls on educators and faculty to incorporate critical race pedagogy to expose normative racist and sexist privileged values and practices in the academy that marginalize women graduate students of color in particular. Harris argues that critical race pedagogical approaches require an intersectional understanding of teaching and learning that advocates for justice and equity in education and society. Further, she names the need for faculty and other educators to do the reflective work necessary to engage in such a pedagogical praxis. Offering tangible recommendations throughout the narrative, Harris posits that while the task of deconstructing and rebuilding graduate education may be great, the employment of a critical race pedagogical praxis can expose the oppressive systems that lie beneath our curricula and approaches to teaching and learning and move our educational systems toward liberatory educational experiences.

All of the chapters push back on majoritarian ideologies and practices in higher education that continue to marginalize minoritized communities. This collective body of work is not meant to be prescriptive, but rather illustrative of opportunities to inform knowing, being, and doing from a critical race praxis perspective. Derrick Bell (1989) wrote in *And We Are Not Saved: The Elusive Quest for Racial Justice*, "Rather than offering definitive answers, I hope . . . mainly to provoke discussion that will provide new insights and prompt more effective strategies" (p. 3). We hope to do the same.

REFERENCES

Bell, D. A. (1987). *And we are not saved: The elusive quest for racial justice*. New York, NY: Basic Books.

Bell, D. A. (1992). *Faces at the bottom of the well: The permanence of racism*. New York, NY: Basic Books.

Brayboy, B. M. J. (2006). Toward a tribal critical race theory in education. *The Urban Review, 37*(5), 425–446.

Calmore, J. (1992). Critical race theory, Archie Shepp, and fire music: Securing an authentic intellectual life in a multicultural world. *Southern California Law Review, 65*, 2129–2231.

Crenshaw, K. (1991). Mapping the margins: Intersectionality, identity politics, and violence against women of color. *Stanford Law Review, 43*(6), 1241–1299.

DeCuir, J. T., & Dixson, A. D. (2004). "So when it comes out, they aren't that surprised that it is there": Using critical race theory as a tool of analysis of race and racism in education. *Educational Researcher, 33*(5), 26–31.

Delgado, R. (1989). Storytelling for oppositionists and others: A plea for narrative. *Michigan Law Review, 87*(8), 2411–2441.

Delgado, R., & Stefancic, J. (2001). *Critical race theory: An introduction.* New York, NY: New York University.

Delgado, R., & Stefancic, J. (2012). *Critical race theory: An introduction* (2nd ed.). New York, NY: New York University.

Delgado-Bernal, D. (2002). Critical race theory, Latino critical theory, and critical raced-gendered epistemologies: Recognizing students of color as holders and creators of knowledge. *Qualitative Inquiry, 8*(1), 105–126.

Ford, C. L., & Airhihenbuwa, C. O. (2010). Critical race theory, race equity, and public health: Toward antiracism praxis. *American Journal of Public Health, 100*(S1), S30–S35.

Freire, P. (2000). *Pedagogy of the oppressed* (30th Anniversary Ed., M. Bregman Ramos, trans.). New York, NY: Continuum. (Original work published 1970)

Harper, S. R., & Patton, L. D. (Eds.). (2007). *Responding to the realities of race on campus.* New Directions for Student Services. San Francisco, CA: Jossey-Bass.

Harper, S. R., Patton, L. D., & Wooden, O. S. (2009). Access and equity for African American students in higher education: A critical race historical analysis of policy efforts. *The Journal of Higher Education, 80*(4), 389–414.

Hughes, R., & Giles, M. (2010). CRiT walking in higher education: Activating critical race theory in the academy. *Race Ethnicity and Education, 13*(1), 41–57.

Ladson-Billings, G. (2000). Racialized discourses and ethnic epistemologies. *Handbook of Qualitative Research, 2,* 257–277.

Ladson-Billings, G. (2005). The evolving role of critical race theory in educational scholarship. *Race, Ethnicity, and Education. 8*(1), 115–119.

Ladson-Billings, G., & Tate, W. F. (1995). Toward a critical race theory of education. *Teachers College Record, 97*(1), 47–68.

Lather, P. (1986). Research as praxis. *Harvard Educational Review, 56*(3), 257–277.

Lawson, R. (1995). Critical race theory as praxis: A view from outside to the outside. *Howard Law Journal, 38,* 353–370.

Solórzano, D. G. (1997). Images and words that wound: Critical race theory, racial stereotyping, and teacher education. *Teacher Education Quarterly, 24*(3), 5–19.

Solórzano, D. G. (1998). Critical race theory, race and gender microaggressions, and the experience of Chicana and Chicano scholars. *International Journal of Qualitative Studies in Education, 11*(1), 121–136.

Solórzano, D. G., & Delgado Bernal, D. (2001). Examining transformational resistance through a critical race and LatCrit theory framework: Chicana and Chicano students in an urban context. *Urban Education, 36*(3), 308–342.

Solórzano, D. G., & Yosso, T. J. (2001). Critical race and LatCrit theory and method: Counter-storytelling. *International Journal of Qualitative Studies in Education, 14*(4), 471–495.

Solórzano, D. G., & Yosso, T. J. (2002). Critical race methodology: Counter-storytelling as an analytical framework for education research. *Qualitative Inquiry, 8*(1), 23–44.

Stovall, D. (2004). School leader as negotiator: Critical race theory, praxis, and the creation of productive space. *Multicultural Education, 12*(2), 8–12.

Sweeney, K. A. (2006). The blame game: Racialized responses to hurricane Katrina. *DuBois Review, 3*(1), 161–174.

Tate, W. F. (1997). Critical race theory and education: History, theory, and implications. *Review of Research in Education, 22,* 195–247.

Yosso, T. J. (2005). Whose culture has capital? A critical race theory discussion of community cultural wealth. *Race, Ethnicity, and Education. 8*(1), 69–91.

CHAPTER 1

THE IMPORTANCE
OF RACIAL LITERACY
AND RACIAL DIALOGUES
IN EMERGING RACE SCHOLAR
IDENTITY DEVELOPMENT
FOR GRADUATE STUDENTS
OF COLOR

Blanca E. Vega, Dianne Delima, and Kendall N. Williams

A professor regularly invites doctoral students to her class to speak on current issues in education policy. The professor, upon speaking with an es-
tranged doctoral student about her topic, decides to invite the student to her
master's class. This is a first for the student. She works full time and because
her research interests are about racial incidents in educational spaces, she
felt that she did not have an audience for her work in this particular academic program. She never received negative messages about her work—but
she never felt completely comfortable talking about race in this academic
space either. Throughout her time in the program she received many covert

Envisioning Critical Race Praxis in Higher Education Through Counter-Storytelling, pages 1–20
Copyright © 2016 by Information Age Publishing
1

messages about what her peers thought about race. When race was brought into discussions, some rolled their eyes, others made comments like, "Here she goes again," and others would sigh or giggle. These messages caused the student to reconsider her presentation on campus racial conflict. Therefore, when the professor invited her to speak in the class, she offered to speak on a different topic. The professor insisted that she speak from her dissertation work on racial conflict in educational spaces. So the student did. As she began her presentation, her concerns became greater as she saw how many White students were in the class. How would they react, she wondered. Would she get eye rolls as she did when she was a student in these classes? She plowed through anyway. When she finished, she thought, "It wasn't that bad." The professor also spoke to her after class and gave the student some recommendations for more literature to review. But she did not expect what happened next. She received several emails from students in the masters program in which she presented. They asked, "Is it possible to study race in this program?" "Who is your advisor? Are there any professors willing to support students who want to study race in higher education?" "Can we meet sometime to talk?" It was then that she realized that like her, others desired to be race scholars and they too were looking for educational spaces to not only discuss race in higher education, but develop into scholars whose work centers race and racism in postsecondary education.

The narrative above demonstrates the importance of understanding the identity development of emerging race scholars among graduate school students. Because race is often a taboo topic to discuss in the classroom (Tatum, 1992), graduate students who desire to become race scholars often find themselves without the necessary academic and peer support to help them develop their race scholar identity. While exploring racial identity development and developing tools to combat forms of racism are necessary, equally important is exploring how scholars create knowledge about race, learn how to do race research, and become race scholars. This exploration of race scholar identity development builds upon work that focuses on the psychological impact of racism in educational spaces (some examples include: Hwang & Goto, 2008; Smith, Allen, & Danley, 2007; Smith, Hung, & Franklin, 2011; Solorzano, Ceja, & Yosso, 2000).

The purpose of this chapter is to work toward a conceptualization of race scholar identity development through the use of racial dialogues (Sue, Lin, Torino, Capodilupo, & Rivera 2009) and racial literacy (Sealey-Ruiz, 2011). The authors employ transformational resistance theory (Solórzano & Delgado Bernal, 2001) as a conceptual framework or lens toward this work and use critical race counternarratives as their methodology to understand the ways race, as a scholarly topic, is marginalized in graduate school classrooms. While the narrative began with a doctoral student, the counternarratives center students in a master's program who are exploring their interest in studying race and identify as emerging race scholars in race-neutral environments. This chapter will conclude with exploring the counternarratives of graduate students who identify as emerging race scholars; discuss ways that counter-spaces can become normalized or institutionalized so that students, staff, and faculty are simultaneously creating these spaces as well as supporting other emerging race scholars; and put forth a call for understanding an emerging race scholar identity to help nurture this in students who wish to continue on this path. By doing so, the chapter will discuss and uphold a goal set out by those who have employed critical race theory in their work—that is, to put forth a framework for social transformation that can lead toward internal and external forms of transformational resistance (Solórzano & Delgado Bernal, 2001). The chapter will aim to achieve the following: (1) to understand how graduate students seek ways to develop their scholarship on issues related to race; (2) to discuss the importance of racial dialogues and racial literacy in the identity development of emerging race scholars; and (3) to begin to conceptualize a framework of race scholar identity development. We conceptualize this framework by using research that race scholars across disciplines have contributed to theoretical frameworks that centers race in educational issues and helps us understand how race operates as a structural element in our society. This chapter is written in the spirit that most individuals in our society desire more understandings about race, albeit at varying levels, but do not know how to access this "race knowledge."1 We believe the mere act of accessing race knowledge in classrooms that provide very little information on it is one form of transformational resistance.

> Teachers who engage in an educational practice without curiosity, allowing their students to avoid engagement with critical readings, are not involved in dialogue as a process of learning and knowing. They are involved, instead, in a conversation without the ability to turn the shared experiences and stories into knowledge. (Freire & Macedo, 1995, pp. 51–52)

LITERATURE REVIEW AND CONCEPTUAL FRAMEWORK

To work toward a conceptualization of race scholar identity development (RSID), we will use transformational resistance theory as a lens to explore the counternarratives presented in this chapter. The authors use racial dialogues (Sue et al., 2009) and racial literacy (Sealey-Ruiz, 2011) to help the reader understand dimensions of *racial transformational resistance*. Together, these elements can begin to provide a conceptualization of RSID that strives to reverse what Troy Duster (1991) calls "the impoverished vocabulary of racism" (p. 17). Students who wish to become scholars on issues of race not only find that there is little discussion about how race operates in educational institutions, but also find it difficult to engage peers in racial dialogues. Racial dialogues are defined as "conversations or interactions between members of different racial or ethnic groups" (Sue, Rivera, Watkins, Kim, Kim, &Williams, 2011). Such lack of dialogical experiences ultimately stunts racial literacy development for race scholars. Defined as "a skill and practice in which students probe the existence of racism, and examine the effects of race and other social constructs and institutionalized systems which affect their lived experiences and representation in U.S. society," racial literacy can be an important factor in the identity development of race scholars and their learning of theories of race and racism (Sealey-Ruiz, 2011, p. 42).

Racial Dialogues

The absence of racial dialogues in postsecondary classrooms contributes to a dearth in race knowledge that is vital to understanding how race functions in our society. In her article, "Silence as Weapons: Challenges of a Black Professor Teaching White Students," Ladson-Billings (1996) reflects on the difficulties that both White tenured faculty and White students have speaking to her about topics related to race. She writes that this silence, while a protective measure, stunts learning about how race is understood in society. She sees these types of dialogues, while difficult, as an important tool to constructing new understandings about race and new understandings of the people engaged in racial dialogues. The absence of these dialogues suggested to her that there was fear of a backlash, particularly by White students, who were not accustomed to racial dialogues. She also reflected on the ways people of color, who have often been silenced themselves, handle these racial dialogues. Ladson-Billings also noted that her formal training in intergroup discussions have helped her facilitate these dialogues. Thus, she found that racial dialogues were important to explore and facilitate, and she believes that those who know how to facilitate racial dialogues should teach others how to engage in them.

While there is no classification system currently to describe and categorize racial dialogues, we believe that racial dialogues are a specific form of *intergroup dialogues*, which provide college students of diverse backgrounds with the necessary tools to help communicate and collaborate with each other through group work. Gurin, Nagda, and Sorenson (2011) found that intergroup dialogues have helped students increase their understanding of social differences, augment interaction between diverse students, and also motivate them to participate in political movements. However, these inter-group dialogues are not always mandatory, thus suggesting that students who are already interested in social justice related work might be more likely to participate in such formal events.

Racial dialogues often occur spontaneously, in classrooms, residence halls, and other spaces on college campuses. One way this manifests itself is in student of color organizations on college campuses. Duster (1991) found that White students expressed an interest to befriend students of color for personal cultural enhancement—in other words, White students were often interested in learning about the cultural aspects of the lives of people of color. On the other hand, students of color often sought friend-ships with same-raced individuals because of a greater likelihood that these students shared a similar value system of participating in activities that pro-mote institutional advancement on behalf of students of color (e.g., en-couraging policies that promote the increase of more students of color on campuses; courses that are more inclusive of the histories and epistemolo-gies of people of color). These varying levels of desiring knowledge about race demonstrate the importance of racial dialogues in college campuses to minimize conflict. Thus, as Sue and colleagues (2011) suggest, racial dia-logues are often difficult conversations that a professor or a student may or may not know how to facilitate or handle when they arise. Students' access to racial dialogues can be important sources for how they develop an un-derstanding of the experiences of people of color. This, then, has implica-tions for administrators and faculty members as they think about and create inclusive spaces for such dialogues to occur.

Racial Literacy

Students who choose a racially literate orientation may do so not only to understand how race works in our society but also to engage in political action to promote racial justice. According to Sealey-Ruiz (2011), racially literate people should be able to have informative exchanges about race that both develop antiracist values and agendas while empowering people of color to resist the racial status quo. An example of racial literacy build-ing can be found among students who engage in what Harper (2013) calls "peer pedagogies," which he defines as "methods minoritized students use to teach others about the racial realities of predominantly White col-leges and universities, as well as how to respond most effectively to rac-ism, racial stereotypes, and microaggressions they are likely to encounter in classrooms and elsewhere on campus" (p. 208). Harper suggests that peer pedagogies not only serve as instruments of socialization for students of color, but peers also actively seek to help their more recently admitted peers know how to respond to racism on campus. Interestingly, peer pedagogies can positively contribute to the leadership development of students of color by informing and creating counterspaces, particularly in predominantly White institutions. Peer pedagogies can help students of color move beyond racial dialogues and effectively build racial literacy, which can help them navigate hostile climates. This teaching and learning that occurs on college campuses among students may also provide the seedlings for faculty and administrators to help create more knowledge about how race and racism functions in society.

Transformational Resistance and Race Knowledge

Racial literacy and peer pedagogies in which information about race and racism could be exchanged among students could also ultimately lead to *racial transformational resistance.* According to Solórzano and Delgado Bernal (2001), transformational resistance "refers to student behavior that illustrates both a critique of oppression and a desire for social justice" (p. 319). What is more, Solórzano and Delgado Bernal affirm that students who experience transformational resistance must learn how to question the oppression that affects them as individuals and their communities to actively critique this oppression. They go on to explain that this critique can be manifested both externally and internally—the explicit forms that are more visible such as student protests and the less overt forms such as seeking knowledge that could build into careers with a social justice orientation.

Thus, we argue that these dialogues, skills, practices, and pedagogies could ultimately contribute to the production of knowledge of race in higher education institutions, which is necessary for transformational resistance in the identity development of emerging race scholars. In essence, this chapter prompts the following questions: If there is an absence of racial dialogues, how are students who desire to engage in race dialogues developing the necessary skills to handle and facilitate them? For students who wish to work in student affairs, where do they learn to build competencies for handling and facilitating racial dialogues? Finally, what role do racial dialogues function in the lives of students who wish to be race scholars one day? Although our society and our college campuses are becoming increasing racially diverse, it is important to understand and accept that not everyone will desire racial literacy, but most will engage in, or hear about, racial dialogues at some point in their lives. This acknowledgement, however, should not preclude us from noting that some *will* desire to move beyond racial dialogues and racial literacy and want to work on race knowledge and scholarship. This chapter will focus on those individuals who seek to become race scholars, who have engaged in racial dialogues and continue to develop their racial literacy. Much of the literature focuses on the psychological impact of racism in postsecondary settings (see: Hwang & Goto, 2008; Smith, Allen, & Danley, 2007; Smith, Hung, Franklin, 2011; Solórzano, Ceja, Yosso, 2000). While this is important, we find that this is only part of our story, particularly as we navigate the academic pipeline, into graduate programs, with few of us culminating in doctorates. These counterstories should help higher education constituents and activists become more aware that students may desire to become more competent as race scholars, and thus, need more rigorous "race-work" in their curriculum and overall academic environment.

SCHOLARLY SIGNIFICANCE OF TOPIC

While identifying as a Race Scholar is not race specific, because the counter-stories for this chapter belong to two graduate students of color, it is important to explore data that pertain to students of color, the role of graduate programs in higher education in RSID, and finally the relationship between racial identity development and RSID. This section will review these three areas.

Graduate Students of Color

The racial and ethnic makeup of higher education institutions has changed along with the greater society (e.g., Maramba & Velasquez, 2012), and thus we are seeing an increase in the representation of students of color. According to the 2009–2010 data from the National Center for Educational Statistics (NCES), since 1999–2000 the population of graduate students of color (e.g., Black, Hispanic, Asian/Pacific Islander, and American Indian/Alaskan Native) has increased in significant numbers. NCES data also demonstrate that between 1995 and 2011 there has been an increase in students of color attaining a master's degree or higher; however, as previously discussed, the percentage of increase has been small, within one to two percent in the last 16 years (NCES, 2011). The small number of graduate students of color can lead to feelings of inferiority and isolation in their programs and/or institution of study. Griffin, Muniz, and Espinosa (2012) found that while underrepresented minorities constitute 28% of the U.S. population and approximately one third of individuals 25–40 years of age—the range within which most graduate students fall—only 11.9% of all doctoral degree recipients in 2006 were awarded to underrepresented minority students. Based on these data, Griffin and associates suggest that this has led to a demand that higher education institutions put more effort into admitting more students of color to their institutions. In order to become attractive to students of color, scholars indicate that universities and colleges must be committed to institutional change and inclusion of these students, through rhetoric, visible support, and financial resources demonstrating that an increase in diversity is a priority for their campuses (Griffin et al., 2012).

The data and literature on graduate students of color indicate tensions in the graduate degree experience for people of color. The feeling of isolation and inferiority is reiterated in the research literature. For example, in their case study of three graduate students of color, Gasman, Gerstl-Pepin, Anderson-Thompkins, Rasheed, and Hathaway (2004) find that graduate students of color often feel isolated from their class discussions, and they are often made to feel inferior in their research interests. In addition, Gardner (2008) finds that students of color are often forcibly socialized into the intellectual and social ideologies and structures that dominate their department. With a sample of 40 graduate students of color in the fields of history and chemistry, Gardner found that graduate students of color often thought of leaving their studies due to their feelings of intellectual inferiority and social and cultural isolation. Moreover, Gardner found that the participants often had to establish social and intellectual connections outside of their department in order to find the will to continue with their studies. These authors, thus, indicate that the small numbers of graduate students of color can impact not only their academic persistence, but also their emotional and mental state.

The Significance of Graduate Programs in Encouraging Racial Dialogues and Building Racial Literacy Among Graduate Students.

Pope and Mueller (2011) emphasize that graduate programs should provide opportunities for future practitioners to develop and/or enhance multicultural competency; as such, graduate courses can provide the historical context, theories, and opportunities for discourse that can allow future practitioners to be multiculturally competent, allowing them to assist in the cultivation of these students' ethnic identities. Furthermore, Pope and Mueller (2011) argue that practitioners should develop a sense for the dynamic model of student affairs competence, which allows practitioners to have a framework for conceptualizing "multicultural competence as both a distinctive category of awareness, knowledge, and skills and as an area that needs to be effectively integrated into each of the other six core competencies" (p. 341).

However, as Gayles and Kelly (2007) find, graduate preparation programs in higher education often provide limited courses in which students can develop multicultural competency. In their qualitative study of 37 higher education practitioners (23 who identified as persons of color and 6 who identified as multiethnic) from different regions of the United States, coming from various types of institutions, Gayles and Kelly found that the participants often learned about diversity and multicultural issues outside of the class and outside of their department. In an updated analysis of the data, Kelly and Gayles (2010) found that the participants often encountered resistance from their classmates during discussions of diversity issues in higher education. Specifically, Kelly and Gayles found that the intersectionality of diversity (e.g., class, gender, gender expression, sexual orientation, immigration status, and race) were often left out of the classroom curriculum. Moreover, Kelly and Gayles find that when issues of race and racism were raised, the students of color in the classroom often felt that they were the spokesperson for their racial group. Findings from this study suggest that the participants often did not feel comfortable having open dialogue about diversity and multiculturalism in the classroom. Gay (2007) also adds that when graduate students of color initiate discussions of diversity issues in the classroom, they often do not receive support from their peers and faculty. Thus, Gay states that graduate students of color are isolated in different fronts of their graduate school experiences, particularly in terms of intellectual and cultural interests and experiences. Kelly and Gayles raise the issue of resistance to learning opportunities and open discussions regarding diversity in graduate school as an impediment to the learning experiences of higher education professionals. An important point that this data highlights, however, is that within the graduate school experience for students of color, these students often feel isolated from the classroom experience and from their classmates. This is further substantiated by Gasman et al. (2004), who also found that faculty members often misinterpret the work and the views of students of color. They also found that when researchers attempt to connect with students of color, they often do so by considering their backgrounds, which are largely based on overarching stereotypes, rather than using the same approach they would with their White students: get to know them as individuals. Davidson and Foster-Johnson (2001) suggest that in order to be an effective faculty mentor, the faculty must have an understanding of their mentee and their background, but also be able to assist them in creating a positive experience in spaces that are hostile.

The Relationship Between Racial Identity Development and Race Scholar Identity Development

The literature on graduate students of color largely shows that students of color are less likely to receive certain types of support, such as mentorship and general inclusion, as compared to their White peers (e.g., Gonzalez, Marin, Figueroa, Moreno, & Navia, 2002; Turner & Thompson, 1993), which can be an effect of poor multicultural competency. Mentorship, or supportive faculty, has been identified as an important aspect in graduate students of color's success in academia (Van Stone, Nelson, & Niemann, 1994), the others being personal ambition and supportive family or community. While it is common to have a mentorship component in a graduate program, it is imperative to the success of graduate students of color that those faculty and staff are fully committed to mentoring those students in a visible and concrete way. Additionally, for students of color, personal ambition and supportive families or communities can often be rooted in their cultural or ethnic identity. Maramba and Velazquez (2010) suggest that knowledge and salience are two dimensions of ethnic identity that influence how students of color interpret their reality, inside and outside of academia. Many student development theories, consider "identity is both an outcome of college student development as well as a door that facilitates the development of other critical outcomes" (p. 296).

However, if Duster (1991) is right, and if we do have an impoverished vocabulary of racism, then how do we jump from racial identity to *race scholar* identity? It is here that we find that students who wish to become race scholars in race-neutral environments make another leap. To become race scholars, students must somehow acquire race knowledge and learn how to conduct race research in environments where programs often lack the expertise. A closer look at narratives from two master's students demonstrates that these students acquire race knowledge through racial dialogues that helped them build racial literacy skills. Because these processes occurred in race-neutral environments, these students engaged in transformational resistance. Becoming a race scholar, we argue, is therefore an internal process of transformational resistance.

METHODOLOGY

To understand how race scholar identities develop, we use critical race theory in education (Ladson-Billings & Tate, 1995) and the following tenets: (1) race continues to be significant in the United States; (2) United States society is based on property rights rather than human rights; and (3) intersection of race and property creates an analytical tool for understanding inequity. Critical race counter-narratives (CRCN), or counterstories, will also be used as they are useful tools to describe the experiences of people of color, particularly in environments where their identities and their knowledge continue to be marginalized (Solórzano & Yosso, 2002). Counterstories are a method to share the experiences from those individuals whose histories are often ignored, not taught, and even banned from academic discourse. They are also a tool to analyze and challenge the majoritarian story. Counterstories function to build community among marginalized groups, challenge the status quo, and build agency. Solórzano and Yosso (2002) write: "While a narrative can support the majoritarian story, counter-story, by its very nature, challenges the majoritarian story or that 'bundle of presuppositions, perceived wisdom and shared cultural understandings persons in the dominant race bring to the discussion of race'" (p. 475). Counterstories also provide an opportunity for marginalized and oppressed individuals to see possibilities that are not depicted in mainstream narratives and rewards that are structurally more difficult to access for people of color.

COUNTERSTORIES

The following section will explore the counternarratives of two graduate students of color in a Master of Arts program in higher education administration. They will be followed by analyses using a transformational resistance lens to understand the role of racial dialogues and racial literacy in emerging race scholars.

Out-of-Classroom Racial Dialogues and the Space for Scholar-Practitioner Reflection and Growth

Tara Yosso (2006) defines a counterstory as one's personal story that "recounts experiences of racism and resistance from the perspectives of those on society's margins" (p. 2). This understanding of a counterstory has been an important part of my own thinking and development as a practitioner and scholar, particularly as I reflect on my own personal experience as an immigrant Filipina working in the field of higher education. As a higher education professional in multicultural affairs, having a counterstory allows me to reflect on my learning experiences in a higher education graduate school program, my work experiences with diverse students, and my progress as a scholar-practitioner.

My academic and work background has always drawn me to working with students from underserved backgrounds. During college, I worked with 4th to 8th grade first-generation and underserved students in a college preparatory class, and with first-generation college-going students in an English and writing workshop. My academic background as a political science major further propelled me to work with young people, as I learned about historical and perpetuated injustices towards students of color. Particularly, I learned the theories (e.g., critical race theory), histories (e.g., Indigenous populations in schools), and narratives (e.g., counterstories of Latino students in United States schools) that have impacted people of color in the United States. Such knowledge led me to have a foundational understanding of my own experiences in school and college, and it further drove me to become involved in changing the experiences for youth of color.

After college, I was drawn to working as an educator because I felt that this would be a way for me to apply what I have learned into a real-world setting. I also believed that I could be a vessel by which small changes for social justice could manifest itself in the classroom. In the following years after college, I worked as a teacher in an urban school, with college students in an ethnic studies course, and conducted research that examined minority college student experiences in college. With this academic and professional background, I was drawn to a graduate degree in higher education because I wanted to explore further how underrepresented students were making the most of their college experiences.

I entered graduate school with the mindset that my colleagues and peers would have an understanding of multicultural competence and social justice issues that affect higher education today. However, what I experienced as a graduate student was much different. I was not expecting the extent to which practicality, rather than theoretical frameworks and studies, was becoming a learning emphasis for the majority of the students in the class. Put more frankly, the students in my cohort were not interested in or pushed to talk about what theoretical frameworks and studies could help explain the historical and current phenomena happening in the field of higher education. Particularly, the issue of race, racism, and the various intersectionalities of class, gender, and immigration status that related to diversity and multicultural competencies were not prevalent in class discussions.

As someone who sought to work in higher education institutions, I felt that multicultural competence for practitioners was missing. Multicultural competence entails that my peers and I, as future higher education practitioners, have an understanding of the history of race, class, gender, and higher education access in the United States and the ways in which education professionals can change the conditions that are systematically and systemically embedded in the educational experiences of underrepresented students (Zamudio, Bridgeman, Russell, & Rios, 2009). I lacked the kind of class discussions that would enable me to engage with my classmates in multicultural competency. In particular, I could not engage with my classmates in the theories, histories, and experiences that impact the college-going experiences of diverse students. As such, I often engaged with others outside of the classroom in conversations that enhanced and furthered my work with underrepresented youth in higher education.

From these out-of-classroom discussions, I was not only able to find a safe space where I could freely talk about my own personal frustrations in the learning that was occurring in the classroom, but I was also able to gain more knowledge and resources that further enhanced my understanding of multicultural competency and the role of such competency on the cognitive growth and development of students of color. I believe that having these out-of-the-classroom conversations fueled the work I do now as a higher education scholar-practitioner. I feel the need to advocate for underrepresented youth, and also to educate colleagues in the history, research, and literature of this student population.

Analysis

In this counterstory, we find that the author already had knowledge about race prior to entering graduate school and was prepared to engage in more racial dialogues to increase her racial literacy. The desire to learn more in graduate school was met by a lack of racial dialogues in the classroom, dialogues the author expected to have with her peers and even faculty at the graduate level. The author notes that while understanding the "practicalities" of race is important, it is not sufficient for students who not only have a background on race scholarship, but also desire to learn more about race. This is especially important for student affairs programs to note: Perhaps one diversity course is not enough and more courses within the program and outside of it should be made available and encouraged for students who desire to learn more theoretical frameworks about the study of race. It is important to note the role of faculty in the facilitation of these racial dialogues in the classroom. Given the student's background and familiarity with CRT and histories of people of color, the author demonstrates that she had hoped to engage in more racial dialogues in graduate school. However, we see that, in a graduate program preparing higher education practitioners, she became more aware of the *need* for racial literacy in the classroom.

This counterstory sheds some light on the academic needs that students of color have when they have a need for more race knowledge. The author was very specific in describing that she was interested in theories and histories, epistemologies that would help her carry out her work with underserved populations in higher education. These desires, not being met in the classroom, were met outside of the classroom, counterspaces that are not formally structured by graduate level programs. Seeking experiences outside of the classroom in order to fulfill the need for more racial dialogues also speaks to a student's agency and point of transformational resistance. While some may see this as courageous, this also speaks to a specific cost to the student's education: Students may wonder, where is their tuition money going? With this in mind, higher education administrators and faculty might consider figuring out how to be more knowledgeable and inclusive of epistemologies of race and other diversity work. Higher education administrators and faculty should also be encouraged to either create those counterspaces or establish relationships with them, relationships that Griffin (2012) explains can be beneficial for faculty, and especially faculty of color.

Education as a Form of Liberation—The Necessity of Race Work and Scholarship for Race Scholar Identity Development

Growing up in a predominantly White middle-class neighborhood, I was often the only Black student, male or female, not only in my advanced classes but also, more noticeably, at the school at large. Luckily, I had parents, an elder sibling, and a community where college was always the plan to drive my academic success. But for all the positive effects that my upbringing had on my educational opportunities, it largely left me isolated from the Black community and my sense of self and self-confidence underdeveloped. As an undergraduate student, I had a transformational experience, inside and outside of the classroom. Like many others, I stumbled onto American studies and ethnicity, and the connection, the excitement that I felt, led me to immediately change my major. It was in those first classes that I began to understand the world I had been living in. Suddenly, I had professors, peers, literature that helped me to contextualize my experiences as a woman of color and gave me the knowledge and the voice I needed to navigate my world with confidence. It was in those classes that I first became a race scholar, engaging with people who were just as curious as I was about why the world is the way it is, and how we got here. From these experiences, I became drawn to the work of racial identity development so that I could ensure as many students as possible have that opportunity to understand themselves as racial beings, something so crucial to living in a multicultural world and environment. Solórzano and Yosso (2002) ground their critical race methodology in the understanding that for students of color, race will always intersect with the different elements that shape their experiences, and thus, identities. Particularly, I wanted students of color to have the opportunity to expose their minds to intellectual thoughts, develop different points of view, have the courage to question what is around them, and ultimately to develop their own consciousness while speaking their mind. In my mind's eye, education was, and continues to be, a means of liberation.

However, my experience as a graduate student woke me to the issues still facing students of color in higher education spaces. From my graduate experience, I realized that higher education remains a polarizing climate for marginalized groups where the quality and topic of conversation concerning race and inequality in the U.S. is superficial, or surface level, and does not really seek to introduce a multidimensional understanding of how race and inequality affect access, retention and matriculation within education, or a myriad of other aspects. This was a drastic shift from my undergraduate experience wherein I was taught and engaged by professors who were not afraid of where those "difficult" conversations would lead but rather encouraged us to express our minds and feelings with the understanding that our perspective was equally valuable to the objectives of the curriculum. In short, we were learning to read the world around us in all of its mediums. I graduated with a Bachelor of Arts degree in American studies and ethnicity, with plans to pursue a master's degree in higher education, believing I would be challenged in a graduate program to the same extent. However, this was not the case, and I found that many of my graduate peers had not yet opened their minds to the harsh realities of institutionalized racism and its effects in the U.S. today and that my professors were hesitant to even allow that space to exist in the classroom. I often sat in lectures where the literature presented one experience of a particular group as opposed to different resources painting a well-rounded picture, suggesting that there is no diversity among the diverse. The readings, sources, literature, and conversations brought into the classroom by the faculty, in addition to myself and other students of color, were being tokenized. Where my expectation was to be challenged to engage and explore in the hopes of becoming a better higher education practitioner, I was challenged by the lack of perspective, acknowledgment, and interest in what diversity really means or looks like and how to support those students.

The result was paralyzing. I soon became disconnected from my graduate program, frustrated with feeling that the education I was receiving was subpar, and depressed from the continuous microaggressions I endured. Some of these were directed towards me, but it became just as hurtful to watch my White classmates roll their eyes as other students of color would add to the conversation. Knowing that these different experiences exist, I, like many race scholars who are truly passionate about their work and knowledge, cannot turn a deaf ear to cries of discontent, whether they are my own cries or those of my peers and future generations. What's difficult is that in higher education the cries are often silenced within the classroom. My entry into the community of race scholars and dialogue formed outside of the classroom in casual and professional settings. The casual conversations I had with my peers expressing our frustrations about a class discussion led to participating in conferences that centered on diversity and inclusion. This then led to an exposure to other race scholars, their work, and the liberation I was seeking regarding my interests that were not a part of my program's curriculum. The need for race discussions, literature, and active-minded individuals participating in a collective goal of liberation and enlightenment would help higher education practitioners address the changing face of education and, more importantly, support the students who attend their institutions. Although all higher education practitioners and community members may not engage in racial dialogue, it can none-theless help practitioners who decide to engage in this work to develop positive experiences by creating spaces for students to engage, speak, and question the status quo both inside and outside of the classroom. Often knowing you have the space to speak can be the stepping stone to a positive experience in an otherwise daunting climate.

Analysis

In this counterstory, the author reflects on her disappointment with her educational experiences because there was not only a mismatch in what she hoped to learn and what she actually did, but also because some of her peers were not even aware of racism as it manifests itself in education. The absence of racial dialogues contributes to a hostile racial climate and, for this student specifically, created a "paralyzing" moment that led to feelings of disconnect from her graduate program. The student also questions the goals of higher education and wonders how student affairs practitioners are able to meet the needs of an increasingly diverse population if they are not even aware of educational inequities that several populations in higher education face to-day. Words such as "creating," "address," and "support" as used by the author also suggest that student affairs practitioners, not just those who aspire to be race scholars, need more than just to engage in racial dialogues, but they also need to build racial literacy if they want to work in higher education environ-ments that are increasingly becoming more diverse.

It is important for student affairs staff and faculty to recognize that stu-dents who desire to become race scholars, practitioners, or even scholar-prac-titioners may choose to leave the field all together if disappointed with their educational opportunities related to race. The field of higher education may be losing brilliant scholars who could provide the field with a deeper under-standing about the role of race and racism in the lives of students, faculty, and administrators. Student affairs programs should be mindful that some students, while starting off as practitioners, may also be emerging scholars and need different types of academic support and encouragement.

IMPLICATIONS FOR FUTURE RESEARCH AND PRACTICE

Since the counternarratives focused on two students from Master's programs in student affairs, the implications for research and practice will focus on this area. More exploration is necessary to understand graduate students' academic needs who identify as emerging scholars. Exploring the skills nec-essary to facilitate effective racial dialogues, building racial literacy as a core value among graduate students, and engaging in race research can provide an academically supportive environment for emerging race scholars.

Research

Understanding who race scholars are and how they developed into this identity is important to explore further, in order for student affairs programs to provide these students with proper support beyond the psychological approach or only one diversity course. Structuring the curriculum to be more inclusive of epistemologies and histories of people of color could enhance the skills and knowledge of all student affairs professionals and encourage emerging scholars to pursue careers in faculty and research. While multicultural competence has been noted as an important aspect to the training of all student affairs professionals regardless of interests or backgrounds, programs must find ways to support those students who want to enhance their racial literacy skills and pursue scholarship that includes how to study race in higher education.

One way for student affairs programs to meet the needs of their emerging race scholars is to understand who their students are and what areas they are interested in pursuing in the field of higher education. Specifically, more research is needed to understand who these emerging race scholars are, how their identities as race scholars develop or shape over time, and what support they need in order to be further encouraged along in their scholarship. Additionally, it is equally as important to learn more about the paths and journeys current race scholars endured to achieve their scholarship and the moments when these scholars experienced transformational resistance, as these moments may provide rich information about how race scholars conceptualize how race and racism functions in our society. Their lives may provide a road map for others who wish to undertake similar paths and encourage future emerging scholars to engage in race scholarship.

Practice

As mentioned earlier in this chapter, racial dialogues are almost inevitable to witness or participate in today. Higher education professionals and other community members can begin to understand how to engage in racial dialogues by establishing relationships with student of color organizations, faculty who identify as race scholars, or practitioners who do race work. Student affairs programs, if not able to restructure the program to be more inclusive of the epistemologies of people of color, could invite current students who are doing work in race scholarship to their classrooms. Round tables and special reading groups that address race scholarship could also be formed to enrich the program, highlight the work that is being done already by students at the master's or doctoral level, and could also provide faculty and administrators an opportunity to highlight their work on race in higher education as well.

CONCLUSION

On November 3, 2011, family, friends, students, and admirers of Professor Derrick Bell gathered together for his memorial service at Riverside Church in Harlem, New York. Throughout the memorial service, the term "race man" kept being used to describe the great professor. Indeed, the body of Professor Bell's work demonstrates that his race scholarship, his race work, was geared toward racial justice in law and in education. Although he was not a student affairs administrator, he often did the work that many of us perform in our lives in higher education—advise students, provide them with the tools to combat racism in the classroom and in their daily lives, and create knowledge about the ways race operates in society, specifically in our legal system and in our educational institutions. Professor Bell left a legacy of race knowledge and race scholarship that another generation of race scholars are urged to continue. As we face yet another battle over affirmative action at the Supreme Court level and debate the existence and effects of racism in our everyday lives in our classrooms, and as we work with students struggling with their racial identities and how to interact and work with one another cross-racially, let us remember that it is absolutely necessary to engage with race scholarship in order to better inform higher education practitioners and encourage another generation of race scholars and scholarship. We firmly believe that student affairs and higher education programs have already demonstrated a commitment to practicing and researching multicultural competencies and they are therefore an excellent place to continue this work.

NOTE

1. For the purposes of this chapter, race knowledge is defined as the scholarship of race, the role it plays in our society, and how it manifests itself in our everyday lives; race knowledge is also understanding how to engage in racial dialogues (Sue et al., 2009) and build racial literacy (Sealey-Ruiz, 2011) not just to learn how to engage in dialogues and promote racial literacy, but also to create more knowledge about race in the U.S. and beyond.

REFERENCES

Davidson, M. N., & Foster-Johnson, L. (2001). Mentoring in the preparation of graduate researchers of color. *Review of Educational Research, 71*(4), 549–574.
Duster, T. (1991). *The diversity project: Final report. Institute for the Study of Social Change.* University of California, Berkeley.

Freire, P., & Macedo, D. (1995). A dialogue: Culture, language, and race. *Harvard Educational Review, 65*(3), 377–403.

Gardner, S. K. (2008). Fitting the mold of graduate school: A qualitative study of socialization in doctoral education. *Innovative Higher Education, 33*(125), 125–138.

Gasman, M., Gerstl-Pepin, C., Anderson-Thompkins, S., Rasheed, L., & Hathaway, K. (2004). Negotiating power, developing trust: Transgressing race and status in the academy. *Teacher College Record, 106*(4), 689–715.

Gay, G. (2007). Navigating marginality en route to the professoriate: Graduate students of color learning and living in academia. *International Journal of Qualitative Studies in Education, 17*(2), 265–288.

Gayles, J. G. & Kelly, B. T. (2007). Experiences with diversity in the curriculum: Implications for graduate programs and student affairs practice. *NASPA Journal, 44*(1), 193–208.

Gurin, P., Nagda, B. A., & Sorensen, N. (2011). Intergroup dialogue: Education for a broad conception of civic engagement. *Liberal Education, 97*(2), 46–51.

Griffin, K. A. (2012). Black professors managing mentorship: Implications of applying social exchange frameworks to analyses of student interactions and their influence on scholarly productivity. *Teachers College Record, 114*(5), 1–37.

Griffin, K. A., Muniz, M. M., & Espinosa, L. (2012). The influence of campus racial climate on diversity in graduate education. *The Review of Higher Education, 35*(4), 535–566.

Gonzalez, K. Marin, P., Figueroa, M. A., Moreno, J. F., & Navia, C. N. (2002). Inside doctoral education in America: Voices of Latinas/os in pursuit of the PhD. *Journal of College Student Development, 43*, 540–557.

Harper, S. R. (2013). Am I my brother's teacher? Black undergraduates, peer pedagogies, and racial socialization in predominantly white postsecondary contexts. *Review of Research in Education, 37*(1), 183–211.

Hwang W, Goto S. (2008). The impact of perceived racial discrimination on the mental health of Asian American and Latino college students. *Cultural Diversity and Ethnic Minority Psychology, 14*, 326–335

Kelly, B. T., & Gayles, J. G. (2010). Resistance to racial/ethnic dialog in graduate preparation programs: Implications for developing multicultural competence. *College Student Affairs Journal, 29*(1), 75–85.

Ladson-Billings, G. (1996). Silences as weapons: Challenges of a Black professor teaching White students. *Theory into Practice, 35*(2), 79–85.

Ladson-Billings, G., & Tate IV, W. (1995). Toward a critical race theory of education. *The Teachers College Record, 97*(1), 47–68.

Maramba, D. C., & Velazquez, P. (2012). Influences of the campus experience on the ethnic identity development of students of color. *Education and Urban Society, 44*(3), 296–317.

National Center for Education Statistics (NCES) (2011). *Postsecondary completions: 1980–2011 degree attainments.* Retrieved from http://nces.ed.gov/programs/coe/tables/table-eda-1.asp.

Pope, R. L., & Mueller, J. A. (2011). Multicultural competence. In J. H. Schuh, S. R. Jones, S. R. Harper, and Associates (Eds.), *Student services: A handbook for the profession* (5th ed., pp. 337–352). San Francisco, CA: Jossey-Bass.

Sealey-Ruiz, Y. (2011). Learning to talk and write about race: Developing racial literacy in a college English classroom. *The English Quarterly. The Canadian Council of Teachers of English Language Arts, 42*(1), 24–42.

Smith, W. A., Allen, W. R., & Danley, L. L. (2007). Assume the position . . . you fit the description: Psychosocial experiences and racial battle fatigue among African American male college students. *American Behavioral Scientist, 51*(4), 551–578.

Smith, W. A., Hung, M., & Franklin, J. D. (2011). Racial battle fatigue and the miseducation of black men: Racial microaggressions, societal problems, and environmental stress. *Journal of Negro Education, 80*(1), 63–82.

Solórzano, D. G., & Bernal, D. D. (2001). Examining transformational resistance through a critical race and LatCrit theory framework Chicana and Chicano students in an urban context. *Urban Education, 36*(3), 308–342.

Solórzano, D., Ceja, M., & Yosso, T. (2000). Critical race theory, racial microaggressions, and campus racial climate: The experiences of African American college students. *Journal of Negro Education, 69*(1/2), 60–73.

Solórzano, D. G. and Yosso, T. J. (2002). Critical race methodology: Counter-storytelling as an analytical framework for education research. *Qualitative Inquiry 8*, 23–44.

Sue, D. W., Lin, A. I., Torino, G. C., Capodilupo, C. M., & Rivera, D. P. (2009). Racial microaggressions and difficult dialogues in the classroom. *Cultural Diversity and Ethnic Minority Psychology, 15*(2), 183–190.

Sue, D. W., Rivera, D. P., Watkins, N. L., Kim, R. H., Kim, S., & Williams, C. D. (2011). Racial dialogues: challenges faculty of color face in the classroom. *Cultural Diversity and Ethnic Minority Psychology, 17*(3), 331.

Tatum, B. D. (1992). Talking about race, learning about racism: The application of racial identity development theory in the classroom. *Harvard Educational Review, 62*(1), 1–29.

Turner, C. S. V., & Thompson, J. R. (1993). Socializing women doctoral students: Minority and majority experiences. *Review of Higher Education, 16*(3), 355–370.

Van Stone, N., Nelson, J. R., & Niemann, J. (1994). Poor single-mother college students' views on the effect of some primary sociological and psychological belief factors on their academic success. *Journal of Higher Education, 65*, 571–584.

Yosso, T. (2006). *Critical race counter-stories along the Chicana/o educational pipeline.* New York, NY: Routledge.

Zamudio, M., Bridgeman, J., Russell, C., & Rios, F. (2009). Developing a critical consciousness: Positionality, pedagogy, and problems. *Race, Ethnicity, and Education, 12*(4), 455–472.

CHAPTER 2

TIGRE DEL MAR

A Boricua's Testimonio of Surviving
a Doctoral Science Education

Lisette E. Torres

Marine Tiger[1]

Prowling through open waters
Bouncing along crashing waves
Determined to reach *la Tierra de Oportunidad*[2]
Clawing, struggling, alone
Tratando de sobrevivir[3]
Drowning is not an option
You are in the hands of Yucahù,[4]
God of heaven and father of life and death

Yemayá,[5]
Goddess of the moon and seas,
Guide this Marine Tiger safely across your rolling surfs
From *la Isla del Encanto*[6]
To the towers of *Nueva York*[7]
Keep this Marine Tiger afloat
Protect it from the undertows of despair
Defend it from the jaws of defeat

Envisioning Critical Race Praxis in Higher Education Through Counter-Storytelling, pages 21–41
Copyright © 2016 by Information Age Publishing
All rights of reproduction in any form reserved.

* * *

With trembling small, brown hands, I manage to slip the hotel key card into its awaiting door slot. As I open the hotel door, my emotions rush through me like ocean waves; I start to feel sick to my stomach. I'm drowning. I walk to the edge of my bed and sit, trying to take a deep breath. The first attempt results in a shallow gasp, but as I focus on relaxing, the breaths become deeper... and I begin to cry. It is cathartic. I am not sure if my tears are out of relief that I am finally alone, away from the predominantly White conference space I was stuck in for more than eight hours, or if they are the culmination of the severe emotional and psychological trauma (e.g., extreme fatigue, anxiety, sleeplessness, hypervigilance, loss of confidence) that I have endured during my time in a hostile White graduate program (Smith, 2004; Smith, Allen, & Danley, 2007). It's probably both. Like many people of color, I experienced years of stress due to racial microaggressions that eventually led to racial battle fatigue. Racial battle fatigue can be defined as physiological and psychological trauma brought about by the need to cope with persistent, racially hostile interactions in unsupportive environments. Chronic symptoms develop, such as tension headaches, upset stomach, fatigue, depression, and anxiety, which make even small stressors burdensome (Smith et al., 2007). So physically removing myself from the conference space seemed like the only way to reduce (yet not completely alleviate) my pain.

Several minutes pass as I sit in the dark hotel room. I reach over and turn the bedside lamp on, my face flushed and eyes red. Wiping the tears away with the back of my sleeve, I try to compose myself enough to call the one person I can always confide in—my sister, Caridad. The cell phone hums as it tries to make its connection. A familiar friendly voice greets me on the other end, "Hey! How's Tahoe?"

"Cari, I want to go home. I can't take it anymore. I can't wait until this science conference is over," I respond, trying to keep myself together.

Immediately concerned, she asks, "Why? What happened?"

I begin to relay the events of that day—how I was the only person of color there, how I felt isolated and unwelcome (Turner, 1994), how no one wanted to talk to me, how my contributions were ignored, how I was an "outsider within" the field of science (Collins, 1986), and how I was regarded as less than human. The more I share, the more I recall other situations in which I have been treated poorly during my doctoral program. As hard as I try, I cannot fight back the tears. Cari patiently and calmly listens to my ramblings. When there is a pause in the conversation, she poses a question to me that I have asked myself a thousand times before: "If the scientific community is treating you so badly, then why are you still pursuing a PhD?"

Why am *I doing this?* It is an excellent question with no easy answer. I used to think that I wanted a doctorate because I loved science and working with animals since I was a child. I can recall being five years old and sitting on the stoop of our Victorian home in New Jersey, feeding ants bread and observing them for hours, much like the biologist E. O. Wilson. I was inquisitive, and my favorite channel was the Discovery channel. My mom even bought me an old microscope kit that I believe she found at a garage sale, despite the fact that she had no idea how to use it or why I wanted one in the first place. That early passion and the drive my parents instilled in me at an early age to get an education stayed with me through high school and college. What I was not aware of until now was how much that passion had eroded during graduate school.

Confused and anxious about the meaning behind this realization, I tell Cari, "I honestly don't know why I am still doing this. Maybe it's stubbornness. You know how our family is full of *cabezas duras*[8]!" We both laugh. "Or maybe I'm afraid of failing or losing my sense of direction," I add in a more serious tone.

Being a very spiritual woman, Cari warmly says, "Whether or not this is the path that God wants you to take, He will guide you. You just have to have faith. The answers will come to you."

"I know. You're right. I just feel so lost," I reply.

"Why don't you sleep on it? Maybe if you pray and get some rest, then you will have clarity in the morning," Cari suggests.

"Maybe you're right. I am exhausted. Good night. I love you."

"Love you, too. Good night, monkey," she caringly responds. *Click.* Silence falls on the other line. I am alone once again, but I am glad that I could have an honest conversation with my sister without the presence of my White roommates. Luckily, they are still at the conference reception.

Tired and emotionally drained, I make preparations to go to bed. As I get into bed and close my eyes, I mentally call out for guidance. *Please, God, help me. Send me a sign.* I soon fall fast asleep, my mind being unexpectedly swept away into a realm of dreams.

Whoosh. Crash. Splash.

I wake up with a start, coughing up seawater and gasping for what feels like my first breath of air. The cool, salt-filled air fills my lungs as I stand up and wipe the sand off of my face and body. It is still dark with the exception of the full moon overhead, which casts enough light for me to see the water's edge and the waves coming in. Confused, I look around me to try to find my bearings. In the distance, I notice a giant wall of a structure that seems familiar to me. It is *El Morro* (or more formally called *Castillo San Felipe del Morro*), the 16th century fort of San Juan. "How the heck did I end up here?!" I say out loud, though I cannot see anyone for miles around me.

Tired and soaked, I look up at the moon. *What am I going to do?* I begin to notice the moon becoming increasingly brighter and seemingly larger. The ocean waves suddenly begin to part, and I see a graceful figure moving towards me. As the figure comes into full view, I realize that it is a beautiful Black woman with a white, Ghanaian open crown hat with light blue trim sitting atop long, flowing braids. Her long-sleeved dress is a brilliant shade of white that sits along her womanly curves and is just as stunning as her smile. With sparkling eyes, she greets me with a warm embrace and a kiss on the cheek as if she has known me for years.

"Oh! It is so great to see that you are okay. I was afraid that you might have given up and drowned! There is only so much that I can do to protect you."

"Wait, wait. I'm confused. Who are you and what am I doing here in Puerto Rico? How did I get here?"

Releasing me from her grip, she looks up to the sky and then back at me. She shares, "My name is Yemayá. I am the Goddess of the Ocean and spirit of your ancestors. I represent womanhood and have command over the moon. I have brought you here to reconnect with your true self and to guide you in your time of need."

"Time of need?" I ask, though deep in my heart I know what she means.

"Yes. You are trying to make a decision that could potentially change your life forever. You want to know if you should stay in the field of science, and *mija,*[9] I am here to help you make a decision." Yemayá is sincere in her offer, but I am still confused. *Is this a dream?* Feeling tired and defeated, I plop myself down in the wet sand.

Yemayá can see that I am struggling. She buries her bare feet in the sand, playing with the grains between her toes before she decides on her approach. She sits next to me and places her long arm around my shoulder. "Let's start with what happened at the science conference. From there, we can move on to other scenarios that have made you question your chosen profession, perhaps looking at threatening situational cues present in the academic environment that have caused you to begin to dis-identify with your science identity (Murphy, Steele, and Gross, 2007)."

Reliving the conference, I begin to cry uncontrollably. Yemayá holds me, softly whispering, "You have been through a lot, haven't you?" I apologize, confessing that I normally keep my feelings bottled up, especially in front of people that I have just met. "No worries, *mija,*" Yemayá says with a smile. "Sometimes you just need to cry, and I know that you have been suffering in silence. Why don't you tell me about your dilemma?"

"Yemayá, I am thinking about quitting my doctoral program. I have always questioned my presence in graduate school and I have found myself increasingly questioning my abilities and intellect. Intellectually, I know that my current self-perception is potentially destructive (Rendón, 1994; Vasquez, 2007), but I keep finding myself in situations in which I am constantly asking, 'Am I going crazy?!' (Gildersleeve, Croom, & Vasquez, 2011)."

"What do you mean?" Yemayá asks, adjusting her long, white dress.

"Well, I am the only domestic student of color in my program, so, when I experience racism (Sue et al., 2007; Smith et al., 2007), I have no one to turn to, no one to validate my experience. I am hyper-aware of how my race and gender are perceived and how these social identities intersect and impact my interactions with White men and women (Hurtado, 1989). However, the conference is a perfect example of how salient race becomes when I am placed in a White, normative space that was not historically constructed for me (e.g., Evans, 2007). I become a '[guest with] no history in the house [I] occupy' (Turner, 1994, p. 256)."

Yemayá's eyes widen, and she asks me to continue. "So, I was given the opportunity to attend a conference in Tahoe, as you may know, and on the very first day of the conference I knew something was wrong. I knew that it was going to be a small conference (less than 100 people), but I was not expecting to be the only person of color in the room! All of the other participants were either White Americans or White Europeans. Since the conference was more intimate, we were asked to place ourselves into topics of interest that addressed the ways in which the field was changing, what research still needed to be conducted, and how the research could be disseminated to the public. Every time I would try to share my thoughts, I would be interrupted or talked over, usually by a White female."

Agitated, Yemayá exclaims, "So much for an all-inclusive sisterhood (Dill, 1983)!"

"I agree! The worst part of the conference, though, was when we were divided into groups to discuss ways in which we could educate the public about global warming. Everyone in my group was excitedly sharing their thoughts. Without letting my previous silencing keep me down, I decided to speak up and suggested that we make brochures in both English and Spanish given the growing number of Latino/as living in the U.S. My idea was greeted by 30 seconds of complete silence. It was in that moment that I asked myself why I was still in science."

Yemayá sits quietly, staring into the distance at the glimmering waves of the sea. She seems deep in thought. After a few moments, she speaks, "¡Perdón![10] There is just a lot to process from what you shared with me. However, the first thing that came to my mind was Whiteness as property (Harris, 1993)."

"What does that mean?" I ask. It was something that I never heard of, but my intuition and experiences as a woman of color were telling me that I knew what Yemayá meant.

"Well, it seems to me that the scientists at the conference were surprised by your presence and would interrupt you because of their (un)conscious belief that science is meant for only White people to engage in. Science knowledge production is viewed as being the sole property of Whites, where Whites have the right to use and enjoy (Harris, 1993) scientific research. They believe that they are the only ones allowed to engross themselves in the scientific method and should have the power to determine what research is valuable and how it should be used. Because science is theirs and theirs alone, they feel that they have the right to exclude (Harris, 1993) you and other people of color from the scientific community. That is why they made you feel unwelcome by silencing you during the conference, and it is also the reason why they were shocked by your suggestion to communicate and work with Spanish-speaking and bilingual members of the Latina/o community. You essentially confronted them with their own White privilege (McIntosh, 1989)."

"Wow. I never thought of it that way!" I respond. I stand up and take a few steps in the water. I love the cool sensation on my bare feet; it is a nice distraction from the heaviness of our conversation. I turn to Yemayá and ask, "And what about how the White women treated me? I think I was more shocked by how aggressive they were towards me than by the treatment I experienced from their male counterparts. Perhaps it was my naïve assumption that we had an invisible bond as women that would trump any racial differences between us."

Yemayá sighs. "*Mija*, you are not naïve. You are trusting, and you could not have predicted that they would treat you in such a way. It seems like your interactions with the White female scientists at the conference are dictated by their own relationship with White men. I think one of my favorite spirited authors, Audre Lorde, sums up my thoughts on your situation when she writes,

> White women face the pitfall of being seduced into joining the oppressor under the pretense of sharing power. This possibility does not exist in the same way for women of color. The tokenism that is sometimes extended to us is not an invitation to join power; our racial "otherness" is a visible reality that makes that quite clear. For white women there is a wider range of pretended choices and rewards for identifying with patriarchal power and its tools. (Lorde, 1984, pp. 118–119)

"The White women scientists have been seduced by the notion of having equal participation in science, with the possibility of having full and fruitful careers. They are 'blinded by the privileges offered to them by their male counterparts and do not recognize their positions as oppressors/oppressed' (Torres, 2012, p. 41)."

Frustrated, I slap the water with my hand, which visibly surprises Yemayá. I quickly apologize to her because the anger was not directed towards her.

"So, why should I put up with that for the rest of my life just so that I can do science?" I pose more to myself than to Yemayá.

Yemayá quickly responds, "You don't have to, *mija*! You were not put on this earth to be mistreated and dehumanized. We have yet to even discuss your experiences in your doctoral program, and I can already see the spiritual and emotional toll that trying to fit in to a White, masculine space has taken on you. You need a career that will help you to thrive, and you need to find mentors, family members, and friends who will support you unconditionally. Most importantly, we need to get you on a path to healing so that you can love yourself again and recover your self-confidence!"

Suddenly, a booming male voice reverberates in the air coming from the direction of the *El Yunque* rainforest way off in the distance. "So, she should just give up then? Just throw everything that she has worked for away? She should let ignorant people drive her away from her dreams?"

Yemayá stands and turns in the direction of the voice, visibly annoyed. The ocean waves, which were once placid, begin to pick up speed and height, crashing violently on the shore. The air unexpectedly becomes hot and humid, and a thick fog begins to form. I can barely see Yemayá, who is only a few feet away from me. She approaches the voice, which has now morphed into a shadowy, nonhuman form. The creature hops out of the murky darkness. It is now before me as the fog dissipates to reveal the moonlight.

As my eyes fall upon the figure before me, I am taken aback by a man with frog-like legs and webbed hands. Dressed in tropical leaves and vines, he is tall and lean with a crown of feathers atop his long black hair. With a warm smile, he grabs Yemayá, hugs her, and spins her around. Yemayá does not look very happy.

"¡*Buenas noches, mi amiga!*[11]" he says to her, giving her a kiss on the cheek.

"*Buenas noches*," was her begrudging reply. "Are you planning to introduce yourself? Or are you just going to keep interjecting and providing unwarranted advice?"

"Oh, *hermana*,[12] don't be that way!" He turns to look at me with his big, circular, brown frog eyes. Walking/hopping over to me with his arms outstretched, he surprises me with a bear hug and kiss on the cheek. Placing me back on the ground, he finally introduces himself, "Lisette, my name is Yúcahu Bagua Maórocoti, the Celestial God, but you can just call me Yúcahu. I live within the *El Yunque* rainforest and sustain human life through agriculture. I am the protector of the people and the essence of life itself. I embody all energy, including heat, fire, and the rays of the sun."

"Are you done providing her with your résumé?" Yemayá says to Yúcahu sarcastically.

Yúcahu lets out a loud laugh while Yemayá rolls her eyes. "Aw, don't be that way!" he replies mockingly. "I am here to help Lisette just as much as you are. I want to show her that she has the strength within her to stay in her doctoral program to become the scientist of her dreams. I want her to gain the skills to protect herself and survive!"

Yemayá scoffs with derision, "But at what cost, Yúcahu? Your message is very masculine and ignores the pain that she has been through!"

Apologetically, Yúcahu states, "My message is that of a protector, one of my roles as the Celestial God. I do not mean to hurt or offend. Yemayá, I understand your argument. In my role as a provider of sustenance, I understand that Lisette needs to be nourished and cared for. I want her to be happy and to experience and enjoy the essence of life." As he says this, he walks/hops over to me on webbed tip-toes, grabs my face, and looks into my eyes. "I see great unhappiness and tension in those brown eyes... but I also see great strength."

Yemayá sighs, looking extremely annoyed at her male counterpart. "Of course that is what you see! The tension arises from her positionality as a woman of color in a field dominated by White men. She is stuck in the classic 'double bind' (Malcom & Malcom, 2011), which is the complex intersection of her gender and race/ethnicity resulting in her unique experiences of gendered and racialized inequality. Her intersectionality is 'greater than the sum of racism and sexism' (Crenshaw, 1989, p. 140)."

Yúcahu smiles, his moist skin shining in the moonlight. "Ah! I see you are quoting Kimberlé Crenshaw's work, and, yes, I understand what you are saying. However, Crenshaw also wrote that '[i]ntersectional subordination need not be *intentionally* produced' (Crenshaw, 1991, p. 1249). So, Lisette's experiences of marginality should not be taken too personally; she could and should rise above these experiences...."

"Whoa, whoa, whoa!" Yemayá interrupts, looking as though she is about to hit Yúcahu. "What you just said seems kind of sexist and lets the individuals with power in her doctoral program get away with not addressing institutionalized racism and sexism."

Slightly offended and tired of being a spectator, I place myself in between Yemayá and Yúcahu and ask Yúcahu, "Are you saying that I need to be more confident, more thick-skinned? Because that sounds a lot like what the men on my PhD committee told me after I took the oral section of my comprehensive exams. They never made such statements to my male colleagues!" I found myself getting teary eyed again.

Yúcahu quickly apologizes. "¡Ay, perdóname![13] I did not mean to offend. What I wanted to emphasize was that sometimes people unintentionally say and do things that hurt others, but you have the strength within you to ignore them and make it as a scientist."

Seeing that he has dug himself into a hole, Yúcahu sighs and, for the first time, his wide grin disappears. "The authoring of a scientific identity unfortunately requires that you *perform* like a scientist, which is challenging when the scientific identity begins to conflict with your racial and gender identity

(Johnson, Brown, Carlone, & Cuevas, 2011). There have been other strong women of color who have figured out 'how to balance competing identities; how to orchestrate a credible bid to author a science identity without compromising components of their precious racial and gender identities' (Johnson et al., 2011, p. 360). They survived because they developed *la facultad*[14] to excel at science while mediating competing identities (Johnson et al., 2011). I believe that you are one of those exceptional women."

Yemayá's face softens. She opens her arms wide and suddenly hugs Yúcahu, planting a big kiss on his slightly green-tinted cheek. Moved by what Yúcahu said and by the show of emotion, I join the embrace. I look up tenderly at Yúcahu and say, "I understand you now, *hermano*.[15] However, I do not know how much more I can do to reconcile my multiple identities."

I look away into the distance and continue, "Like many women of color in science, I have tried multiple forms of racialized and gendered passing in order to be viewed as a competent member of the scientific community (Ong, 2005). I have dressed in loose, more masculine clothing, and I don't wear make-up. I avoid using slang or Spanglish, and I make sure to articulately explain and discuss scientific concepts. I even . . . and I am ashamed to say this, but I . . . I have even tried to smooth my hair so that I could appear . . . less 'ethnic.'" I look down at my feet, embarrassed by this last point.

Yemayá gasps while Yúcahu stands in silence. After taking a moment, Yemayá softly tells me, "*Mija*, fragmentation (i.e., racial and gendered passing) and multiplicity (i.e., stereotype manipulation and performances of superiority) strategies can only help you to persevere for so long (Ong, 2005). By engaging in those strategies, you are compromising who you are as a woman and as a *Boricua*.[16] They will take a costly toll on the physical, emotional, and spiritual self. You know that it can destroy you."

Knowing that she is telling the truth, I begin to sob. Yúcahu leaps over to me and puts his arm around me. "It's okay, *mjia*. What we are dealing with is the essentialization of not only what it means to be a scientist, but also what it means to be a woman and a woman of color in the context of science. By casting issues of race and gender aside and by trying to appear objective and value-neutral (Harding, 1986), the scientific community tricks itself into believing that all scientists have similar experiences, training, opportunities, and support during their educational journeys (or that there are special programmatic interventions to 'fix' individuals lacking these things). However, this essentialism causes the fragmentation of a woman of color's sense of self (Harris, 1990) as she attempts to become a respected member of that community by molding her racialized and gendered identities to fit a 'scientific' (i.e., White and male) one. So, the challenge you must face is that you must 'weave the fragments, [of your] many selves, into an integral, though always changing and shifting, whole: a self that is neither [female] nor [Latina], but both-and' (Harris, 1990, p. 604)."

Yemayá chimes in, "Yes, that is the challenge, but it is an unfair burden being placed on your shoulders. By essentializing what it means to be a scientist (let alone a woman and person of color in science), they are silencing your voice (Harris, 1990) and making you invisible."

Wiping tears away from my eyes, I say, "You are both right. The weird thing, though, is that I feel both invisible and visible. It is obvious that I am the only domestic woman of color in the department and I am treated differently because of that fact. Yet the White graduate students and faculty members in my department are so committed to the epistemology and sacredness of science (Harding, 1986) that they all try to lay claim to color-blindness, attempting to make my race/ethnicity and gender no more than background information (Gallagher, 2003)."

There is a long pause as Yúcahu and Yemayá digest what I just said. Yúcahu responds, "Interesting. Can you give us some examples of how you have seen colorblindness used and how it relates to your (in)visibility?"

After thinking for a couple of minutes, I reply, "Well, as the only domestic female graduate student of color in a predominantly White science department, it is obvious that I stand out. People stare at me when I enter a room, and faculty members know when I am absent from class. However, despite my obvious presence, everyone tries to adhere to the unspoken rule that science 'sees' no color. The only time my peers engage in conversation with me is when the topic is related to science, particularly if they need assistance with research design or have questions regarding course content. They never ask me about my family, my interests outside of science, my background. I am a 'fellow scientist' and nothing more. When I do want to speak about my cultural background or issues of race, I am met with increased rhetorical incoherence and avoidance (Bonilla-Silva, 2010). That kind of talk apparently does not belong in the 'realm of science'; yet, I sometimes hear male graduate students quietly share racist and sexist jokes (Solórzano, 1998) in their offices."

"UGH!" Yemayá exclaims in disgust.

"Wow," Yúcahu whispers. "So, by trying to ignore your outward appearance (i.e., your racialized and gendered identities), they make you feel like you are not really there. They are disregarding and marginalizing you . . . not to mention being obviously racist and sexist behind closed doors!"

I respond, "Yes, and I believe that the abstract liberalism frame of color-blindness (Bonilla-Silva, 2010), particularly the concepts of equal opportunity and myth of meritocracy, as well as racial and gender microaggressions, specifically low expectations (Solórzano, 1998), simultaneously contribute to my feelings of marginalization."

"How so?" Yemayá asks.

Sighing, I sit back down on the wet sand. Twilight is upon us now, and I can feel that my time is growing short, though I do not know how I will get home. I proceed to share, "This is really hard for me to talk about, but the best example of how abstract liberalism (i.e., equal opportunity and myth of meritocracy) and microaggressions (mainly low expectations) is my relationship with me previous advisor."

"You mean, you switched labs?" Yúcahu queries.

I take a deep breath. "Yes. In a desperate attempt to stay in my doctoral program, I switched to another lab. My previous advisor was a well-published and well-funded scientist that everyone loved. I felt honored because I got the opportunity to work with him. However, the longer I worked with him, the more I got to see his true colors. On the surface, he seemed kind and appeared to treat everyone equally. Yet, what I discovered was that other students in his lab were provided with project ideas, undergraduate field help, and funding, while I had to come up with my own projects and look for my own funding and help. Some people would think that it was my fault that I did not get the assistance or funding (myth of meritocracy), but I believe that he had low expectations of me and did not view my work as significant because I am a woman of color (racial and gender microaggressions; Solórzano, 1998)."

I can see Yemayá and Yúcahu carefully listening, so I continue my story: "He basically had an open-door policy where anyone could stop by and talk to him (equal opportunity). I would meet with him on a bi-weekly basis, and each time, he would forget what I was working on! But the worst interaction that I had with him was after a presentation I gave to the department regarding my proposed dissertation research. He asked me to have lunch with him to discuss the presentation. I was thrilled because it was the first time that he actually showed interest in me and my research. As we were eating at a local restaurant, he told me that 'the best part of the presentation was that it was organized.' He then proceeded to criticize my ideas and tried to convince me to change research topics. His words shattered me."

Stunned, Yúcahu says to me, "That's horrible! The sad thing is that, in his mind, he probably thought he was doing you a favor. He didn't have confidence in your abilities (low expectations; Solórzano, 1998). How wrong was he!? Never underestimate the power of Puerto Rican women!"

Yemayá explodes with laughter, and I cannot help but to join her. As we compose ourselves, I share, "I guess you are right, Yúcahu, because after I left his lab, I found out that he slightly modified my project and gave it to two graduate students in his lab. So, my ideas could not have been that bad!"

Placing a hand on my shoulder, Yemayá declares, "In all seriousness, though, your advisor's lack of guidance and support caused you a great deal of stress and forced you to question your competence and identification with the scientific community. This was not a case of benign neglect; it was a cruel act of 'pushing out' (Gildersleeve et al., 2011, p. 96)."

Yemayá's words hit me like a brick. Yúcahu quickly tries to make me feel better. Trying to be cheerful, he says, "Imagine how much you have endured, and you are still in science! Like a phoenix, you should rise from the ashes of this bad experience and see your new lab as a new beginning!"

Yemayá rolls her eyes a little. We sit in silence for a bit. I continue to reflect on my graduate education in the sciences, and suddenly I am struck with a realization. "After all that I have been through thus far, I have come to realize that graduate students of color are just exploited labor," I verbalize with more resentment than I care to admit. I simultaneously feel sadness and sheer anger as I think about my last statement.

Yemayá, with her soulful eyes, asks, "Why do you feel that way?"

"Well, I feel that often graduate students of color are used by their institutions as symbols of all things diversity. We are only asked to be a part of committees or programs when it is an opportunity for the department or the university to demonstrate their so-called commitment to diversity and equality. For example, I was asked to be on an ad hoc diversity committee for our department, which I was extremely excited about. I wrote a list of initiatives that we could use to attract more students of color to the sciences. When I shared my list with the committee chair, she said that there was 'too much red tape' and that it would be 'extremely difficult' to do. Ultimately, the committee only met a handful of times and then it was forgotten. What hurt the most about that situation was that the committee chair was a woman of color."

"Wow. It sounds to me that the committee chair already bought into the culture of the department. Perhaps she knew that anything you tried to do would be met with resistance and she was protecting you from the political backlash?" Yemayá suggests.

With a scoff, Yúcahu chimes in, "Please, Yemayá. This all has to do with interest convergence (Bell, 1980). The department and the committee chair were doing things for their own self-interest. They saw that Lisette was interested in being more involved in the department, and they were being required by the institution to demonstrate their commitment to diversity. So, they created an ad hoc committee to show the institution that it was trying to do something without actually taking action."

"Doesn't interest convergence usually deal with the material reality of people of color versus those of Whites (Delgado & Stefancic, 2001)?" Yemayá countered.

"I think Yúcahu is referring to political interests, but I agree that there are material and economic interests at play as well," I posit. "In that same scenario, I would also add that the department wanted to appeal to the institution and to potential graduate students by feigning an interest in diversity because they would be financially rewarded for accepting graduate students of color."

Yemayá asks, "How so?"

"Well, I was informed by the graduate college (rather than my own department) that there is a financial incentive for departments to recruit students of color. Basically, graduate students of color are half-price. If a department gets a graduate student of color, the graduate college will pay for half of the student's tuition with the expectation that the department will pay the other half. This saves the department money and allows them to invest that money in White students who they deem more valuable."

"That's horrible!" Yemayá laments.

Yúcahu approaches her, placing a webbed hand on her shoulder. "Horrible, but true, and it is all the more reason to survive and fight!" he declares. "Racial realism exists (Bell, 1992). Racism is a permanent facet of life, and it is something that we have to come to terms with. Lisette, that is why you need to hang in there. You need to stick with your doctoral program because racism exists everywhere. You cannot escape it. So, why let go of your dream of becoming a scientist? Fight for what you want!"

I am shocked to hear the truth that was already in my heart, and I can feel my eyes well up with tears. "Then, where is the hope?" I manage to ask without sobbing. Instinctually, Yemayá holds me close, running her hand through my hair to soothe me much like my sister used to do when I was upset as a child. Yúcahu joins us, and looking straight into my eyes, tells me, "There is hope in the struggle itself (Bell, 1992)."

We stand in silence, the waves crashing against the shore. I grab hold of the hands of Yemayá and Yúcahu, and for the first time in a long time, I have clarity. "I know what I must do," I say to them barely above a whisper. "Yúcahu, I know that you mean well and want the best for me just as much as Yemayá. However, after speaking with the two of you tonight about my experiences, I have come to the conclusion that I have lost my passion for science research because of the toxic environment that has slowly drained my spirit. I do not think that I can commit myself to a life of marginalization. I have to leave the sciences."

Yemayá hugs me tightly. Yúcahu seems disappointed, but I can also see in his deep, dark brown eyes that he accepts my decision and understands my reasons. I let out a sigh, feeling relief as a burden is lifted from my shoulders. Yemayá notices the first rays of the sun beginning to creep over the horizon. "It's time for us to get you home," she tells me sadly.

"How am I going to get home? I don't even remember how I got here," I honestly reply.

"You were sinking in the ocean waves and managed to struggle to the shore. Now, Yúcahu and I will guide you home. Your ship awaits you," Yemayá explains.

A large steam ship, approximately 496 feet long and 72 feet wide, mysteriously appears before us. *Marine Tiger* is written on the side of the ship, and I recall that it was a steam ship that took many of my people to start new lives in New York back in the late 1940s. Yúcahu and Yemayá both hug and kiss me goodbye, and Yúcahu produces a spiral of hot air that lifts me onto the ship. As I stand on the deck, I watch as Yemayá uses her powers to force the ship out into the open ocean and Yúcahu helps to produce the steam that propels the ship. I take a seat on a deck chair. The long hours of deep conversation suddenly overwhelm me, and I find myself exhausted and being rocked asleep by the movement of the water. When I awaken, I am back in my hotel bed. I smile, and for once, I feel at peace.

* * *

This testimonio, or counterstory, is my truth—it is my way of continuing the tradition of speaking against White supremacy through creative prose (e.g., *And We Are Not Saved*—Bell, 1987) that honors not only my epistemology as a person of color but also the feelings and experiences of my ancestors. Being a mixture of religious folklore and nonfiction, it is only a snapshot of my doctoral experience that I have chosen to share. It has been locked away inside me for a long time because the hurt was too deep. The times when I did try to articulate my experiences, I was met with denial and negation. However, now I offer my story to those graduate students of color in the sciences to show them that they are not alone and that the "Am I going crazy?!" narrative (Gildersleeve et al., 2011) is more common than the scientific community would like to acknowledge. Yes, there is a lot of pain in these pages, but there is also a lot of hope stemming from the knowledge and strength of our ancestors as well as the opportunity for "exposing, analyzing, and challenging the majoritarian stories of racial privilege" (Solórzano & Yosso, 2002, p. 32).

Though I chose to give up my dream of becoming a faculty member in the sciences, I feel that I have been blessed to find a new path in the field of education that is more in tune with my values, my cultural background, and the legacy I want to leave on this earth. Despite the positive change, I must confess that I have a lot of anger still bottled inside me. Meditation has helped as well as conversations with my loving husband and sister. Yet I also find it extremely useful to use my anger in my scholarship and activism because "anger expressed and translated into action in the service of our vision and our future is a liberating and strengthening act of clarification" (Lorde, 1984, p. 127). Through my counterstory and other scholarship, I hope to expand CRT praxis (Lawson, 1995; Parker & Stovall, 2004) to the realm of science and reach out to other graduate students of color struggling in their science doctoral programs while shedding light on how scientists, institutions of higher education, and funding agencies (such as the

National Science Foundation) can change organizational culture, policies, and practices to move toward greater racial and gender equity.

Thus, I would like to end this chapter with some implications and recommendations for leaders within higher education, particularly those individuals engaged in science, technology, engineering, and mathematics (STEM) disciplines. First, I believe my counterstory highlights and validates the experiences of many doctoral students of color by providing an example of the "Am I going crazy?!" narrative (Gildersleeve et al., 2011). As described by Gildersleeve et al. (2011), doctoral students of color, in general, have "tentativeness, insecurity, and doubt" (p. 100) projected on to them by White faculty members. I experienced this firsthand, as years of isolation in the lab, a lack of meaningful peer relationships, and an unsupportive advisor–advisee relationship left me questioning my abilities, intelligence, and purpose (Gay, 2004; Gildersleeve et al., 2011).

I agree with Gildersleeve et al. (2011) in their call to recognize "the racialized 'Am I going crazy?!' narrative in the culture of doctoral education" (p. 109) and to rectify the injustice this narrative imposes on graduate students of color. Therefore, STEM faculty and administrators must first and foremost recognize that the "sacredness of science" (Harding, 1986, p. 38) is a mirage and that science is a social activity whose practices need to be critically examined (Harding, 1986). STEM faculty and administrators must also learn to identify ways in which they perpetuate this narrative at their own institutions (e.g., college viewbooks highlighting STEM— Osei-Kofi & Torres, 2015) and develop new intersectional initiatives to address the racially gendered injustices faced by students of color. This would require particular attention to how scientific discourse, socialization, and imagery perpetuate and privilege the values and norms of Whiteness and maleness while "rendering the needs and contributions of women of color (in)visible" (Torres, 2012, p. 41). STEM faculty and administrators must learn to recognize the master narratives enacted within science, encourage the voicing of counterstories, and leverage those counterstories into actions that address inequity.

For example, master narratives within science blame the low retention of students of color in science fields on their lack of academic preparation in high school (Seymour & Hewitt, 1997). Others say that students of color are stigmatized by affirmative action initiatives (Seymour & Hewitt, 1997; Wise, 2005) and their ensuing self-doubt results in students not pursuing graduate degrees in the sciences. This assertion has been especially applied to women, who are often said to struggle with work–life balance (Ceci & Williams, 2011). One could also say that the science curriculum is too hard and that students of color do not have the mentoring or resources to succeed (e.g., Aschbacher, Li, & Roth, 2010; Seymour & Hewitt, 1997). Yet it is my experience that the main problem within science is the racism and sexism embedded within the structure of the field.

Science faculty and administrators must be willing to see the racism and sexism perpetuated in science research, in science curricula, in science classrooms, and during scientific conferences in order to truly address the low retention of students of color. Syllabi and course policies need to be (re)examined to see if they are catering to the interests and needs of White students with the assumption that students of color will "learn 'by default' or come into the learning environment with what they already need to succeed" (Milner, 2008, p. 338). Faculty members also need to reflect on whether they silence students of color and how that silencing protects the unearned advantages of the dominant group. They must question how White privilege (McIntosh, 1989) and power is exercised within the academic curriculum (Cammarota & Romero, 2006). Science privileges males (Carlone, 2004), while the absence of race in coursework, discourse, and literature normalizes Whiteness. Heidi Carlone (2004) reminds us that "[s]cience carries a powerful sociohistorical legacy and is reproduced as an objective, privileged way of knowing pursued by an intellectual elite" (p. 394). This legacy is often ignored by the scientific community, and science students are typically unaware of its existence. By hiding the truth about inequities and racialization in the sciences, the field of science silences the history and personal narratives of female scientists and scientists of color. Thus, it is up to STEM faculty and administrators to use their power to reimagine and restructure syllabi, courses, discourses, pedagogy, research, programs, policies, and practices to inspire the scientific community to become more inclusive and equitable.

I believe that CRT can be used as an effective lens to unveil injustices within the sciences, but it would entail a dramatic cultural shift. STEM students, faculty, and administrators must be willing to learn about how science has been used in the past to oppress people of color and to critically examine how science is oppressing people of color today. They must be able to occasionally put aside their linear, quantitative, and objective epistemologies and embrace a postmodern, critical race, feminist perspective to understand the experiences of scientists of color. This also means committing to continuous reflection on Whiteness and its pervasiveness within science that allows for the "cumulative advantages" (Merton, 1968, 1988) experienced by established scientists who tend to be White and male (Rossiter, 1993). If the scientific community truly wants to diversify the field, it must confront Whiteness as property (Harris, 1993) and the realization that making decisions that lead to "more equitable policies and practices might mean that they lose something of great importance to them, including their power, privilege, esteem, social status, linguistic status, and their ability to reproduce these benefits and interests to their children and future generations" (Milner, 2008, p. 334).

Change requires honest self-reflection and a commitment to a shared vision (Morgan, 2006). If science departments wish to diversify the field, they need to improve upon the culture and mindsets of its members. A first step would necessitate scientists engaging in praxis, allowing each member to reflect, question, and act to enhance institutional practices and policies (Freire, 1998). Scientists must be critical of their assumptions and mental models (Senge, 2007). This is especially important in the creation and evaluation of diversity initiatives meant to encourage women and people of color to pursue science careers. The scientific community must be willing to ask if these programs are truly addressing inequities in the sciences as well as how the "culture of competition" and politics in the sciences may be creating barriers for certain groups of people.

Similarly, a national dialogue (Morgan, 2006) regarding diversity in the sciences needs to be promoted. There are too many White scientists who do not want to acknowledge the inequality that is present in the field, and there are not enough voices of color in the sciences to fight the "culture of silence" (Freire, 1998). Several well-publicized dialogical sessions are needed to bring together scientists from various races/ethnicities to engage in open dialogue, deliberative processes of inquiry, and prejudice reduction (Larson & Ovando, 2001). These sessions would force scientists to reflect on "the societal, cultural, and institutional roots of discrimination" (Larson & Ovando, 2001, p. 203) in the sciences and recognize that historic "quick-fix" solutions are not sustainable or effective. Lastly, STEM faculty must teach their students through problem-posing, codification, and dialogical instruction so that all students can come to know science through their own epistemologies (Freire, 1998).

As indicated earlier, cultural change in the sciences would also necessitate a fundamental change in the field's use of language, since language ultimately symbolizes and embodies culture (Henze & Arriaza, 2006). Language is a powerful mechanism by which to challenge and change the mental models of others. Science discourse tends to avoid "warm and fuzzy" terminology in favor of words and phrases that maintain objectivity, logic, or a competitive mindset, such as "publish or perish." Meanwhile, terms such as "collaborative," "interdisciplinary," and "scientific community" are never deconstructed and analyzed. I believe that critical visual and textual discourse analysis and awareness could aid in revealing the underlying assumptions that scientists hold and in reframing the questions that are asked about diversity programming and inequities in the sciences (Henze & Arriaza, 2006).

Science departments need leaders to establish a sense of community based on ethical behavior and compassion. All future scientists, regardless of race or gender, must have mentors who will foster caring, personal relationships with them while at the same time challenging them intellectually (Cammarota & Romero, 2006; Ong, Wright, Espinosa, & Orfield, 2011; Torres, 2008). What scientists forget is that science education and research is a social activity and, by definition, involves the participation of *humans*. To truly be a scientific *community* and to diversify the field, they must reduce feelings of isolation and create a supportive environment where greater communication, trust, and social adjustment will attract new students and give current graduate students a sense of belonging.

In closing, I want to tell my fellow women of color who exist, as I do, within a "symphony of anger" (Lorde, 1984, p. 129) in academia—though I do not know you, I am with you. I hurt when you are in pain; I feel the fury that tears both of us apart. I mourn the loss of my fallen sisters and I rejoice in your triumphs. For those of you who are still in the sciences and are barely surviving, you are not alone. Use your fury as strength; do not be silenced. Do not allow your humanity to be marginalized. For those of you who are still in the sciences and are thriving, do not forget us, your sisters in the struggle. Fight for us. Fight for the next generation of scientists of color.

NOTES

1. Marine Tiger—A 1945 steam ship that transported Puerto Rican migrants to the U.S. mainland
2. *La Tierra de Oportunidad*—The Land of Opportunity
3. *Tratando de sobrevivir*—Trying to survive
4. Yucahù—The Celestial God of the Taino people who was a deity of the land and sea said to live in the *El Yunque* Rainforest and sustaining and protecting life through agriculture
5. Yemayá—The Goddess of the Ocean from the Candomble and Santeria religions of West Africa who is associated with womanhood, the moon, and the sea
6. *La Isla del Encanto*—The Island of Enchantment (i.e., Puerto Rico)
7. *Nueva York*—New York
8. *Cabezas duras*—Hard heads
9. *Mija*—i.e., *mi hija* or my daughter
10. *Perdón*—Sorry
11. *Buenas noches, mi amiga*—Good evening/night, my friend
12. *Hermana*—Sister
13. ¡Ay, *perdóname!* —Oh, forgive me!
14. *La facultad* was coined by Gloria Anzaldúa (1999) to describe a latent ability of some marginalized individuals to sense deeper realities and to be more aware of the world around them. Johnson et al. (2011) used this term to describe how some women of color in science are able to navigate barriers to success.
15. *Hermano*—Brother

16. *Boricua*—a Taino term meaning a person from the island of *Boriquen*, currently called Puerto Rico.

REFERENCES

Anzaldúa, G. (1999). *Borderlands/La frontera* (2nd ed.). San Francisco, CA: Aunt Lute.

Aschbacher, P., Li, E., & Roth, E. (2010). Is science me? High school students' identities, participation and aspirations in science, engineering, and medicine. *Journal of Research in Science Teaching, 47*(5), 564–582.

Bell, D. A. Jr., (1980). *Brown v. Board of Education* and the interest-convergence dilemma. *Harvard Law Review, 93*(3), 518–533.

Bell, D. (1987). *And we are not saved.* New York, NY: Basic Books.

Bell, D. (1992). *Faces at the bottom of the well.* New York, NY: Basic Books.

Bonilla-Silva, E. (2010). *Racism without racists: Color-blind racism & racial inequality in contemporary American* (3rd ed.). Lanham, MD: Rowman & Littlefield Publishers, Inc.

Cammarota, J., & Romero, A. (2006). A critically compassionate intellectualism for Latina/o students: Raising voices above the silencing in our schools. *Multicultural Education, 14*(2), 16–23.

Carlone, H. B. (2004). The cultural production of science in reform-based physics: Girls' access, participation, and resistance. *Journal of Research in Science Teaching, 41*(4), 392–414.

Ceci, S. J., & Williams, W. M. (2011). Understanding current causes of women's underrepresentation in science. *Proceedings of the National Academy of Sciences, 108*(8), 3157–3162. doi:10.1073/pnas.1014871108

Collins, P. H. (1986). Learning from the outsider within: The sociological significance of Black feminist thought. *Social Problems, 33*(6), S14–S32.

Crenshaw, K. (1989). Demarginalizing the intersection of race and sex: A black feminist critique of antidiscrimination doctrine, feminist theory and antiracist politics. *The University of Chicago Legal Forum, 140,* 139–167.

Crenshaw, K. (1991). Mapping the margins: Intersectionality, identity politics, and violence against women of color. *Stanford Law Review, 43*(6), 1241–1299.

Delgado, R., & Stefancic, J. (2001). *Critical race theory: An introduction.* New York, NY: New York University Press.

Dill, B. T. (1983). Race, class, and gender: Prospects for an all-inclusive sisterhood. *Feminist Studies, 9*(1), 131–150.

Evans, S. Y. (2007). *Black women in an ivory tower, 1850–1954: An intellectual history.* Gainesville, FL: University Press of Florida.

Freire, P. (1998). Reprint: Cultural action for freedom. *Harvard Educational Review, 68,* 471–521.

Gay, G. (2004). Navigating marginality en route to the professoriate: Graduate students of color learning and living in academia. *International Journal of Qualitative Studies in Education, 17*(2), 265–288.

Gallagher, C. A. (2003). Color-blind privilege: The social and political functions of erasing the color line in post-race America. *Race, Gender & Class, 10*(4), 1–17.

Gildersleeve, R. E., Croom, N. N., & Vasquez, P. L. (2011). "Am I going crazy?!": A critical race analysis of doctoral education. *Equity & Excellence in Education, 44*(1), 93–114.

Harding, S. (1986). *The science question in feminism.* Ithaca, NY: Cornell University Press.

Harris, A. P. (1990). Race and essentialism in feminist legal theory. *Stanford Law Review, 4*(3), 581–616.

Harris, C. I. (1993). Whiteness as property. *Harvard Law Review, 106*(8), 1707–1791.

Henze, R., & Arriaza, G. (2006). Language and reforming schools: A case for a critical approach to language in educational leadership. *International Journal of Leadership in Education, 9*(2), 157–177.

Hurtado, A. (1989). Relating to privilege: Seduction and rejection in the subordination of White women and women of color. *Signs, 14*(4), 833–855.

Johnson, A., Brown, J., Carlone, H., & Cuevas, A. K. (2011). Authoring identity amidst the treacherous terrain of science: A multiracial feminist examination of the journeys of three women of color in science. *Journal of Research in Science Teaching, 48*(4), 339–366. doi:10.1002/tea.20411

Larson, C. L., & Ovando, C. J. (2001). *The color of bureaucracy: The politics of equity in multicultural school communities.* Belmont, CA: Wadsworth/Thomson.

Lawson, R. J. (1995). Critical race theory as praxis: A view from outside the outside. *Howard Law Journal, 38*(2), 353–370.

Lorde, A. (1984). *Sister outsider.* Freedom, CA: The Crossing Press.

Malcom, L. E., & Malcom, S. M. (2011). The double bind: The next generation. *Harvard Educational Review, 81*(2), 162–171.

McIntosh, P. (1989, July/August). White privilege: Unpacking the invisible knapsack. *Peace and Freedom,* pp. 10–12.

Merton, R. K. (1968). The Matthew effect in science. *Science, 159*(3810), 56–63.

Merton, R. K. (1988). The Matthew effect in science, II. *ISIS, 79,* 606-623.

Milner, H. R. IV, (2008). Critical race theory and interest convergence as analytical tools in teacher education policies and practices. *Journal of Teacher Education, 59*(4), 332–346. doi: 10.1177/0022487108321884

Morgan, G. (2006). *Images of organizations.* Thousand Oaks, CA: Sage Publications.

Murphy, M. C., Steele, C. M., & Gross, J. J. (2007). Signaling threat: How situational cues affect women in math, science, and engineering settings. *Psychological Science, 18*(10), 879–885.

Ong, M. (2005). Body projects of young women of color in physics: Intersections of gender, race, and science. *Social Problems, 52*(4), 593–617.

Ong, M., Wright, C., Espinosa, L. L., & Orfield, G. (2011). Inside the double bind: A synthesis of empirical research on undergraduate and graduate women of color in science, technology, engineering, and mathematics. *Harvard Educational Review, 81*(2), 172–208.

Osei-Kofi, N., & Torres, L. E. (2015). College admissions viewbooks and the grammar of gender, race, and STEM. *Culture Studies of Science Education, 10*(2), 527–544.

Parker, L., & Stovall, D. O. (2004). Actions following words: Critical race theory connects to critical pedagogy. *Educational Philosophy and Theory, 36*(2), 167–182.

Rendón, L. I. (1994). Validating culturally diverse students: Toward a new model of learning and student development. *Innovative Higher Education, 19*(1), 33–51.

Rossiter, M. W. (1993). The Matthew Matilda effect in science. *Social Studies of Science, 23*(2), 325–341.

Senge, P. M. (2007). *The fifth discipline: The art and practice of the learning organization.* New York, NY: Doubleday.

Seymour, E., & Hewitt, N. M. (1997). *Talking about leaving: Why undergraduates leave the sciences.* Boulder, CO: Westview Press.

Smith, W. A. (2004). Black faculty coping with racial battle fatigue: The campus racial climate in a post-civil rights era. In D. Cleveland (Ed.), *Broken silence: Conversations about race by African Americans at predominately White institutions* (pp. 171–190). New York, NY: Peter Lang.

Smith, W. A., Allen, W. R., & Danley, L. L. (2007). "Assume the position...You fit the description": Psychosocial experiences and racial battle fatigue among African American male college students. *American Behavioral Scientist, 51*(4), 551–578.

Solórzano, D. G. (1998). Critical race theory, race and gender microaggressions, and the experience of Chicana and Chicano scholars. *Qualitative Studies in Education, 11*(1), 121–136.

Solórzano, D. G., & Yosso, T. J. (2002). Critical race methodology: Counter-story-telling as an analytical framework for education research. *Qualitative Inquiry, 8*(1), 23–44.

Sue, D. W., Capodilupo, C. M., Torino, G. C., Bucceri, J. M., Holder, A. M. B., Nadal, K. L., & Esquilin, M. (2007). Racial microaggressions in everyday life: Implications for clinical practice. *American Psychologist, 62*(4), 271–286.

Torres, L. E. (2008). Fixing the leaky pipe—Increasing recruitment and retention of underrepresented groups in ecology. *Frontiers in Ecology and the Environment, 6*(10), 554–555.

Torres, L. E. (2012). Lost in the numbers: Gender equity discourse and women of color in science, technology, engineering, and mathematics (STEM). *The International Journal of Science in Society, 3*(4), 33–45.

Turner, C. S. V. (1994). Guests in someone else's house: Students of color. *The Review of Higher Education, 17*(4), 355–370.

Vasquez, P. L. (2007). *Achieving success in engineering: A phenomenological exploration of Latina/o student persistence in engineering fields of study* (Unpublished master's thesis). Iowa State University, Ames, IA.

Wise, T. J. (2005). *Affirmative action: Racial preference in black and white.* New York, NY: Routledge.

CHAPTER 3

BEING IN THE BLACK–WHITE BINARY

Admission Letter to an Asian American Graduate Student

Joyce Lui

This chapter focuses on how I, as an Asian American woman, navigated the Black–White binary during my graduate school experience at a predominantly White institution. According to Delgado and Stefancic (2012), the Black–White binary requires "nonblack minority groups [to] compare their treatment to that of African Americans to redress [racial] grievances" (p. 75). In this chapter, I present a personal narrative counterstory (Solórzano & Yosso, 2001) in the form of a response to an admissions letter received from a graduate program. Throughout, I highlight my experiences of racism and how the treatment of other racialized groups in my program impacted my experiences as an Asian American student. Although I identify as an immigrant, Chinese American, woman, woman of color, I use the umbrella term Asian American to acknowledge the social construction of my racial identity and how others view and racialize me (Lewis, 2003;

Envisioning Critical Race Praxis in Higher Education Through Counter-Storytelling, pages 43–54

Pyon, Cao, & Li, 2007). In my experience, the Black–White binary created a hierarchy in which White supremacy created chasms between myself and other racially minoritized groups. Some believe that Asian Americans do not recognize racism because it does not happen to them and cannot comprehend it when others (specifically Black or Latino/a communities) experience and identify racism (Chou & Feagan, 2008). This counterstory is a cautionary tale meant to illuminate racial realities for Asian American graduate students. Additionally, it provides a narrative for administrators and faculty of graduate schools to better understand how certain models of funding, classroom environments, and opportunities reinforce the Black–White binary, differential racialization, the model minority stereotype, and the myth of meritocracy.

* * *

Dear Joyce,

We are pleased to inform you that the academic program has recommended you to the graduate college that you be admitted to the Doctor of Philosophy (PhD) program.

Congratulations! You have gotten accepted into a doctoral program. I know you weren't sure you would be admitted and questioned whether your letters of recommendation, grade point average, GRE scores, and personal statements were enough. You hoped a program would take a chance on you given your lack of full-time work experience, and they did! All of this uncertainty feels strange, and if a non-Asian American were reading this, they might assume that all your fear was for nothing, simply based on the fact that you are Asian (Pyke & Dang, 2003). Little do you, or they, know that your doctoral program will bring you pain from racial marginalization and that the systemic culture of the experience will cause tension and do harm to you and other racially minoritized groups (Gildersleeve, Croom, & Vasquez, 2011).

FUNDING

We are pleased to offer you a graduate assistantship in conjunction with this offer of admission. The assistantship is half time (20 hours/week) with a stipend of $1800/ month for the nine months of the academic year (mid-August to mid-May). In addition, the assistantship provides a tuition scholarship equal to the amount of your appoint (e.g., 100%) for each semester. This scholarship will be applied to your bill each semester. The initial letter of intent will be for one year, renewable for up to one additional year, after which we will assist you in exploring other funding options.

The admissions offer includes how your doctoral education will be funded in the first year, which is all very exciting! Your short-term advisor is a top scholar in the field, and the letter will encourage you to contact her with any questions you may have. Thanks to several mentors' advice, you will try to find assistantships that will fund your degree and provide you with good experience. Your mentors have shared with you that as a person of color there is likely funding for you to visit campus and maybe even funding for your education overall. You email your short-term advisor with a few questions about assistantships, coursework, and funding to visit the campus.

Her response is helpful, yet awkward. She shares that there is a program dedicated to diversifying graduate minority students at this predominately White institution and you are elated! "That's great!" you'll say. She explains that the program will provide funding for assistantships and admitted students to visit the institution; however, *you* do not qualify for the funding. Despite the name (Graduate Education for Minority Students—GEMS) and vision (diversifying the institution and graduate education) of the program that provides the funding, is only for African Americans, Hispanic Americans, and Indigenous Americans. Asian Americans are excluded from this resource.

You will not able to visit the campus or ever have access to this funding resource. You will feel left out, confused, and not surprised all at the same time. As an undergraduate, you knew certain programs welcomed Asian Americans while others did not. If not spoken or written, it was intentional in their flyers which students were being targeted. You will feel awkward about the whole situation and will turn to your mentors who will not know what to say. They both will believe you should have access to the funding but will know there is nothing anyone can do about it. As you reflect on this experience, you will be grateful for the advisor's candor because she did not have to share the information about the program. She could have said there were no resources and left it at that. You will reread her response several times feeling rejected, even though you never sought out GEMS funding.

You'll want to say, "As an Asian American, I should have access to the resources provided by this program!" You will get frustrated as you learn from your peers who receive GEMS that this is a state-funded program, and faculty members shared that the institution chooses to follow federal policy. The institution could have created a policy that reflected its definition of diversity, which could include Asian Americans. You'll recall a resource your mentors provided you that described how Asian Americans are left out of educational policy debates or not viewed as part of the diversity rhetoric (Poon, 2009).

You eventually will recognize that this program chooses to ignore or overlook Asian Americans, which reinforces the Black–White binary and differential racialization (Delgado & Stefancic, 2012). In this context, Asian

American is viewed as "White" or having similar experiences to more privileged groups (Sue, Bucceri, Lin, Nadal, & Torino, 2007). In conversations with your peers, you'll discover that the power of race, racialization (Lee, 2006), and racism can manifest through programs such as GEMS that restrict resources to certain racialized groups and that racialized power relations have always been about resource allocation (Weber, 2006). You'll become more frustrated with how the institution simplifies race and disregards the differences among and between racially minoritized groups—a student is either White or a minority with no consideration of intersectionality with class, gender, ethnicity, or educational opportunities. Yes, you are Asian American, you're other things as well; the institution, however, chooses to follow federal policy that places Asian Americans outside of the diversity discourse because Asian Americans are not considered a minority group with respect to federal affirmative action regulations (Museus & Kiang, 2009; Suzuki, 2002). This will only reinforce the model minority myth (Kawai, 2005; Lee, 1994; Ng, Lee, & Pak, 2007; Suzuki, 2002). The GEMS policies and practices will communicate that "Asian Americans (YOU) do not need financial support. Asian Americans (YOU) are not underrepresented. Asian Americans (YOU) are smart and will make it on merit alone." These meritocratic ideals embedded within the model minority myth will be overall problematic. Throughout your experience, you will notice that some students in your classes seem to be understand the diversity within the Asian American label, but they will also identify new stereotypes. "Indians and East Asians are rich. All Asian international students are very well off" (Kahlenberg, 2012; Takaki, 1989; Teranishi, 2010). Further, in discussions about race in class, the "yellow peril" argument will present itself. "Joyce, you don't need GEMS! Asians are overrepresented in higher education and before you know it *they* will dominate the economic resources" (Lee, 2006). You will have many experiences with these types of microaggressions, and every year as new cohorts of students of color come in you will be constantly reminded that GEMS is not for you, that you do not contribute to the diversity of the institution, that you are Asian American.

CLASSROOM ENVIRONMENTS

Dr. Martinez will be serving as your short-term advisor as you begin your studies. Please contact him/her at (Martinez@doc.edu) or 555-123-4567 for assistance in selecting courses and course registration. We encourage you to explore the graduate college website to learn more about graduate programs.

You will be very excited to start taking doctoral-level classes and will ask your advisor what courses to register for. You'll be excited to be exposed to literature and new theories. You will expect to read about race and how it impacts education, but you won't be prepared to experience first-hand how race and racism will impact your learning, how you interact with your peers, and how you are perceived by your instructors.

You came from a racially diverse place and as someone with little experience with predominantly White institutions, you will be in awe of how race is socially constructed in an extremely White institution (80% White; Margolis & Romero, 1998; Museus & Truong, 2009). You think about race frequently and won't know what to do with classmates who rarely think about race—or have the privilege to not think about racism (McIntosh, 1990). One of the most painful moments in your doctoral program will happen in the first semester in a seminar that your advisor tells you is "required."

The seminar will include all full- and part-time students from across academic areas in the department. You will be taken aback on the first day when you notice that the racial diversity that is touted throughout the program's marketing materials feels a bit inaccurate given the number of White bodies present in the seminar. The second meeting of seminar will focus on ethics and leadership, and the conversation will shift to race. As one of your peers (a budding friend), a Black woman, is sharing her racialized experiences in education, she will be cut off (Martinez-Aleman, 2000) by a White, male student who proclaims "Racism does not exist!" The conversation will grow louder, harsher, and tenser as White students will argue that poor White people have it worse than Black people. Your friend will be verbally attacked continuously and you will sit there frozen in your seat, face hot from frustration.

Others will react—sharing their opinions, looking uncomfortable, and some White students looking embarrassed (Morrison, 2010). People of color in the room will look like they are in pain. Women of color in the room will tear up. The senior scholar, a White man who preaches diversity, will sit in silence. You will wish for him to say something, anything. Some students, including you, will walk out of the room, refusing to listen anymore. You will be shaking and your eyes will well up with tears; you will want to scream. You will want to contribute to the conversation and validate that as a person of color, racism exists. But you won't because you will be fearful that just like the institution, your classmates will argue that Asian Americans do not face racism and even more you will worry that the other people of color will not acknowledge your racialized self. In those moments you will worry that no one will understand that within the field of education (and society) Asian Americans experience racism in a way that has been framed differently because of the Black–White binary (Lee, 2006). The worry and fear will be overwhelming. You will go back into the class but everywhere you look you will see someone who frustrates you, and you will write a plan in your notebook to leave this place. On the list you will include, "sell furniture, find a job, create good excuse for leaving, pack car and leave." The remainder of the class session you will sit with your arms wrapped around your torso, as if you need to be physically held up. This experience will make you question if doctoral education is for you (Gildersleeve et al., 2011).

Fear is how Whiteness keeps communities of color from coming together. The lack of cohesion between communities of color is a tool for Whiteness to expand its reach (Harris, 1995). That night, you will go to dinner with some of your colleagues, but you all won't say much. The sadness will be noticeable to all. Even though you don't drink alcohol now, you will have your first glass of wine this night and wonder why—and will you need to drink to get through this experience? You'll want the memory removed and you will tell yourself that you expected too much from the faculty member. You will learn a lot from that day, such as the fact that you need to speak up and out too, faculty won't speak up, and privilege is very real. The faculty will try and clean up the damage that will be done but they will fail miserably with their "Diversity Seminar." This will be it though, that will be the only response, no further dialogue about race and climate, and no accountability for anyone's behaviors. You will learn the difference between managing racial tensions and confronting them. The department will manage the tension, faculty will be divided on how to proceed, and the incident will become gossip. Seminars will be seen as a joke instead of the learning opportunities they were meant to be.

You will hear your dad in your head, "Education is a field for White people. Why would students go to you for advice or assistance?" Your mom will sense a change in you and check in. You worry that you can't share your pain with them because they never went to college. You won't actively decide to stay, but you won't leave. You will instead protect yourself from racial battle fatigue as much as possible (Smith, Yosso, & Solórzano, 2006). You will become robotic. Breakfast, work, school, dinner, television. Repeat. The pain, discrimination, and isolation will overwhelm you (Lee et al., 2009; Lee & Kumashiro, 2005). It will also push you to understand Whiteness and build relationships with other people of color in the program (Hartlep & Hayes, 2013).

OPPORTUNITIES AND RELATIONSHIPS

The assistantship you are being offered is a research assistantship with Dr. Hemi. Congratulations on your admission to the graduate program. If you have any questions, please contact your short-term advisor.

Do you have a question? Do you see racism? How do you talk to your White advisor about the racism in your department? How do you tell her when you're seeing and witnessing racist actions towards others? Are you in pain? These aren't the questions they want you to ask, but they will be the questions that flood your mind from the first semester. As you continue to progress through graduate school, you will finish coursework and should be more focused on your research. You may be invited to work on several different projects with faculty members. As you begin working on these projects, you should feel more comfortable being in the doctoral program. As a research assistant, you should take the opportunities that are presented to you. You should be elated. You will be invited to participate in different projects and you may feel like you are finding your space in academia. When you think about your experiences being at a predominantly White institution, the faculty members are, in large part, responsible for your persistence. The relationships you will build with trusted advisors and learning about their experiences will make you want to continue your academic progress. At this point in your academic journey, you will feel accepted.

You will, however, observe when your closest friend in the program, Ashleigh (a Black woman), has a different experience than you. You will notice that Ashleigh is not asked to be on projects, not encouraged to seek out publication opportunities, not told she is a strong writer. You will witness Ashleigh struggle to set up meetings with faculty members. You will wonder why your experiences are so different given your educational backgrounds and skill sets. You will acknowledge that she is equally as intelligent and hardworking and by far a better writer than you. You will struggle with understanding why Ashleigh is not being mentored or included in the same ways you are. You want to believe that hard work will get you to the next step and that those around you will get similar opportunities. However, that won't be the case. Differential racialization, model minority stereotype, and the meritocracy myth (Chou & Feagin, 2008; Suzuki, 2002; Teranishi, 2010; Teranishi, Behringer, Grey, & Parker, 2009; Wang, 1995; Wu, 1995) will once again rear their ugly heads.

You will witness your friend crying and questioning her worth and wondering why her experience was so different than yours. You will be angry and you will eventually name this racism. At the same time, you will feel paranoid. You will wonder if your actions perpetuated a "*nice Asian girl*" stereotype, if your mentoring relationships were connected to you as a scholar or to the perception of you being a "*nice Asian girl*"—an industrious, quiet, scholar (Chou & Feagin, 2008). You will be grateful for all the opportunities and will acknowledge that you could not have navigated through the doctoral program without them. You will struggle, however, because you won't be able to discern between your effort/hard work and their beliefs about (and therefore actions towards) Asian Americans (Cole, 2009). You'll be constantly torn between gratitude and frustration with the racialized structure of graduate education (Gildersleeve et al., 2011). You will know that relationships with faculty are incredibly important (Margolis & Romero, 1998; Weidman, Twale, & Stein, 2001), but the thought that these faculty are helping you because of their preconceived notions about your intelligence, diligence, and docility as an Asian American woman (Chou & Feagin, 2008; Pyke & Dang, 2003; Suzuki, 2002) will linger and fester.

You will hate what you see happening with your Black and Latino friends in the program and you will want to shout, "Stop it!" although faculty and peers may want you to dismiss Whiteness and embrace colorblind ideology (Kawai, 2005). You must refuse! To accept is to not only further marginalize your friends but to accept the microaggressions you will experience as an Asian American doctoral student (Sue, Bucceri, Lin, Nadal, & Torino, 2007). Don't limit who you are or what you stand for. Your friends will experience microaggressions that include continuous perceptions of less desirable traits related to hard work or intelligence (Delgado & Stefancic, 2012). When you witness these, it will be painful and awkward. You will recognize racism and yet you still will not know what to do. All you will be able to do is tell your friend that she's not crazy (Gildersleeve et al., 2011), that she did not imagine it, that these assaults are happening. And while consoling her, you will question how your socialization is being affected by differential racialization and how that process is creating a divide between different communities of color in the program.

EXPERIENCE NEEDED

Once your full admission to the program has been approved by the graduate college, you can begin your coursework in the fall semester. We look forwarding to hearing from you soon and we appreciate your interest in pursuing graduate studies here.

However painful, you will need this experience of being an Asian American graduate student at a PWI. You will graduate, miss your graduate school community, and you will need time to heal from the experience. The experience will bring about a great deal of internal struggle and you will grapple with how you view yourself. As Gildersleeve et al. (2011) posited, the graduate education experience will make you question who you are as opposed to what you know, and in the end, you will meld these two questions together. You will reflect on the moments you felt graduate school ignored your needs, your pain, and the ways systemic racism impacted your friends and colleagues. You will remember those times you were too scared to deal with the pain because you worried that if you thought about it, you would drop out.

Graduate school will be challenging and enlightening. As your mom says, "Education is worth it! No one can take it away from you. They can take your money, your time, and your energy. However, your education is fully yours." And she's right, because when you finish the credential will open doors and allow you a place in the conference room and in closed meetings that you would not have been aware of otherwise. This experience will help you speak up in predominantly White spaces and call out how people, White and of color, reinforce Whiteness. Being aware of the Black–White binary will give you a desire to understand how complex race relations can be and dismantle Whiteness. Further, you'll understand that you not only face racism, but sexism, class differences, and many other systems of oppression (Crenshaw, 1991; Weber, 2006), and those too must be dismantled. Your struggle and actions make it easier for the next Asian American and the following generations of diverse scholars who enter graduate school and exit with a degree in hand.

Sincerely,

[Your Future] Joyce Lui, PhD

ENDURING QUESTIONS AND IMPLICATIONS

As an Asian American, I provide facts about my identity on a regular basis.

   My English level is comparable to yours.

   I consider myself an American.

   Yes, I enjoy Asian food as much as French fries.

   No, I do not know that one other Asian person on this campus, or maybe I do.

When I was an Asian American graduate student, I felt tense. I was a swinging pendulum between great joy and pain. I grew from professional opportunities that led to publications and presentations. I have been frustrated with feeling overlooked. I felt valued and overworked, which is a hallmark of graduate studies.

For Asian American students, higher education leaders need to understand their needs and the diversity within the Asian American community (Takaki, 1989). Also, institutional leaders should take the time and consider how different policies affect different Asian American communities. Racialized policies need to move beyond the Black–White binary. Demographics have changed in the United States with the increasing numbers of different ethnic groups in Asian American and Latino communities. Racially connected policies must be proactive and be reflexive to change in demographic trends.

Further, beyond the foresight of understanding demographic shifts, each institution must be willing to listen to critiques of policies and protocol. There should be opportunities for students to openly share their critiques (through external reviews or surveys). Institutions should use these data to evaluate their policies, which can be stagnant and exclude individuals who should be included. Specifically, leaders should find out why policies have not been updated to be more inclusive and how resources can be reallocated to further develop resources for all students.

I could not have navigated through graduate programs without the support of faculty and fellow graduate students. My faculty advisors and mentors provided me with professional development opportunities. Being in a predominantly White institution and community, the acceptance from faculty members and peers was that much more important. The opportunities given to me made me feel accepted. I want others to understand that one of my most committed faculty members is a White woman. The responsibilities of developing relationships with graduate students of color cannot solely rely on people of color. White faculty members must consider whom they are mentoring, and why.

Institutions should evaluate faculty members' competencies towards multiculturalism and diversity. One of the questions faculty members must answer is, how does one respond when a student makes a derogatory statement towards a minoritized group (race, gender, sexual orientation, citizenship status, class, and many others) or when the learning environment is compromised due to racism? Further, how can the department and the institution provide training and tools to navigate a discussion and documentation of the incidents that pertain to discrimination? Any implications for leadership come down to a few enduring questions which leaders must ask themselves: Why do you want a diverse student body? What are your perceptions, prejudices, and biases towards minoritized groups? What resources have been allocated to provide a safe and secure environment for all students to pursue their academic goals? How do you see yourself as part of the institutional change to create a better campus climate for all students?

REFERENCES

Chou, R. S., & Feagin, J. R. (2008). *The myth of the model minority: Asian Americans facing racism.* Boulder, CO: Paradigm Publishers.

Cole, M. (2009). Critical race theory and education: A Marxist response. New York, NY: Palgrave MacMillan

Crenshaw, K. W. (1991). Mapping the margins: Intersectionality, identity politics, and violence against women of color. *Stanford Law Review, 43*(6), 1241–1299.

Delgado, R., & Stefancic, J. (2012). *Critical race theory.* New York, NY: NYU Press.

Gildersleeve, R. E., Croom, N. N., & Vasquez, P. L. (2011). "Am I going crazy?!": A critical race analysis of doctoral education. *Equity & Excellence in Education, 44*(1), 93–114.

Harris, C. (1995). Whiteness as property. *Harvard Law Review, 106,* 1707–1791.

Hartlep, N. D., & Hayes, C. (2013). Interrupting the racial triangulation of Asians: Unhooking from whiteness as a form of coalition politics. In C. Hayes & N.

D. Hartlep (Ed.), *Unhooking from whiteness: The key to dismantling racism in the United States*. New York, NY: Springer. Retrieved from http://link.springer.com/chapter/10.1007/978-94-6209-377-5_9

Kahlenberg, R. (2012, June 1). Asian Americans and affirmation action. *Chronicle of Higher Education*. Retrieved from http://chronicle.com/blogs/innovations/asian-americans-and-affirmative-action/32649

Kawai, Y. (2005) Stereotyping Asian Americans: The dialectic of the model minority and the yellow peril. *Howard Journal of Communications, 16*(2), 109–130.

Lee, S., Juon, H-S., Martinez, G., Hsu, C. E., Robinson, E. S., Bawa, J., & Ma, G. X. (2009). Model minority at risk: Expressed needs of mental health by Asian American young adults. *Journal of Community Health, 34*, 144–152.

Lee, S. J. (1994). Behind the model-minority stereotype: Voices of high- and low-achieving Asian American students. *Anthropolocy & Education Quarterly, 25*(4), 413–429.

Lee, S. J., & Kumashiro, K. K. (2005). *A report on the status of Asian Americans and Pacific Islanders in education: Beyond the "model minority" stereotype*. Washington, DC: National Education Association.

Lee, S. S. (2006). Over-represented and de-minoritized: The racialization of Asian Americans in higher education. *InterActions: UCLA Journal of Education and Information Studies, 2*(2). Retrieved from http://repositories.cdlib.org/gseis/interactions/vol2/iss2/art4

Lewis, A. E. (2003). Everyday race-making. *American Behavioral Scientist, 47*(3), 283–305.

Margolis, E., & Romero, M. (1998). The department is very male, very white, and very old, and very conservative: The functioning of the hidden curriculum in graduate sociology departments. *Harvard Educational Review: 68*(1), 1–33.

Martinez-Aleman, A. M. (2000). Race talks: Undergraduate women of color and female friendships. *The Review of Higher Education, 23*(2), 133–152.

McIntosh, P. (1989). White privilege: Unpacking the invisible knapsack. *Peace and Freedom*, July/August, 10–12.

McIntosh, P. (1990). White privilege: Unpacking the invisible knapsack. *Independent School, Winter*, 31–36.

Morrison, G. Z. (2010). Two separate worlds: Students of color at a predominantly white university. *Journal of Black Studies, 40*, 987–1015.

Museus, S. D., & Kiang, P. N. (2009). Deconstructing the model minority myth and how it contributes to the invisible minority reality in higher education research. *New Directions for Institutional Research, 14*(2), 5–15.

Museus, S. D., & Truong, K. A. (2009). Disaggregating qualitative data from Asian American college students in campus racial climate research and assessment. *New Directions for Institutional Research, 142*, 17–26.

Ng, J. C, Lee, S. S., & Pak, Y. K. (2007). Contesting the model minority and perpetual foreigner stereotypes: A critical review of literature on Asian Americans in education. *Review of Research in Education, 31*, 95–130.

Poon, O. A. (2009). Haunted by negative action: Asian Americans, admission, and race in the "Color-Blind Era." *Harvard University Asian American Policy Review, 18*. Retrieved from http://www.hks.harvard.edu/aapr/AAPR.pdf#page=91

54 ▪ J. LUI

Pyke, K., & Dang, T. (2003). "FOB" and "Whitewashed": Identity and internalized racism among second generation Asian Americans. *Qualitative Sociology, 26*(2), 147–172.

Pyon, H. T., Cao, Y., & Li, H. I. (2007). Between "what I am" and "what I am not": Asians and Asian Americans in contention and conversation. *Educational Perspectives, 40*(1), 13–18.

Smith, W. A., Yosso, T. J., & Solórzano, D. G. (2006). Challenging racial battle fatigue on historically White campuses: A critical race examination of race-related stress. In C. A. Stanley (Ed.), *Faculty of color teaching in predominantly White colleges and universities* (pp. 299–327). Bolton, MA: Anker.

Solórzano, D. G., & Yosso, T. J. (2002). Critical race methodology: Counterstorytelling as an analytical framework for education research. *Qualitative Inquiry, 5*(1), 23–44.

Sue, D. W., Bucceri, J., Lin, A. I., Nadal, K. L., & Torino, G. C. (2007). Racial microaggressions and the Asian American experience. *Cultural Diversity and Ethnic Minority Psychology, 13*(1), 72–81.

Suzuki, B. G. (2002). Revisiting the model minority stereotype: Implications for student affairs practice and higher education. In M. K. McEwen, C. M. Kodama, A. N. Alvarez. S. Lee, & C. T. H. Liang (Eds.), *Working with Asian American college students* (pp. 21–32). San Francisco, CA: Jossey Bass.

Takaki, R. (1989). *Strangers from a different shore: A history of Asian Americans.* Boston, MA: Little, Brown & Company.

Teranishi, R. T. (2010). *Asians in the ivory tower: Dilemmas of racial inequality in American higher education.* New York, NY: Teachers College Press.

Teranishi, R. T., Behringer, L. B., Grey, E. A., & Parker, T. L. (2009). Critical race theory and research on Asian Americans and Pacific Islanders in higher education. *New Directions for Institutional Research, 142,* 57–68.

Wang, L. L. (1995). Meritocracy and diversity in higher education: Discrimination against Asian Americans in the *post-Bakke* era. In D. T. Nakanishi & T. Y. Nishida (Eds.), *The Asian American educational experience* (pp. 285–302). New York, NY: Routledge.

Weber, L. (2006). A conceptual framework for understanding race, class, gender, and sexuality. *Psychology of Women Quarterly, 22,* 13–32.

Weidman, J. C., Twale, D. J., & Stein, E. L. (2001). *Socialization of graduate and professional students in higher education: A perilous passage?* San Francisco, CA: Jossey-Bass.

Wu, F. (1995). Neither Black nor White: Asian Americans and affirmative action. *Third World Law Journal, 15,* 225–284.

CHAPTER 4

LEADERSHIP, ACCOUNTABILITY, AND DIVERSITY IN HIGHER EDUCATION

A Critical Race Counterstory

Eugene Oropeza Fujimoto and Noemy Medina

Public funding for higher education has seen a precipitous decline in recent years. Simultaneously, the call for increased accountability has been
on the rise. This chapter discusses ways in which such current issues have
affected the direction of a particular four-year, comprehensive state university in the Midwest. Drawing on a composite of administrative experiences at several institutions, a counterstory (Solórzano & Yosso, 2002) was
developed revealing how these larger issues can affect the very mission of
a state institution that was originally intended to serve a particular local
area. By compromising the mission, the role of leaders and their complicity
in perpetuating social and educational inequality based on race and class
becomes evident. An analysis based in critical race theory and the present-

Envisioning Critical Race Praxis in Higher Education Through Counter-Storytelling, pages 55–73
Copyright © 2016 by Information Age Publishing
All rights of reproduction in any form reserved.

ing of a narrative that counters the dominant perspective on administrative decision making helps to effectively interrogate decisions and processes generally hidden from view. The following review of the literature provides a context of some of what we know about the accountability movement and the ever decreasing public funding of higher education in the U.S. along with a brief look at retention issues faced by low-income students of color.

LITERATURE REVIEW

Higher Education and Accountability

When the U.S. economy struggles, states and state departments fight over fewer resources (Bruininks, Keeney, & Thorp, 2010). When resources are allocated, few departments are safe from scrutiny, and the more evidence of productivity and efficiency you are able to provide, the more likely you are to secure both federal and state aid (Webber & Boehmer, 2008). Education is no exception. Accountability has become increasingly important in all levels of education, due in part to new legislation, changing economic trends, and shifting public opinion. Thus, there is increased competition for federal funding, state funding, and student enrollments.

Institutions of higher education no longer rely on consistent public support in terms of their mission or funding and as a result have needed to change quickly in recent years in order to maintain a positive image (Gumport, 2000; Slaughter, 1993). However, as institutions adapt and develop strategies to respond to the changing economy and new public demands, there is an inevitable tension between those who advocate for fundamental change and those who look to protect the traditions of higher education (Gumport, 2000, 2001; Rhoades & Slaughter, 2004). Gumport (2000) stated, "Over the last 25 years, . . . the dominant legitimating idea of higher education has changed from higher education as a social institution to higher education as an industry" (p. 68). With decreased federal and state support (de Oliver & Briscoe, 2011), institutions of higher education have been forced to change and do so rapidly (Gumport, 2000). Increasingly, institutions operate using a business model, viewing students as consumers to whom they sell a product: in this case, a degree (Bruininks et al., 2010). How has this shift in philosophy and practice affected students?

In order to make up for the decreased government support, tuition has been on the rise and financial aid has not kept pace with this upwardly spiraling cost (Webber & Boehmer, 2008). The resulting lack of affordability and increased competitiveness has an immediate negative effect on those students from low-income backgrounds, disproportionately from communities of color, who may otherwise be eligible to attend a college or university (Liu, 2011b; Webber & Boehher, 2008). In order to stay functional and competitive, institutions of higher education have determined that they must increase tuition to cover operational and personnel costs. Thus, the burden of decreased funding is often passed down to the student, slowly but surely leaving out those at the economic, social, and cultural margins (Somers & St. John, 1997).

But colleges and universities are not all the same. As institutions approach these economic challenges, they must plan for the short and long term (Bruininks et al., 2010). For institutions that have a tradition of serving their local community, these shifts in budget allocations and accountability may disrupt that relationship. If institutions look to maintain functionality, much less reputation, they must maintain funding and performance levels. The sources of this funding and the ways in which it is acquired have raised many questions in regards to the maintaining of the educational access mission of such institutions. If there is divestment in the community, the community loses valuable resources with which it could look to solve its own problems (Freire, 1972; Kretzmann & McKnight, 1993). Thus, the pressure for institutions of higher education to "perform" falls largely upon the leadership. And there is perhaps no greater performance challenge than to increase higher education's level of success with the increasingly diverse population of students entering their doors. This chapter examines the response of leadership to this growing pressure.

Underrepresented Students of Color and Persistence

In addition to affecting access, funding shifts that increase tuition can contribute to lowering persistence among underrepresented students of color as well (Carter, 2006). The decrease in federal financial aid grants in the past two decades has left many students who were otherwise eligible to attend public four-year institutions enrolling in community colleges (St. John, 1994) because they are a more affordable alternative. However, low-SES, underrepresented students of color also persist at lower rates as a result of their perceptions of college costs being higher when compared to White students of a similar SES (St. John, 2000). In addition to financial challenges, students from underserved backgrounds are associated with poor academic preparation, for which institutions must also provide opportunities and resources for remediation once they arrive (Bruininks et al., 2010). As a result, administrators such as those featured in the counterstory in this chapter perceive diverse students as responsible for low institutional achievement in terms of accountability measures. Carter (2006) suggests that some institutions may practice inadvertent discrimination when they do not conduct effective research in order to effectively serve the most needy populations. Furthermore, Carter (2006) also asserts that it is the responsibility of campus leaders to work to solve the existing racial achievement and persistence gap by conducting research and developing interventions to assist these students. Some scholars believe "[t]he strength of American higher education comes, in part, from the diversity of students who enroll for study" (Webber & Boehmer, 2008, p. 80).

In her explanation of community cultural wealth, Yosso (2005) presents the differences in students from diverse backgrounds as assets. This asset perspective is one that is difficult for middle-class White people to see as well as those of underrepresented populations who have internalized the deficit and discriminatory actions they have experienced from the dominant culture (Delgado & Stefancic, 2012). Some see this growing diversity as a challenge; others see it as an opportunity to attract underrepresented students with fresh perspectives given their varied life experiences (Solórzano & Yosso, 2002), while still others equate providing access to diverse students with lowering academic standards, leading to continued discriminatory practices that deny access to underrepresented students (Delgado & Stefancic, 2012). If administrators work with the local community, which in the case of this counterstory is highly racially diverse, they may discover that the solution to the issues of enrollment and persistence can be solved in partnership with the community (Freire, 1972) with no need to reallocate or increase personnel costs in order to recruit "better" students. Additionally, pressure for accountability often does not consider the time it takes to make sustainable change. The need for immediate results can distract attention from existing issues and can compromise the mission and vision of an institution.

ANALYTICAL FRAMEWORK

While leadership has been the topic of extensive discussion and scholarship, rarely has critical race theory (CRT) been used as a form of analysis. CRT originated in the 1970s from critical legal studies and radical feminism (Delgado & Stefancic, 2012). From critical legal studies, CRT adopted legal indeterminacy, which argues that "not every legal case has one correct outcome" (Delgado & Stefancic, 2012, p. 5); from radical feminism, CRT adopted "the relationship between power and the construction of social roles" (p. 5). In providing a critique of how the legal system has been complicit in the development of inequitable systems and structures based on race, CRT has been adapted to other disciplines, including the field of education (Ladson-Billings & Tate 1995; Taylor, 1999).

With the understanding that there is no monolithic definition upon which all critical race theorists would agree, several concepts were core in the analysis used in this chapter. These include a recognition of social inequality based on race, class, gender, and other forms of social identity; how issues of power and privilege as socially constructed "realities" maintain such inequalities; that social institutions often can and do serve to produce and reproduce social inequalities; that the manifestation of power and privilege in the service of this production and reproduction of inequality is always contested and unstable; that all research is based in one's values and political orientations; and that the focus of this research should ultimately serve the purpose of dismantling forms of oppression toward a liberatory and emancipatory end (Apple, 2004; Crenshaw, Gotanda, Peller, & Thomas, 1995; Delgado & Stefancic, 2012; Kincheloe & McLaren, 2000).

The "counterstory" is a particularly appropriate method to examine leadership, as those at the top of institutional hierarchies are notable for maintaining an air of caution in public interactions. This caution leads to a sense of mystery around the workings of leadership and the bureaucracy and politics that surround it. This mystery is typically sensed by all except a few "insiders."

Our intention is to uncloak this sense of mystery; therefore this counterstory addresses the following issues: (1) how increased accountability measures impact the allocation of resources during times of budget constraints, (2) how accountability can impact recruitment and service to the community, and (3) the role and responsibility that leadership has in advocating for issues of diversity, equity, and social justice.

* * *

It is a gorgeous fall day in the Midwest, with blue skies and trees turning bright yellow, orange, and crimson. My office is a good-sized one. It is even south facing with a view from the fifth floor, overlooking rows of those brilliantly colored trees, extending out to a residential area. It is one of the "perks" of being an administrator at the university. But it is with a sense of foreboding that I look out over that residential area, as I wonder how well we will continue to effectively serve this community.

FUNDING AND ACCOUNTABILITY

When I decided to come to Midwest University (MU) three years ago as an associate vice president for diversity, I was largely attracted to this mid-sized, comprehensive university by their accurate claim of being the most ethnically diverse campus in the state. Not coincidentally, as the president of MU at the time would often tout, 40% of our students were from the lowest quintile socioeconomically in the country. That means the bottom

20% in terms of income. We served a poor and working-class community, devastated by the departure of manufacturing jobs overseas in recent decades. There were over 20% students of color, the largest segment being African American. As the provost would often say, we were as close to being an "open access" four-year university as you could find. But change was in the air. . . .

"Did you hear the latest on the budget, Henry?" asked Paul, our financial aid director, as I poured hot water for my daily cup of green tea in the cafeteria.

"More good news, I'm sure," I deadpanned, as we found a table together.

"Of course! The governor's proposed budget calls for another $250 million cut to higher education over the biennium. That's $125 million cut for this year and next. It would be about 11% of our total budget!" exclaimed Paul, as he gulped down his tar black coffee.

"Incredible. How many years in a row can we keep this up?" I said, shaking my head.

"Keep what up?" interrupted Sofia, our human resources director.

"Oh, not much, just another 11% budget cut coming up," quipped Paul.

"Oh yeah. I saw the headline this morning too. All part of the 'new normal', right?" said the always sarcastic Sofia. "You should have heard my staff this morning; they were beside themselves."

"Yup. And you know we will just end up passing this on to students through more tuition increases," said Paul.

"And of course, vacant positions that go unfilled," added Sofia. "You know what they say, efficiency is the name of the game; we just need to learn to do 'more with less'!"

"Speaking of doing more, I've got to get to an IE committee meeting. See you folks later," I said.

As I left, I couldn't help but think they were probably right. With the gravity of the cuts to the higher education portion of state budgets around the country (de Oliver & Briscoe, 2011), it wasn't likely we would see any substantial reinvestment from the state for a long time. And in part the "more with less" was related to the accountability movement that would demand results and our ability to show them. We had our work cut out for us. And the value of "efficiency" (Gumport, 1997), as Sofia mentioned, goes almost unquestioned. In spite of the work of people like Weick (1995), Gumport (2000), and others who extended our notions of educational institutions as merely mechanistic, rationally driven organizations, I could not help but think that the functionalist approach as core to leading organizations has never really left us. While our missions have evolved to be more inclusive of the communities that surround institutions, the methods of accountability have not. All institutions are expected to perform similarly even if the populations that they serve are not. And, I wondered, what did this mean for a place like MU and its open-access mission?

RACIAL ACHIEVEMENT GAPS

The inclusive excellence (IE) committee was in its second year. We had done substantial work in analyzing data on student achievement with a focus on closing racial achievement gaps. The committee now knew more than anyone on campus about the key areas that needed addressing to create a more equitable campus environment. And with strong support from the president, things were looking up. It was not long before the committee discussion got heated.

"It is unbelievable to me that in fall 2005 so many of our first-year students were on academic probation," said Mina, a math professor.

"I was surprised as well—23.6% of all of our freshmen students on probation. But what about African American males: 43.3% or 58 out of the 134 are on academic probation in their first year. And Black females right there also at 42.6% on probation. And Latino males at 31.1% is nothing to be proud of either," exclaimed Jaime, a biologist.

Rita, our institutional researcher chimed in: "And don't forget that we had similar numbers in the other two years we looked at as well. So, unfortunately, this is not an anomaly for us."

We mined the data for clues on what could be factors in why this was occurring. Academic preparation was certainly a factor. But interestingly, entering White students with the same ACT scores as Black students at almost all levels were faring better in terms of retention and graduation. It was data like this that spurred our recommendations to ramp up our programming for first-year students. This included hiring two full time advisors to focus specifically on first-year students on probation. Developmental skills courses were examined as well, with recommendations to place more full-time instructors in these courses, and fewer adjuncts. Committee discussions included much more radical ideas, including questioning the existence of developmental skills courses altogether, with evidence that students placing in basic skills levels can make more academic progress by taking college-level English and math courses right out of high school rather than languishing in developmental courses term after term. We also questioned the continued use of ACT scores that have consistently been shown to disadvantage Black and Brown students (Zwick, 2007). But strategically and politically, there was a time and place for these recommendations. And at this time, this report was not it.

Long-term plans discussed by the committee included working in collaboration with local school districts to align curricula with the university in

English, math, and reading, as well as developing collaborations with our teacher education program on culturally relevant pedagogy for the K–12 teachers. As disturbing as the achievement gap data were, the committee was buoyed by the concrete recommendations and hopes for change. And we all knew we were at the point where the real work would need to happen.

AGENDA SETTING

The president's cabinet met every Tuesday morning at 7:30 a.m. The usual early arrivers were always there first, claiming their seats at the long, oblong shaped table. Of course, the seating never varied, regardless of who got there early. President Hope was always at the head of the table, Provost Eleanor Meyer to his immediate left, Vice President of Student Affairs Bill Turner next, then me, and then Associate Provost Michael Cooper. To the right of the president was his special assistant Ellen Iverson, then Vice President of Advancement John Brockmeyer, Vice President of Enrollment Services Tom Snook, and then the new Vice President of Finance and Administration Hector Olivas. The proximity to the president was obviously most desirable. And it was largely dependent upon seniority, except if you were president, provost, or special assistant. Those seats were designated no matter when you took the role. It was a standing joke how the seating never varied, yet we all knew how serious it was as well.

I remember the day well. I entered the room just as the meeting was beginning to see Associate Provost Cooper sitting in my chair. He had apparently decided it was time to move up a seat. I let it go for that meeting, but at the next meeting, "jokingly" let it be known that my place was not up for grabs. There was laughter, but also a clear understanding that it was not OK by me. I kept my place from then on. It was a "game," but a serious one that you could not afford to lose if you were going to be a significant player.

The racial composition of the cabinet was typical for that part of the country. Seven of the nine members were White. Olivas, a Latino from Texas, had just joined us. For as long as folks could remember, the only person of color who had served on the cabinet had been in the diversity position I held. As the only Asian American and person of color in the administration up to the point of Olivas' hire, Hector was a welcome sight for me. But still it was clear that the top five members of the cabinet in terms of seniority and influence were all White, with four of those five being White males. And long-time special assistant Ellen Iverson, although not hierarchically in a position of power, took her "gatekeeping" role very seriously. She was one person everyone knew not to cross.

While the internal group politics of the cabinet were significant, there was an assumed and somewhat odd sense of camaraderie in this group as well. The obvious absence of faculty, student affairs staff, classified staff, and students on this most important body was indicative of the political need for the president to have a trusted body of advisors who were his "team." Yet the air of competitiveness within the group was also unmistakable, and the assumed confidential nature of the discussions lent an air of mystery on the campus as to what happened behind these closed doors.

That next Tuesday at president's cabinet, Rhonda Thomas, the admissions director had been invited to bring the latest enrollment numbers to the cabinet. It was not good news.

"You can see from the chart on your handout that not only is it not looking like we will grow this year, but we have been relatively flat for the last three years," said Rhonda.

"What is happening here? When we last heard from you earlier in the semester, the numbers appeared to be up significantly," said Vice President Brockmeyer.

"Yes, and our projections from previous years told us we would be up in FTES by a fairly comfortable margin," said Vice President Snook.

"We need to get to the bottom of what is going on with our students this semester", said President Hope.

I decided to venture into the conversation. "I don't know if this is connected at all, but the inclusive excellence committee has been uncovering some very interesting information on our first-year students."

"What kind of information?" inquired Vice President Snook.

"Well, it is hard to capture in a nutshell, but the numbers of students who end up on academic probation in their first year on campus is very high, particularly for our African American and Latino students. About one-fourth of new students overall, and over 40% for some groups of color," I explained.

"OK, if those numbers are a factor in our overall enrollment decline, why does it appear to be worse this year?" asked Provost Meyer.

"Well, I'm sure there are multiple factors. But I can tell you we have had advisors leave that have not been replaced. And two full-time lecturers in our developmental skills courses retired, with more courses now being taught by new adjuncts with little experience," I offered.

"I'm sure we can all speculate on possible reasons, but we need solid data to get at this. Henry, work with Rhonda to try and bring your data together to see what we can find out. Report back to us next week," said President Hope.

Rhonda and I nodded to each other in understanding. There were a few glances and smiles around the table. Everyone knew this was no small task the president had just given us. And we all knew from previous meetings that the pressure from system administration to grow was never more intense. With the ever-present budget cuts to our bottom line, the "doing more with less" adage took on an ominous tone. But the president wasn't done.

"And Tom, I want you and Hector to pull together the integrated marketing team to work on a strategy to increase our reach with short- and long-term goals for this enrollment issue right away. Let's hear from both of you in two weeks." The President was in no mood for equivocation this time around. The IMT was a relatively new committee, and President Hope clearly saw them as key players in providing direction. And those of us on the IE committee knew those players had a very different agenda than we did. This move by the president also placed Vice President Snook in a particularly powerful position. We all knew that Snook had become a favorite of the president. Snook was smart, capable, and he understood budgets better than anyone on the cabinet, including the president. And it did not hurt that he graduated from Penn State, which was also President Hope's alma mater.

We knew as well that all presidents were under tremendous pressure to grow our campuses—and that this relatively small and exclusive group that made up the cabinet would make decisions over the next few weeks that would greatly impact not only the campus, but the community as well. The agenda had been set, and those of us advocating for diversity had our work cut out for us.

THE NEW NORMAL

Over the next couple of months, the pressure was intense to develop and implement a plan. In many ways, it may have been an ideal time for the recommendations from the IE committee to be taken seriously. With the growing ethnic diversity of the state and local population (over 50% of K–12 students in our local area were now students of color, with Latinos and Blacks making up the largest groups), we had to close this racial achievement gap. We could not increase our success rates overall until we figured this out. At least that's what I thought at the time. I heard footsteps approaching my door quickly. It was Mina. She closed the door behind her. She was clearly agitated.

"Hi Mina. What is going on? You look like you just saw Michael Jackson," I said.

"Much worse than that, Henry. I just came from the integrated marketing team meeting," Mina blurted out, as upset as I've ever seen her.

"OK, take a deep breath. What on earth happened? Was Michael moonwalkin'?" I asked. "OK, that's enough, funny guy. Remember two weeks ago when I told you it looked like the IMT was going to adopt much of the IE committee recommendations into their plan? Well, that just went out the window." Mina shook her head in disgust.

"They can't do that. They don't even have a long-range plan that will serve our students. All they have are those cockamamie ideas to extend recruitment to affluent White areas and raise ACT requirements," I exclaimed.

Mina stared at me without saying a word.

"No, don't tell me that is what they decided on today? Wasn't there any challenging of the direction that would take us as a campus?" I was appalled.

"Of course, but you know how this works," said Mina. "Snook knows exactly what he is doing. He knows that to overtly decide to change focus on recruitment to areas outside our catchment area and to raise ACT requirements would be politically very difficult. So, instead, remember the one-year-only positions to recruit out of the area students into our new residence halls?"

"He wants to make them permanent," I said.

"Exactly. Under the guise that they have been 'so successful' and we cannot afford to stop this effort given the growth pressures we are under," said Mina. "He even had the nerve to say these positions could spend time locally as needed as well, even though we know *that* will never happen."

"This is exactly what I warned against when the one-year positions were approved in the first place," I interjected. "And the admissions requirements. Now our recent discussion at president's cabinet makes sense. Rhonda presented information on the students at different levels of ACT scores and their retention rates. Of course, not disaggregated by race. I insisted on that, but she said she will get that to us next month. And of course, the lower levels of ACT scores are not succeeding at the same rates."

"But that is who our students are!" exclaimed Mina. "We are failing at getting them through, so instead of figuring out what we can do more effectively, let's go get new students? Unbelievable!"

I shook my head in disgust. "And we know the admissions process is much more subjective than most people realize. We recently have been espousing this idea of holistic admissions, looking at the whole student, not just test scores and high school GPAs. But ultimately, we revert to those test scores. Even though we know that the best predictor of success in higher education is family income! (Carter, 2006). Well, what about Hector—as co-chair, did he say anything?"

"Very little. I could tell he was disturbed, but he is new enough, it is pretty difficult for him to oppose something like this. And I am not sure he has been around long enough to understand the politics that Tom is playing," said Mina.

With the rising pressure for accountability, the vice president of enrollment management position has become increasingly important. And Tom Snook, after seven years at MU, is a seasoned and smart administrator who knows the System and the institution very well. As a White man, he is also smart enough to know that he must at least appear to support diversity efforts to survive the racial politics on the campus. Snook has spent the last couple of years developing strong relationships with key faculty of color. We all knew who his lunch buddies and golfing partners were, and Snook's cultivating of relationships with the current and past chairs of the Minority Faculty and Staff Association (MFSA) were no accident. And the MFSA had remained silent on many key diversity issues in which Tom was a part.

The next day, our fears began to be realized. The two forms came across my desk in the late morning. They were requests to turn the two previously approved one-year only positions for outreach into the northern and western parts of the state into permanent positions. They were originally approved for the short-term goal of recruiting to fill the new residence hall for the following fall. Now they would become permanent positions, with a focus outside the area. What this meant was a focus into more White, more affluent areas, with schools that produced higher test scores than our local schools. When I expressed my outrage to my supervisor, he tried to tell me that the recruitment office would keep up their focus on the local schools as well. Even he knew his argument sounded hollow.

I refused to sign the approvals for the two positions. And I made my argument in writing to attach to the form. I knew when it got to the provost, she would call me in, give her explanation, and sign regardless of my objection. After running this around in my mind, I knew it was time to get some sage advice.

A CRITICAL RACE THEORY ANALYSIS

I caught Dr. Thomas on the phone, just returning from his Saturday walk with his wife. Deron Thomas was a semiretired vice president at two different institutions, and a long-time friend and mentor. I say semiretired because he seems constantly busy with speaking, writing, and consulting gigs as a result of his long and esteemed career in higher education. I was fortunate to have him to call on when I felt stuck.

"Dr. T, did I catch you at a bad time?" I asked.

"No such thing as a bad time to talk with you Henry. The wife and I are just putting a few things away we picked up at the market. They had some beautiful greens for this time of year. How is the family? How is that beautiful daughter of yours?" Dr. Thomas was as welcoming as ever.

"We're all doing very well. Maia's in her second year of college and loves it; Samuel is almost as tall as I am already. And Maria and I are fine. You and Mrs. Thomas are well?" I asked.

"Couldn't be better. Old age catchin' up with us a bit, but just part of life. So what can I do for you?" said Dr. Thomas. I heard the rustling of bags and cabinet doors opening and closing on the other end of the phone.

"Well, I've run into a few obstacles at MU that I thought I might get your thoughts on," I replied.

"Nothing like a few obstacles to get my juices goin', Henry. Let me grab my iced tea here . . . tell me what's been happening." I could hear Dr. T getting settled in to his chair.

Dr. Thomas was one of the few upper-level administrators I have met in higher education who rose through the ranks to become a vice president while truly maintaining his sense of integrity and passion. He had many offers to move to the presidency, but he saw the ways in which presidents' roles were increasingly focused on fundraising and public relations. His main interests were maintaining scholarly pursuits while focusing on the campus and the community it serves. And he did that better than anyone I know.

I had spoken to Dr. T enough over my time at MU that he knew the players, the history and mission of the campus, and some of the politics as well.

"Well, as you know, Dr. T, we have been making concerted effort to address the racial achievement gaps on our campus. And our inclusive excellence committee has done a great job of uncovering very important data on what is happening with our students. We have a strategy with short- and long-term goals that we are convinced will move us in the right direction. And with President Hope's support, we have been in a very good place to move forward," I explained.

"I know that this effort has been a main focus for you lately. It sounds very promising. What's getting in the way? Is Hope backin' off on his support?" asked Dr. T.

"Yes and no. That's part of what I want to talk with you about." I explained the situation in detail to Dr. T. There was a long pause on the phone before Dr. T responded.

"What you are experiencing, Henry, is one of my greatest fears regarding the direction of higher education in recent years. We already know that when there is a large-scale public divestment in education, as has been the case for some time in our colleges and universities, change is coming soon. What's the saying, 'nature abhors a vacuum'? Well, so does capitalism. So 'academic capitalism' (Gumport, 2000; Kezar, 2004; Rhoades & Slaughter, 2004) is well upon us, as privatization has quickly filled the vacuum left by this public divestment," Dr. T. opined.

"OK, there has been recent increase in campus, particularly faculty, involvement in 'market like behaviors' (Rhoades & Slaughter, 2004, p. 37), but some would argue that higher education has been partnering with industry for a hundred years; that this is not new, in fact it is the market that has been key to the success of colleges and universities" (Gioia & Thomas, 1996; Zemsky, 1993), I replied.

"Fair enough. But only in the last 50 years, and the last 20 in particular, have the neoliberals been successful in moving higher education substantially toward seeing students as 'human capital' and shifting their function to job preparedness (Kezar, 2004, p. 437). And the cost of this move away from developing students' 'higher order thinking skills' (p. 443) toward seeing them as receptacles to receive information as opposed to developing a 'critical consciousness' (Freire, 2007) has been catastrophic. Particularly for oppressed groups, where the priority on individualism has not only led them to historical and cultural amnesia, but moved them toward an ideological vacuum that results in abandoning their communities, and in some cases their own families. The sense of a communal existence is being eradicated," Dr. T. said emphatically.

I needed some time to digest the conversation. I took a deep breath and replied, "If we are that close to 'eradication' of our communities, if privatization has already moved in, don't we need to learn how to work toward equity within academic capitalism? I read a study recently that talked about 'industry-friendly' relationships with academe (Mendoza, 2012), and much depends on the context," I responded.

"I saw the same article. The author makes an interesting argument about the integrity of the faculty research in the context of these 'industry-friendly' departments. I also noted that she does not address the issue of the dramatic shift in funding away from humanities, social sciences, and education, toward business and the STEM fields that has been going on since the 1980s (Slaughter, 1993). So you may well be able to find departments in these areas that are ethically doing what they should be. But these other disciplines that are less able to show themselves as producing industry-ready students, will continue to struggle. 'Industry-friendly' departments in business and the STEM fields will at best maintain the status quo of inequality and, at worst, make it unlikely that research that challenges this status quo will be taking place.

"Also, notice, much of what the author considers benefits are those to the individuals and their job prospects, students learning about the world outside of academe, or even departments and their short-term interests. And the long-term concerns raised by social scientists and education faculty (Gumport, 2000; Kezar, 2004; Slaughter & Rhoades, 2004) that contextualize the issues in a more societal or global context of social justice remain unaddressed. This is also where a critical race theory perspective can provide insight. If we acknowledge that inequities based on race, class, and gender are normative (Delgado & Stefancic, 2012; Ladson-Billings & Tate, 1995)— that is, they are part of the fabric of our society and our institutions—only then can we view these issues from this larger social justice lens," said Dr. T.

"Yes, I can see that the theoretical framework you use to analyze data can impact what you find! But what about the whole accountability movement? In part this is what is pressuring administrators to make decisions that, to me, seem contradictory to the mission of our institutions!" I exclaimed.

"Good question," affirmed Dr. T. "One thing we know is that the Department of Education has been pushing this agenda of measuring higher education through economics and accountability for quite a few years now (Suspitsyna, 2012). As I was saying earlier, this has been happening to the point that some are saying a fundamental change has been going on; the change 'from higher education as a social institution to higher education as an industry' (Gumport, 2001, p. 243). Now this can mean many things. Consistent with the idea of 'academic capitalism,' higher education as an 'industry' is seeing education and knowledge as a commodity; something that can be bought and sold. And in the context of our so-called 'meritocracy', education becomes a privilege for the few. For example, as we continue to use standardized test scores to predict student's ability to succeed in college, those that can afford the privately offered test preparation programs such as Kaplan, will succeed at higher rates.

"Along with this 'myth of meritocracy' (Liu, 2011a) comes the increasing need to clearly define who is deserving of a college education, and who is not. And to ensure 'efficiency' is a top priority in moving students through the system. So, when a business model is used instead of an educational model, the primary measure of success is one of cost-effectiveness. Thus the strong push for 'accountability.' How well are you utilizing the dollars you are being provided to achieve your goal of increased graduates? This is a very different value system from a college education being a right for all people and an emphasis on serving the 'public good' (Nixon, 2011)."

I was getting more incensed the more we talked. "And this is why the MU actions are so troubling. After defending their mission for many years to work to provide educational opportunity for all students who want it in the local area, this push for accountability is being responded to by essentially abandoning the community! And then to act as if this is not what is going on...it's criminal..."

"That's one word for it. And my hunch is that the area you serve is changing demographically as well, am I right?" said Dr. T in a self-assured tone.

"As a matter of fact, our IE committee just looked at those figures. In Lakeview, in the last 10 years, the White population has gone from 63.5% to 53.5%. And in Castlerock, the White population went from 85.7% White in 2000, to 69.5% White in 2010. And the vast majority of the growth has been African American and Latino in both cities. White flight at its finest!" I said.

"And if you had the family income data, I would be confident that this figure has gone down for both cities. From a critical race theory perspective, we would say not only is this not surprising, but is merely part of a long and sordid history of racism in the U.S. As a population becomes more Black and Brown, the opportunities dwindle. In other words, racial segregation in and of itself is not the problem. It is when that racial segregation is accompanied by segregation of opportunities (Reece & Gambhir, 2008) that problems occur," said Dr. T.

"And the actions we are taking at MU are doing just that. Decreasing the opportunities for people of color as the population diversifies," I said.

"I'm afraid you are correct about that," said Dr. T.

"This sounds like a leadership issue to me. It is difficult to move in a different direction unless there is principled leadership willing to speak out strongly on these concerns of 'academic capitalism,' 'myth of meritocracy,' and how 'accountability' can be used to exclude," I said.

"I agree. But don't forget for many White folks, 'interest convergence' (Bell, 1995) is what will drive their decision making. They need to see what is in it for them. And I also believe we often need to expand our view of leadership. It doesn't necessarily mean those in formal positions of power. Or even within the institution," said Dr. T.

"I'm not sure what you mean," I said.

"Historically, remember that social movements are often grassroots movements. So who are the politically and racially conscious people on your campus, regardless of their position? My hunch is there are students, classified staff union members, student affairs folks, and faculty who may fit this category. Remember too, that one of the largest concerns that university presidents have on their minds is the perception of the campus by the community. Building awareness and relationships with key community folks can pay large dividends.

"And this leads me to a final thought on this. Kezar (2004), in her otherwise excellent treatise on the social good versus the industrial good in higher education, focuses on the 'market' forces versus the 'traditional' (p. 454) and the need to rethink the contract between these two forces. Yet she fails in any concrete way to discuss the community itself, which is served by the colleges and universities. The growing research on the overlooked but significant assets that exist in oppressed communities (Carter, 2003; Moll, Amanti, Neff & Gonzalez, 1992; Yosso, 2006) makes these communities the 'missing link' in the discussion. It is in these communities that much of the needed wisdom lies that can move higher education to where it needs to be.... Looks like I have to get movin' Henry. My wife needs my help getting ready for some guests we have coming soon. You keep me posted on how things are shakin' there. Remember that your concerns regarding serving the community are the right concerns. And never give up hope!" affirmed Dr. T.

"Thank you for taking the time, Dr. T. You've given me much to chew on. Best to your wife. I'll be in touch," I said.

* * *

It is clear that this campus' strategy is one way to increase graduation rates, close racial achievement gaps by imposing stricter admissions requirements, and be accountable to the increasing demands from accreditation visits. The story presents the covert, but looming, strategy of finding politically acceptable ways to increase ACT score admission requirements. In part, this is done by disaggregating success data by ACT scores, but not by race. Then one can provide rationale to raise ACT score requirements for admission, without a race-based examination of the impact on access. The resulting increase in ACT requirements for admission shuts out many students of color from being admitted. The campus then may be able to show how the students of color who do get admitted are doing better, more closely approximating rates of success by White students. Further, this divestment from the local service area is also a step toward abandoning the communities the university was intended to serve. The counterstory presented in this chapter is intended to shed light on these areas of possibility:

- Campus leaders learn to identify and challenge subtle shifts in direction that may result in a homogenization of the campus culture.
- Campus leaders use critical race theory as an analytical tool to strategize on how to interrupt and challenge decisions that perpetuate inequalities.
- Campus leaders utilize a "praxis" model (Freire, 1972) of decision making that places "critical consciousness" at the core of their process.

The use of a critical approach to leadership suggested here is intended to counteract the dominant narrative of a meritocratic system of education. The continued use of this mythology of meritocracy (Delgado & Stefancic, 2012; Liu, 2011a; Spring, 2013) to lead our institutions is contrary to the growing body of knowledge of the ways in which institutionalized racism and classism underlie many of our most pressing issues on student access and success. It is our hope that counternarratives such as this one can shed light on the development of more critically informed leadership theory and practice.

REFERENCES

Apple, M. W. (2004). *Ideology and curriculum* (3rd ed.). New York, NY: Routledge Falmer.

Bell, D. A. (1995). Brown v. Board of Education and the interest convergence dilemma. In K. Crenshaw, N. Gotanda, G. Peller, & K. Thomas (Eds.), *Critical race theory: The key writings that formed the movement* (pp. 20–28). New York, NY: The New Press.

Bruininks, R. H., Keeney, B., & Thorp, J. (2010). Transforming America's universities to compete in the "new normal." *Innovation in Higher Education 35*, 113–125.

Carter, P. L. (2003). "Black" cultural capital, status positioning, and schooling conflicts for low- income African American youth. *Society for the Study of Social Problems, 50*(1), 136–155.

Carter, D. F. (2006). Key issues in the persistence of underrepresented minority students. *New Directions for Institutional Research, 130,* 33–46.

Crenshaw, K., Gotanda, N., Peller, G., & Thomas, K. (1995). *Critical race theory: The key writings that formed the movement.* New York, NY: The New Press.

Delgado, R., & Stefancic, J. (2012). *Critical race theory: An Introduction.* New York, NY: NYU Press.

de Oliver, M. & Briscoe, F. M. (2011). U.S. higher education in a budgetary vortex—1992–2007: Tracing the positioning of academe in the context of growing inequality. *Higher Education, 62,* 607–618.

Freire, P. (1972). *Pedagogy of the oppressed.* New York, NY: Continuum Publishing Company.

Freire, P. (2007). *Education for critical consciousness.* New York, NY: Continuum.

Gioia, D. A., & Thomas, J. B. (1996). Identity, image, and issue interpretation: Sensemaking during strategic change in academia. *Administrative Science Quarterly, 41,* 370–403.

Gumport, P. J. (1997). Public universities as a workplace. *Daedalus, 126*(4), 113–136.

Gumport, P. (2000). Academic restructuring: Organizational change and institutional imperatives. *Higher Education, 39,* 67–91.

Gumport, P. J. (2001). Restructuring: Imperatives and opportunities for academic leaders. *Innovative Higher Education, 25*(4), 239–251.

Kezar, A. (2004). Obtaining intergrity? Reviewing and examining the charter between higher education and society. *The Review of Higher Education, 27*(4), 429–459.

Kincheloe, J. L., & McLaren, P. (2000). Rethinking critical theory and qualitative research. In N. K. Denzin & Y. S. Lincoln (Eds.), *Handbook of qualitative research* (2nd ed., pp. 279–314). Thousand Oaks, CA: Sage.

Kretzmann, J. P., & McKnight, J. L. (1993). *Building communities from the inside out: A path toward finding and mobilizing a community's assets.* Evanston, IL: Institute for Policy Research.

Ladson-Billings, G., & Tate W. F. (1995). Toward a critical race theory of education. *Teachers College Record, 97*(1), 47–68.

Liu, A. (2011a). Unraveling the myth of meritocracy within the context of U.S. higher education. *Higher Education, 62,* 383–397.

Liu, A. (2011b). The admission industrial complex: Examining the entrepreneurial impact on college access. *Journal of College Admission, 201,* 8–19.

Moll, L. C., Amanti, C., Neff, D., & Gonzalez, N. (1992). Funds of knowledge for teaching: Using a qualitative approach to connect homes and classrooms. *Theory into Practice, 31*(2), 132–141.

Nixon, J. (2011). *Higher education and the public good: Imagining the university.* London, UK: Continuum.

Reece, J., & Gambhir, S. (2008). *The geography of opportunity: Review of opportunity mapping research initiatives.* Columbus, OH: Kirwan Institute for the Study of Race and Ethnicity, The Ohio State University.

Rhoades, G. & Slaughter, S. (2004). Academic capitalism in the new economy: Challenges and choices. *American Academic, 1*(1), 37–60.

Slaughter, S. (1993). Retrenchment in the 1980s: The politics of prestige and gender. *The Journal of Higher Education, 64*(3), 250–282.

Solórzano, D., & Yosso, T. (2002). A critical race counter-story of affirmative action in higher education. *Equity and Excellence in Education, 35*(17), 155–168.

Somers, P., & St. John, E. P. (1997). Interpreting price response in enrollment decisions: A comparative institutional study. *Journal of Student Financial Aid, 29*(3), 15–36.

Spring, J. (2013). *The American school: A global context from the puritans to the Obama era* (9th ed.). New York, NY: McGraw Hill.

St. John, E. P. (1994). Assessing tuition and student aid strategies: Using price-response measures to stimulate pricing alternatives. *Research in Higher Education, 35*, 301–334.

St. John, E. P. (2000). The impact of student aid on recruitment and retention: What the research indicates. *New Directions for Student Services, 89*, 61–75.

Suspitsyna, T. (2012). Higher education for economic advancement and engaged citizenship: An analysis of the U.S. Department of Education Discourse. *The Journal of Higher Education, 83*(1), 49–72.

Taylor, E. (1999). Critical race theory and interest convergence in the desegregation of higher education. In L. Parker, D. Deyhle, & S. Villenas (Eds.), *Race is . . . race isn't: Critical race theory and qualitative studies in education* (pp. 181–204). Boulder, CO: Westview Press.

Webber, K. L., & Boehmer, R. G. (2008). The balancing act: Accountability, affordability, and access in American higher education. *New Directions for Institutional Research, (S2, Assessment Supplement)*, 79–91.

Weick, K. E. (1995). *Sensemaking in organizations.* Thousand Oaks, CA: SAGE Publications. Yosso, T. J. (2005). Whose culture has capital? A critical race theory discussion of community cultural wealth. *Race, Ethnicity and Education, 1*, 69–91.

Yosso, T. J. (2006). *Critical race counterstories along the Chicana/Chicano educational pipeline.* New York, NY: Routledge.

Zemsky, R. (1993). Consumer markets & higher education. *Liberal Education, 79*(3), 14–17. Zwick, R. (2007). College admissions in twenty-first-century America: The role of grades, tests, and games of chance. *Harvard Educational Review, 77*(4), 419–429.

CHAPTER 5

LA COMUNIDAD
ES LA FUERZA

Community Cultural Wealth of Latina/o
Leaders in Community College

Ignacio Hernández, Jr.

For Latina/os actively engaged in community college leadership preparation, gaining access to the leadership pipeline is a vital component of their
career pathway (Valverde, 2003; Weisman & Vaughan, 2007). In higher education, that pipeline is mediated by professional organizations and leadership preparation programs and institutes (León, 2005; McCurtis, Jackson,
& O'Callaghan, 2009). These organizations typically host annual conventions, regional conferences, and often sponsor and/or endorse a variety
of seminars and trainings for members across the professional spectrum
(León & Nevarez, 2007).

   Since their nascence in 1901, community colleges in the United States
have offered access to an array of educational programs, while only re-
quiring students to have earned a high school diploma or its equivalent
(Cohen, Brawer, & Kisker, 2013; Dougherty, 1994; Vaughan, 2006). This

Envisioning Critical Race Praxis in Higher Education Through Counter-Storytelling, pages 75–88
Copyright © 2016 by Information Age Publishing
75

open-door admissions policy has undoubtedly impacted the composition of the student bodies who enroll in these colleges, resulting in campuses with more working-class, older, and students of color than their four-year counterparts (Dougherty, 1994; Snyder & Dillow, 2011). Trend data since the late 1990s, however, show that four-year universities' and community colleges' administrative teams remain largely the domain of White individuals. White persons predominate the community college leadership pipeline (Eddy, 2010), while Black and Latina/o students compose large proportions of the student population (León, 2005; Snyder & Dillow, 2011).

Data reported by the United States Department of Education's (Snyder & Dillow, 2011) annual *Digest of Educational Statistics* quantify the disproportionate reality of Latina/os as students compared to Latina/os as leaders and administrators. The numbers show nearly 50% of all Latina/o undergraduates are enrolled in a public, two-year community college while Latina/os hold five percent of the executive or managerial positions in these colleges (Snyder & Dillow, 2011). Data collected and disseminated by the American Association of Community Colleges (AACC) confirm this stark reality. Current estimates indicated that six percent of all community college presidents and chancellors identify as Latina/o (AACC, 2013).

Community colleges present an ongoing reminder of the conflicting origins of their founding vision as well as their evolving missions. Because so many Latina/o students enroll in community colleges, one may find it a reasonable assumption to expect parity in administrative representation. Since the statistical data informs us that this is not the case, the stories of Latina/o students and leaders in community colleges deserve to be shared and brought to the center. In this chapter, I focus on Latina/o leaders in community colleges. These leaders face discrimination (Esquibel, 1992), are held to a higher standard than their White counterparts (Haro, 1995), and are often undervalued in the quotidian operations of their institutions (Valverde, 2003). These patterns of discrimination, unfair expectations, and general devaluing are taxing for Latina/o leaders working to hold community colleges accountable to their missions of open access and democratic education.

I present this counterstory to detail the discovery process of five composite characters who are community college leaders. Each is confronting the harsh racialized realities in his or her career pathway. This reality is often in contrast with their idealism and commitment to educational equity for all stakeholders invested in the community college movement. The counterstory is narrated by Gerardo Duarte, a director of institutional research at a mid-size community college in the Southwest. Erica Nuñez, a department chair, and Luis Escobedo, a provost, work in Southwestern Community College District (SCCD), a large, urban, multicampus community college district. Erica and Luis are spearheading an effort to develop a leadership group at SCCD. Martín Archuleta and Analisa Valdez already hold leadership positions and are each eager to learn and develop new skills. All five characters are attending the Community College Association's annual convention. Their story begins during the keynote speech at lunch.

*   *   *

The grilled chicken and baby carrots were typical for these types of professional, banquet-style keynote-lunch sessions. I asked the server for *chile,* really meaning Tapatío, but he instead brought those mini Tabasco bottles along with a sheepish smile that made us feel he wanted the same hot sauce we did. The hum of the room was dotted with the clanking of silverware and the awkward conversations about the schools we worked in and the roles we held. Erica Nuñez was sitting to my left, quietly tapping my forearm to ask which water glass was hers, mouthing "bread, drink?" while making two okay hand signals. I nodded and we giggled just before the high-pitched feedback of the microphone reverberated across the ballroom. We listened intently to the convocation of the Community College Association's (CCA) annual convention. The speech was full of clichéd talking points about how community colleges admit 100% of all applicants while creating jobs for local communities. Erica had been a department chair for nearly a decade now, so her regular attendance at this convention signaled her clear intent to ascend her college's organizational chart. She had reminded me during the cab ride from the airport, "I really feel ready to apply for the dean position that recently opened up." I met Erica the year before when we participated in a fellowship sanctioned by the CCA specifically for Latina/o community college leaders. She introduced me to other Latina/os from the Southwest Community College District (SCCD) who were also on an upward leadership trajectory.

I came to know Martín Archuleta during the CCA fellowship. We quickly developed a friendly bond, discussing community colleges within the broad context of higher education in the United States. Over the past year we stayed in touch, exchanging emails and text messages. Erica and Martín held the same positions in adjacent community colleges within SCCD, so they relied on one another for support in district-wide meetings, where they were often part of a small group of people of color, and usually the only two Latina/os. The lunch keynote presentation was about to end when the speaker closed by imploring the crowd to work more diligently to foster a diverse campus culture. The three of us immediately looked at one another.

President Maxwell of Midwestern Plains Community College is a senior leader in CCA, one of those godfather-ish characters with the monogramed shirts and cufflinks to prove it. He was a tall man with the sort of receding hairline and mix of gray and brown hair that gave him a distinguished appearance. He spoke with a Tommy Lee Jones-like twang that sort of made you feel he was up on stage just telling stories rather than talking about the impending leadership vacuum facing community colleges as more and more of his contemporaries received their AARP cards. During this closing talk, President Maxwell waxed rhetorically about how we could face the diversity crisis. He exclaimed: "I tell you what, we have lots of Hispanics at my college, right near four percent of all the students on campus." He glanced over at his provost who was nodding in agreement. "And you know what?" He stated, "They are very hard working and have decent values, but it's just that too many come from a culture where education is just not that important to them." You could see heads nodding in agreement across the audience. "We have to do something for them so they can see education is the right path. Here's what we're doin'.... We have a partnership with the local welding company who makes drivetrains for Tractors International where our students could get jobs paying upwards of $14 an hour. Quite a decent wage for them if you ask me." Attendees greeted his workforce development story with applause. I looked over at Erica to gauge her reaction as we withheld our applause; her puckered lips made the loudest sound I had heard all lunch.

After the keynote presentation concluded and the long ovation and applause subsided, a throng of attendees made their way to the stage to shake hands with President Maxwell. Erica, Martín, and I made our way to the foyer perpendicular to the ballroom, where Analisa Valdez found the three of us. "*Oh-Em-Gee!*" she exclaimed. "Did you guys hear that crap about us coming from a culture that doesn't value education?"

Dr. Valdez, a vice president of student affairs at a community college in New York and a proud Nuyorican, huddled us together and asked, "How could this guy say his campus has lots of Hispanics and they're only four percent of his students? *Pa' mi que el esta pal carajo.*" We laughed as her Spanglish began flowing like a river downstream. She explained to us that her college is one of the eleven federally designated Hispanic Serving Institutions in New York (HACU, 2013) and that their fall enrollment numbers had shown Latina/os making up nearly 38% of the total student body. Erica, a true practitioner-scholar, reminded us about the most recent iteration of the *Digest of Educational Statistics* data (Snyder & Dillow, 2011), sharing, "*Ustedes saben que de los* 2.5 million Latina/o undergraduates in the United States, *como 1.2 million estan* enrolled in a community college?" I nodded to confirm I had read the latest Digest. Martín did some quick calculations on his iPhone and turned the screen towards us to show 0.48046: "48%," he said. Analisa confirmed our calculation. "I had coffee with CCA's data analysts a month ago and they had estimated that nearly one-in-two Latina/o undergraduates is in a community college. At least that's better college access than we had growing up!" We all shared a similar gaze as we swallowed the bitter pill of access to higher education for Latina/os, which meant community colleges as a *de facto* institutional choice. As we nodded our heads slowly, we decided to skip the breakout sessions, opting for a space in the hotel lobby to collect our thoughts.

As we sat, Erica told a story about how her and other Latina/os from her multi-college district had started an emerging leaders group to challenge the continued lack of representation in administrative positions across the colleges. "Luis Escobedo has been really instrumental in helping put together the leadership group at SCCD. Has anyone seen Luis yet?" Erica asked. We shook our heads to indicate we hadn't.

I learned that SCCD's geographic location—in a state that had once been Mexico—shaped its current demographic realities. While the state was about 38% Latina/o, the county was closer to 49%. SCCD's student population includes 51% Latina/os, 16% African Americans, 18% Caucasians, and 14% Asians. Of these students, 43% were from below the poverty line and 15% came from homes where their parents received no more than an elementary school education. Erica described a culture of apathy bordering on hostility when she described how faculty interacted with the heavily Latina/o student body. Poor academic performance was attributed to students' lack of effort and to uninvolved parents. Erica continued, "The typical shit, you know? Some of these folks I work with swear Latina/o parents actually encourage their kids do perform poorly in school or that I've just been too lazy to get promoted. I guess it feels like the concept of Whiteness as property." Martín turned his head to Erica with a puzzled but intrigued look. "Wait, what? Are you getting all *mechista* on us again?" He chuckled. "Dude, let me explain!" Erica retorted.

LATINA/O LEADERS IN COMMUNITY COLLEGE AND THEIR WEALTH

Analisa ordered a Tuscan flatbread for us to share. It was supposed to be something like a pizza. We laughed as Martín teased her, saying they tricked her into ordering a tostada. Water with lemon and some iced teas soon followed. Analisa took a few sips of the water, crunched an ice cube, and leaned in to listen. Erica looked ready to drop some knowledge. "So I told you we were starting this leadership group right? I helped put together the proposal with Luis Escobedo so we could get some funding from the chancellor's office. One of the major pieces we focused on was that if the district fails to account for the mental models that continue to influence leadership development as a colorblind, race-neutral endeavor, then any gains in Latina/o leadership at SCCD will revert over time." Analisa and Martín listened intently. "In this proposal we really attempted to resist any perspectives that would depict the United States' Latina/o population as this big, single-minded monolithic entity." Analisa smiled and said, "That's wassup since you know people swear Mexico and Puerto Rico are like in the same county or something." Erica nodded quickly, "Exactly, that's the point, you know?"

Luis had found us in the lobby. "*Con las manos en la masa!*" he exclaimed, showing his toothy smile. Each of us greeted him. It was so nice to see Luis. He always was one to talk to us about anything ranging from current politics or the latest article he read in the *Review of Higher Education*. We looked to him for his academic background and his deep commitment to helping more people of color develop their leadership potential. His experiences as a provost had proven beneficial to all of us. I said "Just in time, Luis. Erica was talking to us about that proposal you all put together for the leadership group." He pulled up a chair, leaned in closer and jokingly said "they're serving tostadas now?"

As the laughter subsided, Erica continued: "Well, Luis had been doing some consulting for the regional accreditation agency so when he came back from a trip to Santa Barbara he just couldn't contain his excitement about a conceptual framework he had learned about—community cultural wealth." Luis' smile was expanding exponentially. Erica continued, "I kept thinking how I couldn't quite put my finger on how to explain what I kept referring to as our hustle and street smarts, it's like what psychologists refer to as situational awareness." We could feel how invested Erica was in this leadership group and the concept of community cultural wealth.

She explained, "Community cultural wealth is a model borne out of critical race theory driven by research which highlights the values and resources of marginalized communities that influence persistence and social mobility (Burciaga & Erbstein, 2010; Yosso, 2005). Often, these values and resources are overlooked or obscured in mainstream research focusing on traditional notions of social capital (Bourdieu, 1977) or within the context of leadership development (Ospina & Foldy, 2010). We felt that cultural capital was an important sociological concept to help us understand power, privilege, and social mobility. The unfortunate reality it is that it's usually used in a way that shows Latina/os and other communities of color from a deficit perspective, while masking the various forms of capital that are abundantly employed in ways that promote persistence and social mobility."

Analisa was nodding. "Okay, okay, I'm following you. So you mean cases like ours when we grow up speaking and thinking in two languages but teachers always focused on English only? And I bet those same teachers are the ones buying up all the Rosetta Stones from those commercials!"

We erupted into laughter with Luis wrangling us back to the topic. "Absolutely, Analisa. I think you hit on a key point that Dr. Yosso's conceptual framework means to get at. She describes six forms of capital that make up the concept of community cultural wealth, and one in particular is this idea of linguistic capital."

Erica broke it down quite plainly: "Linguistic capital encompasses the intellectual and social skills attained by, and needed to communicate in, various languages and/or styles (Burciaga & Erbstein, 2010; Yosso, 2005). The concept of linguistic capital also lets us think about the multiple ways Latina/o leaders communicate that are often overlooked across higher education. Think of the linguistic capital you have because of our music, visual arts, as well as all those *cuentos* and *dichos* we know, which essentially come from our oral traditions of passing along our histories."

We all nodded, seemingly fading from the hotel lobby and the convention noise swirling around us. Martín's furrowed brow gave way to this sort of rapid head nod. "Yeah, okay I follow. This reminds me of these students in my trigonometry class a few semesters ago. They had limited English proficiency. So this one time before class they were cracking jokes back and forth. I totally understood and couldn't help but laugh with them so they looked at me and were so surprised, they were like 'you understand Spanish?!' And I was like 'Yeah!' Since then they ask me questions in Spanish and that's fine because we can now communicate at their comfort level. I don't speak it very well but I definitely understand it so we end up speaking a sort of Spanglish." I could see that this concept Erica and Luis were talking about seemed well suited for the leadership group they were involved with.

Luis continued, "Martín, you bring up a good point in your story. As leaders in our colleges our Latina/o students look to us to for a lot more than just academics. I can only imagine that for those students in your trig class, getting some content in Spanglish was a sign of hope. Think of the possible impact we can have in advancing our students' and our own aspirations as leaders."

Erica asked the server for another glass of ice water. "Luis, tell them about aspirational capital." By this time we all were in full-fledged note-taking, missing-the-afternoon-sessions mode. Luis cleared his throat.

"Aspirational capital is made up of the ability to aspire and have dreams despite the immediate challenges at hand. I think we can relate to this resiliency in how our families pushed us to dream of possibilities beyond the circumstances we faced growing up. In our proposal we highlighted aspirational capital as one of the most prominent forms of capital for the leadership group. Not only the aspirations they hold for themselves, but also those placed on them by certain folks in the district who have recognized their capacity to lead."

I slowed down my furious note taking to share a comment. "Even though I have my master's degree I still aspire to learn more. And I can't help but think of my mom when you talk about this aspirational capital." Erica looked at me and asked me talk more about what I meant. "Well, the work ethic I picked up from my mom made me realize that if I was going to progress I needed higher education, and my mom realized that too. She had been working minimum wage jobs but when I was in middle school I remember she took some classes at the adult school so she could learn about being an administrative assistant. I saw that, you know? She got her certificate and applied for some better jobs. I saw how that kind of transformed her and I thought to myself 'wow to advance I really do need more than just a high school diploma,' which I think was all the advice I kept getting at school during that time."

I took a minute to compose myself because whenever I talk about how my mom encouraging me, my eyes get watery. Luis patted me on my left shoulder. "What a powerful story, que no?" He asked rhetorically.

Erica smiled and continued, "As a leader in my community college I've learned to expand my view of what family means to me. And Dr. Yosso's framework gives us some really beautiful ways to weave the role of family into the larger picture of our leadership group. In the proposal we described how familial capital consists of cultural, family, and community histories and knowledge."

Erica paused for a sip of water and gestured to Luis, who described this form of capital. "Familial capital is committed to community well-being and can show up as caring and nurturing traits. We've each discussed situations that include examples of familial capital, like you Martín when you recalled your mom getting her certificate from the adult school. This framework can help us talk about the role of family as it plays out in the development of Latina/o leaders in community colleges."

Analisa cracked the knuckles on her left hand and talked about her experience immediately after receiving her doctorate: "I made it a point to not bolt out of my neighborhood you know? Of course, I had opportunities for other positions but I couldn't do it. Being me and with my Nuyorican identity, I think it's impacted my desire to work in the Northeast, it's my commitment and I don't say it's my responsibility, you know, because I stay local from my own will. It's a commitment I feel to the community I grew up around and to this next generation coming up now."

I looked at my left wrist to check the time. "By the way guys, we have lots of time, the evening receptions aren't for another four hours." Luis adjusted his glasses, saying, "Well, that's good then. Let's continue discussing the leadership group and Dr. Yosso's framework, shall we?"

Analisa sat closer to the edge of her chair and held her empty water glass, saying, "Bueno, if we're gonna keep going with this deep topic I need a little splash of Don Q in with my lemon water!" Martín signaled for the server to come over to our table. We ordered some cocktails and two appetizers to share.

Erica raised her martini glass, saying, "Salud!" I took a long swig from my bottle of Guinness and asked Luis about the moment we were living. "So if I'm following you and the community cultural wealth framework you're sharing with us, can I venture to say that our relationships here at this convention can be a form of capital? Because without you all I don't think I'd keep coming back to this environment year after year."

Chewing on his olive that had garnished his drink Luis continued, "Como no?! The way I've understood it, and Erica can correct me if I'm wrong, but this is a good example of how we've learned to navigate institutional spaces like this annual convention."

Erica nodded. "Oh yeah, Dr. Yosso's article described social capital as component of community cultural wealth. Think of all our mentors and the *padrinos* we've had coming up. Remember at the convention like three years ago when Dr. Villa emceed the awards dinner? We felt so validated when he casually mentioned us over at SCCD as emerging leaders in the community college movement."

I specifically remembered the moment Erica was referring to and I felt so wonderful to be at their table when they were mentioned even if I didn't work at SCCD. Erica went on, "So you mention this relationship we have here, all of us are from across the country yet we've forged meaningful, authentic friendships with one another as well as some of the senior Latina/o leaders here. Just think of how that made you feel."

I could see Analisa begin to get more emotional than she had been all afternoon. She wiped her eye gently holding back tears as she said, "I get a little *llorona* because I could see how this social capital stuff is so important. When I first got my job I used to think that everyone else assumed I was only there for some minority quota. But all it took was some encouragement from the vice chancellor at the time. She was from Panama and would share her stories of triumph and of course all those challenges. I'd listen to her and how she would encourage me to do my best always and I'd imagine the impact on students and my community that I'd like to have. She would tell me that together we accomplish more. And you know her time commitment to me lifted me up so much that I could dare to ask myself all these hypotheticals about my career, like 'what if I become a president?' You know? So I felt like I had this social connection in my corner always supporting me." She stopped and dried the tear rolling down her cheek.

Martín added, "Analisa's comments make me feel like social capital is as much about finding it, like we have, as it is about cultivating it in a way that may consider the needs of individuals and the larger community."

Erica smiled widely as she noshed on a piece of crostini. "I think you read our proposal, Martín!"

As we laughed heartily Luis put his glass down, nodded his head, and adjusted his tie. "You all were at the lunch keynote, right? Ay ay ay! Let's not even rehash that now but I'm sure you all debriefed what President Maxwell said about us being welders. Pues, let's use that for example. Dr. Yosso's framework gives us ways to reflect and account for these interactions with supposed mentors and leaders. I think it's a reminder of how we as leaders are in tune and sensitive to how we're treated by those with positions of authority and who wield power especially when we know the connections we make with them are not meaningful. This raises imperative questions about well-meaning and 'nice' mentors who cannot conceptualize Latina/o community college leaders as holding the social capital they deem valuable. Being able to help others think of Latina/os as capable community college leaders goes hand-in-hand with navigating the leadership pipeline." Luis paused and looked at each of us. "We're good right? We're following."

I looked down and noticed I had been tapping notes into my iPad for so long the battery was quickly draining. Erica offered me a sheet from her portfolio, but she didn't have a pen so I called for the server to ask for one. Luis offered us another round of cocktails to which we quickly obliged. Luis asked Erica to detail the final components of their proposal to fund the leadership group. Erica agreed, "Sure, let's see, I think we have the navigational and resistant capital."

Our next round of cocktails arrived to the table. "To our future," I toasted to which Analisa quickly responded, "No more waiting, to the present!" And that, right there, was why I enjoyed Analisa's company so much. Her keen awareness to our realities as community college leaders was on point. Why wait? We are the present and the future. A million thoughts raced through my head, so I was glad when Erica started talking about community cultural wealth again.

"This afternoon when we heard President Maxwell say those things, remember how you felt? Pretty pissed off, right? But even more we decided to not just ignore it. We convened and skipped some breakout sessions and our conversation this afternoon is indicative of us challenging inequities and subordination. Yosso calls this resistant capital. Can you think of times you've enacted your resistant capital?"

She paused and took a sip of her drink and dipped a carrot stick into the hummus. Luis spoke first, "I think of the historic lack of educational opportunity for my uncles and parents, you know. I guess in a convention like this everyone would say that is a risk factor or some negativity I've had to face. But the reality is that I've used that as a positive motivator for me, and I've been successful at engaging with students and parents whose stories are like mine. White folks, Blacks, and Asians too, you know? They all want and expect the best from their kids and from themselves, so I think I've resisted that idea that I come from a negative family background and it's helped me connect on so many levels."

Luis offered us a wonderful example of his resistance to the assumptions around the lowered expectations of first-generation college students. His statements impacted me because I could see how as individuals, Latina/o leaders in community colleges are more than what we are stereotyped to be—leaders only concerned in helping advance the interests of the Latina/o community. I asked Analisa to share because of her Afro-Latina identity. "Well, I look Black, obviously, but when I talk I think people begin to kinda look at me more confused like they want to guess where I'm from. I think my experiences contribute by offering a different sort of resistance to that idea that all Latina/os do this, say that or that all Black people talk like this. This is dope. I can see this totally! Shoot, I've been resisting since grade school."

"So you've been resisting since you were a kid, huh?" asked Erica. Analisa took a second to gather her thoughts and replied, "Well, I didn't have something like community cultural wealth to let me know I was doing it, but I was doing it. You know how easy it could have been to just listen to all the bad advice out on the streets?" Her rhetorical question seemed to resonate with all of us.

I interjected, "So how did we do it to not get caught slipping and how did we end up here, like today having this talk?" In unison we looked at Luis. "Why are you looking at me? I found you all here in the lobby!" he said cheerfully. "Let me break it down and make a connection to the final piece of Dr. Yosso's framework. By learning to take what some would say are negative experiences and use them as motivators, to rely on our families in a culture that glorifies the lone ranger archetype, and to teach trigonometry in Spanglish to students who need it, we've all been enacting our resistant capital. Resisting those clichéd stock stories of what Latina/os are supposed to be in this space of community college leaders in the larger landscape of United States higher education is an opportunity for all of us to learn how we demonstrate our community cultural wealth."

Luis was on a good roll. I loved when he morphed into our senior scholar figure like this. "Resistant capital is commonly demonstrated in how we challenge inequity or subordination by articulating a vision for rethinking the ubiquitous misconceptions of community colleges. Such capital indicates our active critical thinking, showing us that as Latina/o community college leaders we are not only out for themselves, but rather we are actively engaged in advocacy by resisting negative beliefs about our communities and ourselves."

I was so amped from hearing Luis and Erica drop this concept of community cultural wealth. I was so glad we had this opportunity to convene and that they were in my corner. Their leadership group was sure to be successful and I only prayed that SCCD granted them the seed funding they requested. I was drifting in my own thoughts when Analisa tugged at my sleeve. "Mira, its President Maxwell coming this way."

He came over to us and introduced himself. "John Maxwell, Midwestern Plains Community College. Nice to meet you." I could smell the vodka on his breath. "It's a pleasure although we met at last year's convention," I said. Analisa got up to remind him, "Hi there! We met at the CCA's data analysts meeting last month." President Maxwell licked his lips. "Oh, of course we did, how's it going over here? Looks like you're having a little *fiesta* aren't ya."

Erica exhaled loudly and corrected him, "Well, we're just discussing a conceptual framework that can help us make sense of our experience as leaders." President Maxwell sipped his cocktail while looking right through Erica as if she was not there. His gaze was distant even while he nodded, pretending to listen. "Really?" he said. "Well, you know what we don't need at CCA anymore, it's this radical critical race theory. It's like some liberal pissing contest to help people feel like oppressed victims. I was there you know, I testified in front of a congressional committee in the first Bush administration and I was touting diversity since then, so all this stuff is just too much."

I looked at Analisa, Luis, Martín, and Erica, and we all just looked at President Maxwell in a mix of shock and disgust. Luis politely shifted his body weight. "Well thanks for sharing your point of view. We have a meeting to catch so we'll see you later."

* * *

DISCUSSION AND CONCLUSION

One benefit of using Yosso's (2005) framework to guide this counterstory was that it allowed me to recognize the voices of those silenced or obscured in mainstream leadership research. This framework promotes social justice and transformation by "challenging traditional notions of how to conduct, practice, or rhetorically engage in educational leadership" (Alemán, 2009, p. 295), and is especially relevant to the case of studying Latina/o community college leaders, since most studies on leadership have largely ignored the fact that power and influence largely remain the dominion of White, middle-class men (Lopez, 2003). This power and influence needs to be addressed so that the ideals on which community colleges were founded are not forgotten. Community colleges are supposed to be spaces where all parties are invested in generating new knowledge by developing students who are exposed to different ways of thinking as well as new cultures (Valverde, 2003).

The composite characters in this counterstory demonstrated community cultural wealth resources and values, which they drew upon on the community college leadership pathway. These resources and values add complexity to predominant views of leadership in general and community college leadership in particular. Additionally, the community cultural wealth framework positions Latina/o community college leaders as valuable, contributing members of the higher education community, who have not had equitable access to opportunities at all levels of education, as students, and now as emerging campus leaders.

Through this counterstory, I am advocating for the continued investment of our collective resources to nurture and support the various forms of capital found in Latina/o community college leaders. Leadership programs and professional organizations are wonderful examples of community cultural wealth that was created and is maintained despite the challenges and disappointments Latina/os face(d) along the community college leadership pathway. Many forms of capital are employed every day. As Analisa mentioned in the counterstory, "I've been resisting since grade school." The values and situational awareness inculcated from a young age among communities of color offer invaluable access to stores of cultural stamina. This quotidian occurrence of persistence and resistance may contribute to the continued overreliance on finding the "right" forms of capital. As leaders in service are facing, have faced, and will face more challenges, the composite characters in this counterstory hold critical insight into how to confront a changing higher education demographic landscape. To this end, it is critical for individuals and organizations committed to advancing Latina/o leadership for community colleges to listen to emerging leaders in their own voices. Perhaps we may be surprised to realize that leaders have been leading for a long time—since grade school.

REFERENCES

AACC. (2013). *CEO characteristics.* Retrieved from http://www.aacc.nche.edu/AboutCC/Trends/Pages/ceocharacteristics.aspx

Alemán Jr., E. (2009). Through the prism of critical race theory: Niceness and Latina/o leadership in the politics of education. *Journal of Latinos and Education, 8*(4), 290–311.

Bourdieu, P. (1977). Cultural reproduction and social reproduction. In J. Karabel & A. H. Halsey (Eds.), *Power and ideology in education* (pp. 487–511). New York, NY: Oxford University Press.

Burciaga,R. & Erbstein, N.(2010). *Challenging assumptions, revealing community cultural wealth: Young adult wisdom on hope and hardship.* Healthy Youth/Healthy Regions working paper. Center for Regional Change, UC Davis.

Cohen, A. M., Brawer, F. B., Kisker, C. B. (2013). *The American community college* (6th ed.). San Francisco, CA: Jossey-Bass.

Dougherty, K. J. (1994). *The contradictory college: The conflicting origins, impacts, and futures of the community college.* Albany, NY: State University of New York Press.

Eddy, P. L. (2010). *Community college leadership: A multidimensional model for leading change.* Sterling, VA: Stylus.

Esquibel, A. (1992). *The career mobility of Chicano administrators in higher education.* Boulder, CO: Western Interstate Commission on Higher Education.

Haro, R. (1995). Held to a higher standard: Latino executive selection in higher education. In R. V. Padilla & R. C. Chavez (Eds.), *The leaning ivory tower: Latino professors in American universities* (pp. B32–33). Albany, NY: SUNY Press.

Hispanic Association of Colleges and Universities. (2013). *Hispanic serving institutions definitions.* Retrieved from http://www.hacu.net/hacu/HSI_Definition1.asp

León, D. J. (Ed.). (2005). *Lessons in leadership: Executive leadership programs for advancing diversity in higher education.* New York, NY: Elsevier/JAI.

León, D. J., & Nevarez, C. (2007). Models of leadership institutes for increasing the number of top Latino administrators in higher education. *Journal of Hispanics in Higher Education, 6*(4), 356–378.

López, G. R. (2003). The (racially neutral) politics of education: A critical race theory perspective. *Educational Administration Quarterly, 39*(1), 69–94.

McCurtis, B. R., Jackson, J. F. L., &. O'Callaghan, E. M. (2009). Developing leaders of color in higher education. In A. Kezar (Ed.), *Rethinking leadership in a complex, multicultural, and global environment: New concepts and models for higher education* (pp. 65–92). Sterling, VA: Stylus.

Ospina, S., & Foldy, E. (2009). A critical review of race and ethnicity in the leadership literature: Surfacing context, power, and the collective dimensions of leadership. *The Leadership Quarterly, 20,* 876–896.

Snyder, T. D., & Dillow, S. A. (2011). *Digest of Education Statistics 2010* (NCES 2011–015). Washington, DC: National Center for Education Statistics, Institute of Education Sciences, U.S. Department of Education.

Valverde, L. A. (2003). *Leaders of color in higher education: Unrecognized triumphs in harsh institutions.* New York, NY: Altamira

Vaughan, G. B. (2006). *The community college story* (3rd ed.). Washington, DC: Community College Press.

Yosso, T. J. (2005). Whose culture has capital? A critical race theory discussion of community cultural wealth. *Race Ethnicity in Education, 8*(1), 69–91.

CHAPTER 6

VOICES FROM THE MARGINS

Illuminating Experiences of African American Women Senior Administrators in Higher Education

Brenda Marina, Sabrina Ross, and Kimberly Robinson

VOICE(S) UNSILENCED

If African American women are gauging our success and mobility by the faces that we see at the top, we will soon become discouraged and disillusioned. There is a gross underrepresentation of women of color, particularly African American women, holding senior administrative positions in higher education (Crawford & Smith, 2005; Patitu & Hinton, 2003). Over fifty years have passed since *Brown* v. *Board of Education* attempted to level the playing field for African Americans as a whole; however, African American women continue to face racial inequities beyond the barrier of gender (Nichols & Tanksley, 2004). Despite the cruel treatment people of color endured to prevail over social injustices and discrimination while fighting against the institutionalized practices and structures that created barriers to their advancement, African Americans have persisted (Jean-Marie, 2006).

Envisioning Critical Race Praxis in Higher Education Through Counter-Storytelling, pages 89–106
Copyright © 2016 by Information Age Publishing
89

Despite the steady gains African Americans have made, their voices are still not heard within the sometimes-cold nature of the academy (Holmes, Land, & Hinton-Huston, 2007; Thomas & Hollenshead, 2001; Valverde, 2003). More specifically, the history of African American women details a past of struggles and oppression that resulted from a history of slavery and denial of access to education (Mabokela & Green, 2001). Today, African American women administrators are constantly challenged; viewed as inferior; assumed to be affirmative action hires and thus less qualified; over-scrutinized by peers, superiors, and students; considered tokens; having to work harder than others in order to gain respect; and denied access to resources typically given to someone in such positions (Valverde, 2003). In looking at the current state of affairs for African American women in academe, we found that women continue to face isolation, demoralization, and opposition in attaining equity in university administration (Holmes et al., 2007).

The underrepresentation of African American women in senior administrative positions in higher education and the negative experiences they report when holding senior administrative positions contradicts the presumed ethos of equal opportunity in the United States. Examining the experiences of African American senior administrators in greater detail can yield important information about micro- and macro-level processes that contribute to their underrepresentation; such understanding, in turn, can highlight changes necessary to increase the number of African American female senior administrators in academia. We offer counterstories in this chapter to further the discussions about racism that are missing from critical discourse in higher education. In this chapter, we employ critical race theory as a framework for highlighting the counterstories of African American senior administrators and as a guide for deconstructing relationships between race, gender, and inequality in higher education recruitment, hiring, and retention policies for African American women senior administrators.

Critical Race Theory

Critical race theory (CRT) is an interdisciplinary field of study (Matsuda, Lawrence, Delgado, & Crenshaw, 1993; Smith, Yosso, & Solórzano, 2007; Solórzano & Yosso, 2002) developed by scholars of color who challenged the absence of attention to and theorization about race in the legal system and within the field of critical legal studies (Crenshaw, 1988; Iverson, 2007; Yosso, Parker, Solórzano, & Lynn, 2004). CRT draws on diverse sources such as critical theory, women's studies, sociology, history, and ethnic studies, and analyzes and challenges manifestations of racism in United States society and abroad (Smith et al., 2007; Yosso et al., 2004). CRT theorists examine how social systems (law, education, media, etc.) reproduce and normalize racism (Ladson-Billings & Tate, 1995; Lopez, 2003). Like other critical theories, the goal of CRT scholarship is social transformation through the empowerment of marginalized groups and the elimination of interconnected structures of oppression (Matsuda et al., 1993; Parker & Villalpando, 2007; Smith et al., 2007; Solórzano & Yosso, 2002).

Critical race theorists identify a number of central tenets in their scholarship that include: (1) a primary focus on race and racism (Solórzano & Villalpando, 1998); (2) recognition of how other forms of oppression interact with racism (Smith et al., 2007); (3) challenging dominant ideology (Lynch 2006); (4) validating and learning from the experiential knowledge of persons of color (Parker & Villalpando, 2007); (5) using interdisciplinary approaches to analyze oppression (Solórzano & Yosso, 2002); and (6) a commitment to social justice (Parker & Villalpando, 2007). The relation of several of these tenets to understanding the experiences of African American women in senior leadership positions will now be discussed.

Validating and Learning from the Experiential Knowledge of Persons of Color

Several researchers have made the argument that stories from persons of color come from a different frame of reference. These voices, so dissimilar from those of the dominant mainstream culture, should be heard and shared (Delgado & Stefancic, 2001; Tate, 1996). CRT scholars document the stories of individuals who experience racial oppression and view those stories as both pedagogical and counter-hegemonic. While majoritarian stories, or dominant stories about the workings of the world, help to maintain existing social relations, stories of the oppressed provide insight on surviving and transcending racial oppression and also call into question dominant ways of understanding the world (Ladson-Billings & Tate, 1995; Matsuda et al., 1993; Parker & Villalpando, 2007; Solórzano & Villalpando, 1998; Solórzano & Yosso, 2002). We use the storied vignettes of African American senior administrators as the primary source of data for this study. Having navigated, and ultimately survived, the challenges associated with their pursuit of senior administrative positions, these women possess knowledge about the inner workings of higher education that can help to explain and challenge the underrepresentation of African American women in these positions.

Challenging Dominant Ideologies

CRT practitioners deconstruct rhetoric of colorblindness and race-neutrality that conceal dominant ideologies with pretenses of equality and homogeneity (Ladson-Billings & Tate, 1995). Through deconstruction of purportedly race-neutral laws and policies, CRT scholars reveal ways in which Whiteness is normalized and privileged relative to racial/ethnic minorities (Lynch, 2006; Matsuda et al., 1993; Parker & Villalpando, 2007; Solórzano & Yosso, 2002). By highlighting the stories of senior African American women administrators, this chapter will deconstruct hiring policies in higher education that, on the surface, appear to be race-neutral, but nevertheless function to isolate, alienate, and disqualify African American women, making them appear to be unfit for senior administrative positions.

Commitment to Social Justice

By shedding light on the ways in which social constructions of race intersect with other forms of oppression to produce inequality, CRT makes invisible structures of oppression visible so work to eradicate those structures can be done (Ladson-Billings & Tate, 1995; Parker & Villalpando, 2007; Yosso et al., 2004). Considering that we have previously worked in a predominantly White higher education institution, we agreed that we must carefully consider the attainment of a leadership position juxtaposed to exposure to microaggressions (conscious, unconscious, verbal, nonverbal, and visual forms of insults) that are pervasive for African American women in higher education institutions. Covert racial acts can be difficult to investigate in institutional settings and can cause a great deal of anxiety for those who experience this type of racial oppression. Thus, we use critical race theory to examine the internal factors affecting educational organizations and how institutional policies have adversely impacted the hiring, retention, and promotion of African American women in senior level administration. In this chapter, our exploration of the intersections of race and gender that influence the hiring, retention, and promotion of African American senior women administrators holds the promise of making visible micro- and macro-level structures in higher education that disadvantage African American women seeking advancement to senior administrative positions. In this way, our chapter has a social justice focus—to highlight the ways towards more democratic hiring practices for senior administrative positions.

OUR STUDY

We invited and selected African American women who were currently holding senior level positions in predominantly White higher education institutions in both academic and student affairs to share their lived experiences with us. Senior level positions included those in the positions of deans, provosts, vice presidents, and presidents. This selection was carefully considered with the knowledge that of the 196,324 executive, administrative, and managerial staff in the nation's degree-granting institutions, approximately 51% are women and less than 10% are African American (Snyder, Dillow, & Hoffman, 2007). Additionally, of the 51%, or 101,101, executive, administrative, and managerial women in higher education, only 11% were African American (Snyder et al., 2007).

We initially contacted the two educational organizations whose primary memberships are women of African descent. From that point, we used snowball sampling through various networking groups recommended by higher education faculty or administrators. Each woman interviewed was asked to suggest additional women who met the sampling criteria for interviewing. The snowball sampling method is based on the idea that members of a particular population who might be particularly difficult to locate know one another, and therefore, can provide a researcher with additional members of that target population (Creswell, 2009). We considered each woman as an expert because each one had been exposed to the institutional climate and culture of academe, had successfully navigated the obstacles to obtain senior administrative positions in higher education, and had held her position for at least three years.

Eight of the women in our study were between the ages of 40 to 59, two were between the ages of 30 to 39, and two were over 60 years old. Eight of the women were married, three divorced, and one was widowed. Nine of the women had one or two children, while three others had three to four children. Similar to our own stories, most of the women have had families the majority of their educational career and had to learn how to balance the demands of the career with the needs of the home. Interestingly, several of these women came from families with married parents, four were reared by their mothers only, and one was raised by an aunt. We thought that it was important to mention that the highest level of education achieved by any of the participants' parents, both male and female, was a Master's degree, and the lowest level of education completed by any of the women's parents was high school. We also found that one of the participants considered her family class growing up to be upper middle class and all the others considered their family class to be middle class.

The process of data analysis involved a review of the data from the interviews. It was advantageous to have the interviews transcribed by a professional transcriptionist. Initially, a basic interpretive process was employed with three iterations of coding. First, the data were reviewed for commonalities or patterns from the exact words of the participants recorded during the interview. Second, we reviewed the commonalities or patterns and grouped the data into themes. Third, the themes were analyzed and the dominant concepts from the data were interpreted. Finally, through the use of imaginative variation we were able to analyze the information and reach conclusions from the perspective of the participants. According to Merriam (2009), imaginative variation seeks to ascertain possible meanings through the use of the imagination. The intent of this approach is to try to obtain meaning by looking at different roles, functions, or positions in addition to the underlying or precipitating factors that could account for reasons as to why the women felt marginalized thus lending to their underrepresentation.

VOICES OF AFRICAN AMERICAN WOMEN SENIOR ADMINISTRATORS

During the process of exploring institutional factors contributing to the underrepresentation of African American women in higher education and strategies that were used to overcome perceived barriers, four dominant concepts became apparent. These concepts are "leadership preparation," "perception of race and gender," "institutional challenges," and "success strategies."

Leadership Development

One senior administrator stated:

Obtaining credentials through receiving a doctoral degree is very important and necessary in ascending to leadership positions in higher education. After obtaining the necessary credentials, it is imperative that we participate in leadership programs both within the institution, if available, and other programs located throughout the country.

The women observed that most of the institutions either did not have leadership programs in place or the programs were not authentic in their commitment to diversity. Therefore, they would have to pay to attend credible leadership programs out of their own pockets. African American women typically make less than their White counterparts and therefore the expectation that these women can simply "afford" to do these things is erroneous (Institute of Women's Policy Research, 2013; Nichols & Tanksley, 2004). However, participation in leadership programs was necessary in establishing well-rounded skill sets to expand the knowledge and opportunities in higher education. All of the women agreed that African American women should get as much experience outside of their professional arena through participating on committees or special assignments. This exposure would allow them to learn about all facets of higher education and meet people who may be able to assist them in their career advancement goals.

Mentoring and Networking

In preparing for leadership positions in academe, 11 of the 12 senior administrators emphatically noted mentorship as critical for leadership attainment. We listened intently as one senior administrator testified:

> Securing an advocate or finding a mentor was very vital in my quest in obtaining a senior administrative position. A mentor is someone who can help you both professionally and personally. It is important that you decide early on what type of mentoring relationship you need and who can meet those needs for you. A mentor should not just be a person who validates you or strokes your ego, but also a person who can challenge you and provide constructive criticism.

There was a concern that African American women were not privy to the informal networks that existed among their White counterparts, and thus, information conducive to professional growth and leadership attainment was not shared. The women often felt isolated and left out of the "know" when it came to leadership opportunities becoming available and the skills required to obtain the position. Another senior administrator stated, "It has taken me longer to get where I am because I felt like I was always the last to know about things. Our [White peers] are being groomed early on, but we are left out of the conversation."

The women who have successfully navigated the tumultuous terrain into senior administration have had the assistance of a mentor. Five of the mentoring relationships were with immediate supervisors who were more hands-on in honing their skill sets and potential, as well as recommending them for positions as they became available. There were others who had mentoring relationships with previous faculty members and colleagues who were able to provide a listening ear, sound advice, and a broader perspective of the situation. As we reflect upon the CRT tenet of *commitment to social justice,* we see the mentorship relationships as a commitment and unique partnership to overcome barriers and eliminate racism and sexism.

Perceptions of Race and Gender

Persistence to overcome both race and gender barriers has provided a unique perspective on achievement of higher education advancement. There was consensus that racism and gender differences are still very much a part of the culture of academe; however, it has become very subtle. As one senior administrator stated:

> There is still some gender bias and some old fashioned sexism as to whether or not women should be in these roles. Can they do this? Can they juggle? Can they manage? Can they make tough decisions?

Although ten of the women had the academic credentials in terms of a doctoral degree, they still believed that there was a cultural barrier that contributed to what they referred to as a *double glass ceiling.* One glass ceiling was for their race and the other for their gender. Another senior administrator stated:

> It's not always negating the African American woman but I think that sometimes we're dismissed as not even thought of, I don't think it's taken serious that I have aspirations to be a President. But I did see other people being groomed.... You have to work harder to prove your worth, you are never considered equal.

Zamudio, Russell, Rios, and Bridgeman (2011) asserted that the critical race theory framework dismisses the idea that all individuals have access to the same opportunities and success. Half of the women felt they were denied positions of leadership because they were viewed as less competent or overly aggressive. These women were racialized in ways that allowed domination from their White counterparts to coexist. Overall, their authority as a credible leader was unfairly questioned time and time again. As one senior administrator stated:

> I knew when I got the job as President that some of my colleagues would not like me because I was Black and some because I was a woman and some because I was younger than some of my faculty, but the reality is that I was there and I wasn't going anywhere so they might as well get used to it.{\ext}

Overall, these women constantly felt scrutinized for their actions, lumped together, and accountable for the whole race of African American women. Negative characteristics such as being too loud, too strong, or too aggressive were attributed to their leadership style at the onset of their positions. Another senior administrator said:

> When an African American woman stands her ground and is firm in her tone, she is considered angry or bitter or difficult to work with. On the other hand, when a White woman administrator stands her ground, she is considered to be firm and strong.

One of the women felt that it was necessary to document accounts or encounters in order to be accountable for her actions, defend her position, and explain her reasoning for the decisions she made. These provocative perceptions provide insight on surviving and transcending racial oppression, as suggested by the CRT tenet of *intercentricity of race and racism with other forms of subordination.*

Institutional Challenges

After each woman detailed her journey to leadership attainment, the actual challenges they all faced were explored to get a better picture of their lived experiences while navigating the terrain to higher education administration. All of the women agreed that their governance structure was mostly White and male dominated and there seemed to be an ongoing perception that leaders are supposed to be men. We were not surprised to hear one senior administrator say:

> When you get into higher education senior administration, men primarily make the decisions regarding hiring and advancement. Therefore, they may feel uncomfortable hiring a woman leader or working for a woman, especially an African American woman.

Despite having the credentials, sound work experience, hard work ethic, and ability, the women overwhelmingly agreed that knowing what they know now, they would have pursued getting into administration sooner rather than later. They were under the idea that the skills and preparation that they acquired would translate into job advancement and growth. However, many of them were not able to advance as quickly as their White male and female counterparts after controlling for credentials, leadership preparation, and experience. We were disappointed to hear:

> Even when we [higher education institutions] say diversity is valued, sometimes it doesn't play out when it comes to leadership, and so yeah, I would definitely say that my race and my gender have impacted my ability to move up.

These women felt that their race and gender were factors in the slow pace of job advancement. Several of the women felt as if they could have moved into administration sooner; however, they didn't feel emotionally prepared to take on the mental challenges of the unbalanced expectations (of having to do more and work harder than their majority counterparts) that would be placed on them by the institution. Although these women had the necessary credentials and experience, the undue expectations as African American women in leadership was a source of disenchantment with the institution and the position. As we thought about the CRT tenet, *challenge to dominant ideology*, these unsilenced voices countered the notion that education is the key to advancement.

Personal Strategies for Success

After discussing the challenges to leadership attainment and challenges experienced within the institution, securing a mentor was noted as the top strategy for success. It is important to establish a mentoring relationship with people you can trust and it is also important that the relationship be authentic. As one senior administrator stated:

> Even if you talk to that person once a year ... or you could email that person. You know, you really need to do that. And you really need to observe people and watch people, how they manage.

These women are now "paying it forward" by mentoring other young women desiring leadership positions in academe. It is necessary to have stable and supportive relationships with people who can be trusted. Several of the women in our study did not feel comfortable hanging out with colleagues and going out in the community or town where their university was located. It is important to have a well-rounded support system both inside and outside of the job. We were glad to hear, "I had folks at my institution that would say let's go to breakfast/lunch, let's meet so you can understand politically what happens here." This information allowed this particular administrator the opportunity to learn the culture and climate of the organization and the implications behind the operational dynamics.

Several women agreed that it is essential to not mix the personal with business, as you have to be watchful of what you do and how you behave at all times. Additionally, maintaining a level of professionalism is important in your ascension to higher education leadership. Parallel to maintaining high standards of professionalism, being aware of how they dressed and spoke around their colleagues and subordinates was critical. B ecause they were under so much scrutiny, they could not allow their appearances to become a distraction. The women needed to be aware of the smallest details of their appearance even down to the color of fingernail polish they chose to wear. One senior administrator asserted:

> When you are on vacation, you can wear the acrylic nails as long as you want and any color that you want but you have to make sure that before you go back to work, the nails are off and at an appropriate length and in a neutral shade.

Self-confidence is crucial and vitally important for attaining and maintaining a leadership position in higher education. Self-confidence allowed them to believe in themselves and their abilities as leaders. One of the women attributed her confidence from her early upbringing. Listen to what this senior administrator said:

> And I have always had a sense of confidence that I could do it. I grew up in the Civil Rights Era and I went to a traditionally White institution and there were things heard there that in my estimation that nobody was going to tell me that I couldn't do it because I knew better and if nothing else I was going to prove them wrong.

And finally, other success strategies include: a passion for students and education, keeping up with the trends and best practices in higher education by participating in professional organizations and becoming experts in the field, balancing both family and career, and taking time to rest and relax.

The CRT tenet of *centrality of experiential knowledge* recognizes and legitimizes the lived experiences of these women. It was evident that these women believed their stories had merit and their strategies for success were a way to debunk the ideology of inferiority for women and persons of color. Their stories defy the stereotypical perceptions of women of color as angry and bitter. Their stories, their experiences were cause for introspection as we considered our paths to leadership.

OUR OWN SENSE MAKING AMIDST THEIR EXPERIENCES

Kimberly

At the time of this study, I was a doctoral student with an anticipation and eagerness to enter the realm of higher education as an educator. I was enlightened by the voices of women who detailed challenging experiences and success stories of how they overcame those challenges. Through their journeys, I was able to envision myself persisting through barriers to obtain success in my own quest to leadership attainment.

As I listened intently to each of the women's stories, their words pierced my soul, as their tone changed to one of disillusionment when discussing societal stereotypes of their race and gender. Instead of being gratified by the qualifications and credentials they had persisted to achieve, namely, the doctorate, they felt demoralized. Their joy and fulfillment would be short lived, as the reality of what they looked like seemed to take precedence over who they actually were. As for me, an African American woman beginning my quest to leadership attainment, I began to reflect on my own journey and visualize how my hard work and perseverance could very well turn into years of struggle and disappointment. From a historical perspective, African American women have always had to climb harder and longer to rise to the top. What inspires me most about these twelve women, however, is the fact that they did not allow negative perceptions of the way they were born define their destiny in which they were created to achieve.

Personally, I find great strength in hearing the stories of the twelve women, knowing that despite the odds, they still persisted to leadership attainment.

If I could be brutally honest, as a budding young professional, hearing the women's stories detailing the challenges and barriers that they would face in their quest to succeed caused me to be a little fearful. I began to ask myself: How do I enter into the ivory tower doors of opportunity and promise when the keys of education and experience are not enough to unlock them? The revelations from these women caused me to take an introspective look at what this all means for my journey. After careful consideration, I finally realized that, although I may not be privy to all of the opportunities of leadership attainment, their stories shed some light on the path to leadership success. I understand that I may encounter struggles in my climb; however, those who have gone before me have provided a compass to help guide my route through their experiences.

I would be slighting my goals and dreams if I allowed the institutional barriers to negatively influence my resolve to succeed. As a young woman with dreams of leading in higher education, I faltered when I believed my career path had stagnated. Through their stories my motivation has been renewed and my dream revived with a sense of empowerment to deal with an unwelcoming climate in higher education.

As a doctoral student and an aspiring administrator in higher education who has experienced challenges in my own quest for leadership attainment, I needed to hear the voices of women who looked like me. I needed to listen to their struggles and hear their successes and understand how higher education institutions contribute to those challenges. I felt that their advancement was a victory for me as each woman was willing to share insight into her life's journey in an effort to accelerate my success and support my goals. I have come away with not only tangible strategies for success but with a stronger commitment and resolve as an African American woman to persist despite the resistance. My voice has power and is important. My experiences have merit and are valid. My goals are possible and obtainable.

Sabrina

As an African American assistant professor currently working through the challenges of securing promotion and tenure at a predominantly White university, I have often felt out of place. In analyzing the narratives of the women in this study, I was struck by the similarity of shared experiences, particularly the themes of isolation and/or alienation the women described. To me, these themes also speak to a sense of feeling out of place and not belonging. Further, experiences of isolation and alienation described by African American women in this study speak to the CRT claim of Whiteness as a form of property (Harris, 1993; Ladson-Billings & Tate, 1995), which provides symbolic, psychological, and material benefits to White individuals and simultaneously denies benefits to racialized (and this case, gendered) individuals.

The property value of Whiteness was conveyed in this study through stories of White administrators who were groomed for senior administrative positions and who, upon receiving those positions, were permitted to carry out their jobs with a taken-for-granted presumption of competence not afforded to the women in this study. That African American women in this study had to seek out their own paths to advancement (often self-funding their professional development) and, once hired, were not afforded hospitable environments speaks to their exclusion from the benefits of Whiteness. The chilly climate experienced by these women suggests that they were unwelcomed in their positions—as if they were trespassing on White property (e.g., the senior administrative position).

While the negative treatment experienced by the women in this study was troubling, I found hope in the resistance strategies that they employed (e.g., maintaining separation between public and private spheres of their lives; utilizing family, friends, and support systems as coping resources) to remain psychologically well balanced while carrying out their duties in hostile environments. Ultimately, these resistance strategies enabled the women in this study to persist in their difficult positions; such persistence (in addition to increased numbers of African American women being hired and retained in senior administrative positions) is necessary for African American women to attain senior administrative positions in numbers proportionate to their percentages in the population.

Brenda

As a tenured, associate professor, a female educator and researcher of *African ascent*, I reflect upon our own praxis within the context of the CRT tenet commitment to social justice. Let me explain why I use *"ascent"* before I move on. The term *ascendant* or *ascent*, in contrast to the term *descendent* (a well-established canon of Western thought), is used to articulate how reality is known when based in the roots of African thought. The term *descend* ascribes to falling or tumbling down, which has a negative connotation. In contrast, the term *ascend* can be described as coming up, which has a positive connotation (Marina & Fonteneau, 2012). I account the reflections of this group of women of African ascent, who have embraced their roles as leaders in education and see that they utilize their spirituality in their work as leaders in education, and I see them as social justice agents.

With these reflections, I pause to consider my connections and my purposes—which are teaching and mentoring women for leadership. What would happen to my life (and the lives of my students) if I were to immerse myself more deeply in my spiritual roots of Africa? What would happen to my teaching and my research if I were to immerse myself into an African way of thinking? Several of these women discussed how much of their patience comes from their reliance on their spiritual beliefs. One of the women stated that when she was repeatedly turned down for positions that she felt qualified for: "You know, maybe this isn't the time for it. And I do believe—I'm very spiritual. And I'm just thinking that, you know, God has another plan for me." Their dreams appeared to be rooted and grounded in the construction of their faith in God and support of their family.

I saw women who have demonstrated such great strength of character through their willingness to work hard, stay focused on their goals, persist in their quest to obtain a leadership position in higher education, and maintain their current positions as a leader. One of the women put it best by saying, "If you do not believe in yourself and your capability to lead, no one else will." I was encouraged to see that these women had succeeded despite the challenges they faced. Each woman, so unique in her own individuality, yet with stories so similar, reminded me of my call and purpose as a woman of African ascent.

While pursuing my doctorate degree, I recall the conversations of my peers who were invited to make presentations with their professors. Then I discovered that my peers were also invited to work on scholarly publications with their major advisors and some professors. These opportunities were never presented to me while I worked through my courses and the dissertation process. And so, it is my purpose to mentor young women climbing the ladder in academia. Many of our African mothers and sisters have gone before us, and now I must "pay it forward" through my story and experiences to inspire other young women in their quest to succeed.

SILENCED NO MORE

We used several tenets of critical race theory (CRT) as a lens to help us see the similarities among all of the women interviewed and how their experiences shaped their perceptions. Intercentricity of race and racism with other forms of subordination, challenge to dominant ideology, commitment to social justice, centrality of experiential knowledge, and a transdisciplinary perspective (Yosso et al., 2004) shaped our perceptions of the women in our study. We are able to see and understand the tenets of CRT through the stories of race and how race relations affect marginalized groups. Despite the challenges their race and gender constructed, these women possessed a common desire to invest in themselves and their abilities to obtain success through leadership attainment.

The CRT tenet of *intercentricity of race and racism with other forms of subordination* intersects racism with other forms of subservience. This tenet is interwoven in the stories the women recount based on their experiences of race and gender. The women believed that they had to work harder just to be considered equal to their White counterparts. Their stories detailed accounts of being overlooked for leadership positions for which they were qualified and retained the necessary credentials. There is a level of race consciousness that is evident when an African American woman's quest for leadership attainment takes significantly longer to achieve than her White counterparts holding lesser degrees and experience. In the experiences of these women, their race consciousness extends beyond mere awareness of the color of their skin but can be attributed to their gender as well. It becomes evident that racial stereotypes are a fundamental part of social relations. Race is never divorced from gender due to the distinctive ways Black women experience their race and gender (Pasque & Nicholson, 2011).

The CRT tenet, *challenge to dominant ideology*, was used to explore the challenges or factors that African American women have faced in their quest for leadership attainment. This tenet challenges White privilege and counter claims made by higher education institutions that they are indeed equal opportunity providers. After talking to the women in this study, this claim appears to be hard to substantiate, as their experiences fly in the face of race and gender neutrality claims. However, not all of the challenges experienced by the women surfaced as overt racism or sexism. The women experienced subtle undertones of rejection justified by reasons of not being a good fit for the organization or simply not being privy to informal networks of information sharing. Thus the feeling of isolation, loneliness, and a sliver of despair, perpetuated by the institutional climate towards African American women, made it difficult but not impossible. Climbing the ladder of success to achieve a leadership position in higher education did not necessarily come with a road map for these women. Nevertheless, they did not allow the twists, turns, and roadblocks they encountered to impede their successful advancement in academe.

Considering the CRT tenet of *commitment to social justice*, we were able to see differences in the women's racial identity as well as their corresponding motivations, sense of empowerment, and self-esteem. This tenet suggests working toward eliminating racism and sexism by empowering minorities through authentic gains in education once initiated through civil rights legislation. The idea of these women investing in their own value was significant to persist in overcoming the institutional barriers that attempted to impede their advancement.

Higher education must challenge its White-dominated leadership structures by offering an alternative model for African American women (and women of color overall) to obtain success through leadership attainment. Leadership preparation programming is an area where African American women can receive the training and skills needed to obtain professional expertise. The women in our study who participated in professional leadership training programs or women's leadership trainings were able to meet other women and women of color holding leadership positions. They were able to hear their stories as well as their challenges and opportunities on their journey, as well as specific information about what education institutions are looking for in leadership candidates.

Centrality of experiential knowledge was the CRT tenet used as a lens to explore the strategies used for successful advancement in the academy. The premise of this tenet recognizes that the lived experiences of people of color are indeed legitimate and critical to understanding racial subordination. These women refused to accept their ascribed inferiority status by their majority counterparts and found safe spaces where they could express themselves, provide support to each other, and regain power by defining themselves and their worth (Robinson, 2012). They believe that their stories have merit and are worth sharing. Through CRT, we have examined the ideology of racism, racist injuries were named, and victims of racism shared their voices (Solórzano & Yosso, 2002)—we too have shared our voices. We know that these counterstories are an essential tool for our survival and liberation (Delgado, 1989). We have discovered that those injured by racism and other forms of oppression are not alone in their marginality. We are empowered by hearing the stories of others and listening to our own stories. We will continue to present a space for women's' voices and experiences. As we work from positions in the margin, we will continue to tell counterstories as a strategy to debunk traditionally held social constructions and transform ways of knowing.

REFERENCES

Crawford, K., & Smith, D. (2005). The we and the us: Mentoring African American women. *Journal of Black Studies, 36*(1), 52–67.

Crenshaw, K. (1988). Race, reform and retrenchment: Transformation and legitimating in anti-discrimination law. *Harvard Law Review, 101*(7), 1331–1387.

Creswell, J. W. (2009). *Research design: Qualitative and quantitative, and mixed methods approaches.* Thousand Oaks, CA: Sage.

Delgado, R., & Stefancic, J. (2001). *Critical race theory: An introduction.* New York, NY: New York University Press.

Harris, C. I. (1993). Whiteness as property. *Harvard Law Review, 106,* 1707–1791.

Holmes, S. L., Land, L. D., & Hinton-Huston, V. D. (2007). Race still matters: Considerations for mentoring Black women in academe. *The Negro Educational Review, 58*(1/2), 105–129.

Institute of Women's Policy Research (2013). Retrieved from http://www.iwpr.org/

Iverson, S. V. (2007). Camouflaging power and privilege: A critical race analysis of university diversity policies. *Educational Administration Quarterly, 43,* 586–611.

Jean-Marie, G. (2006). Welcoming the unwelcomed: A social justice imperative of African American female leaders of historically Black colleges and universities. *Educational Foundations, 20*(1–2), 85–104.

Ladson-Billings, G., & Tate, W. F. (1995). Toward a critical race theory of education. *Teachers College Record, 97*, 47–68.

Lopez, G. R. (2003). The (racially neutral) politics of education: A critical race theory perspective. *Educational Administration Quarterly, 39*, 68–94.

Lynch, R. V. (2006). Critical-race educational foundations: Toward democratic practices in teaching "Other people's children" And teacher education. *Action in Teacher Education, 28*, 53–65.

Mabokela, R. O., & Green, A. L. (2001). *Sisters of the academy: Emergent Black women scholars in higher education.* Sterling, VA: Stylus Publishing.

Marina, B. L. H., & Fonteneau, D. Y. (2012). Servant leaders who picked up the broken glass. *Journal of Pan African Studies, 5*(2), 67–83.

Matsuda, M., Lawrence, C. R., Delgado, R., & Crenshaw, K. W. (1993). *Words that wound.* Boulder, CO: Westview Press.

Merriam, S. B. (2009). *Qualitative research: A guide to design and implementation.* San Francisco, CA: Jossey-Bass.

Nicols, J. C., & Tanksley, C. B. (2004). Revelations of African American women with terminal degrees: Overcoming obstacles to success. *The Negro Educational Review, 55*(4), 175–185.

Parker, L., & Villalpando, O. (2007). A race(cialized) perspective on education leadership: Critical race theory in educational administration. *Educational Administration Quarterly, 43*, 519–524.

Pasque, P. A., & Nicholson, S. E. (2011). *Empowering women in higher education and student affairs.* Sterling, VA: Stylus Publishing.

Patitu, C. L., & Hinton, K. G., (2003). The experiences of African American women faculty and administrators in higher education: Has anything changed? *New Directions for Student Services, 104*, 79–93.

Robinson, K. A. (2012). Institutional factors contributing to the under-representation of African American women in higher education: Perceptions of women in leadership positions. *Electronic Theses & Dissertations.* Paper 811. Retrieved from http://digitalcommons.georgiasouthern.edu/etd/811

Smith, W. A., Yosso, T. J., & Solórzano, D. G. (2007). Racial primes and black misandry on historically white campuses: Toward critical race accountability in educational administration. *Educational Administration Quarterly, 43*, 559-85.

Snyder, T. D., Dillow, S. A., & Hoffman, C. M. (2007). *Digest of education statistics 2006 (NCES 2007-017).* National Center for Education Statistics, Institute of Education Sciences, U.S. Department of Education. Washington, DC: U.S. Government Printing Office.

Solórzano, D. G., & Villalpando, O. (1998). Critical race theory, marginality, and the experience of minority students in higher education. In C. Torres & T. Mitchell (Eds.), *Emerging issues in the sociology of education: Comparative perspectives* (pp. 211–224). Albany, NY: State University of New York Press.

Solórzano, D. G., & Yosso, T. J. (2002). Critical race methodology: Counter-story-telling as an analytical framework for education research. *Qualitative Inquiry, 8*, 23–44.

Tate, W. F. (1996). Critical race theory: History, theory and implications. *Review of Research in Education, 22*, 201–247.

Thomas, G. D., & Hollenshead, C. (2001). Resisting from the margins: The coping strategies of Black women and other women of color faculty members at a research university. *The Journal of Negro Education, 70*(3), 166–175.

Valverde, L. A. (2003). *Leaders of color in higher education: Unrecognized triumphs in harsh institutions.* Walnut Creek, CA: AltaMira Press.

Yosso, T. J., Parker, L., Solórzano, D. G., & Lynn, M. (2004). From Jim Crow to Affirmative Action and back again: A critical race discussion of racialized rationalities and access to higher education. *Review of Research in Education, 28,* 1–25.

Zamudio, M. M., Russell, C., Rios, F. A., & Bridgeman, J. L. (2011). *Critical race theory matters: Education and ideology.* New York, NY: Routledge.

CHAPTER 7

CRITICAL RACE MEDIA LITERACY AND CRITICAL INCIDENTS OF RESISTING TEACHABLE MOMENTS

Vonzell Agosto, Zorka Karanxha, and Deirdre Cobb-Roberts

In 2002, the interim dean of the College of Education (COE) appointed a task force whose purpose was to assess efforts to infuse diversity throughout curriculum across the college. In addition to curricular concerns, the interim dean articulated issues related to the recruitment and retention of faculty and students of color and the development of cultural competence in the faculty and preparation of students. On the recommendation of the task force, the interim dean organized a permanent diversity committee (DC) to address concerns within the COE. This chapter centers the work of the DC that illustrates the efforts of the committee co-chairs who attempted to infuse critical theories of race and media literacy into the curriculum of professional development for faculty and graduate students. The committee co-chairs provided faculty and graduate assistants opportunities to learn from modeling and dialoguing about adopting critical race media literacy to analyze critical incidents.

Envisioning Critical Race Praxis in Higher Education Through Counter-Storytelling, pages 107–120
Copyright © 2016 by Information Age Publishing
107

To encourage critical race media as a framework for examining racial oppression, we provided faculty and graduate students with media footage of critical incidents involving race and racism (e.g., video clips from the local news, student generated videos from coursework, library collection of sheet music). Through faculty meetings and a retreat hosted by the DC, we generated and interpreted data using a critical race theory analysis. In addition to the critical incidents involving race and racism in education that we used to facilitate dialogue, responses to these cases (ours as co-facilitators and participants as faculty and graduate students) offer another set of critical incidents. According to Flanagan (1954), "incidents" permit inferences and predictions to be made about the person performing the act, and to be "critical" the intent of the act must be fairly clear and consequences must be definite enough about what the effects are or could be. Readers might use these critical incidents in the development of educators to combine critical media literacy with critical race theory—or what we call critical race media literacy.

Our use of critical incidents poses a critique of "teachable moments" in that we challenge the view that the teachable moment is located in the readiness or receptiveness of the learner as much as, if not more than, the actions of educators. According to Havighurst (1953), "when the body is ripe, and society requires, and the self is ready to achieve a certain task, the teachable moment has come" (p. 7). Van Soest and Garcia (2000) discuss the role of the facilitator who demonstrates cultural competence as one who attempts to transform an issue into an opportunity or a teachable moment for learning. While they place the facilitation of critical incidents along the spectrum of cross-cultural competence (Cross, Bazron, Dennis, & Isaacs, 1989), they do not place the student along the same spectrum. Our view is that both learners and facilitators can operate at different points along a spectrum of cultural competence to create a dynamic experience that can enhance or diminish the teachability of the moment. Waiting for the teachable moment to arise in oneself or others can become an excuse which behind one retreats when unwilling to risk thinking (differently). In other words, the idea that an even more ideal moment of readiness needs to arise can become a strategy to avoid immediate conversations that one finds emotionally and/or cognitively taxing.

In our observations of faculty engagement, we noted the tendency of White faculty, like White students in several media clips, to deemphasize counternarratives in the media and thereby reinscribe White privilege in the context of secondary education and during the preparation of educators and administrators in higher education. Rather than attempt to replace one master narrative with another (e.g., heroic narrative), we address the limitations of committees, workshops, and intermittent activities to change institutional cultures. We also discuss the implications and recommendations for the development of critical race media literacy among faculty and students through diversity committees in other institutions of higher education.

BACKGROUND CONTEXT

The diversity committee's membership was voluntary rather than a standing committee with elected membership. The interim dean appointed four co-chairs, two assistant professors, and two doctoral students to the lead the DC. The mission of the diversity committee reads:

> The mission of the Diversity Committee is to generate and organize opportunities that build community and capacity in support of the continuous improvement of the institutional culture and climate in the COE. The diversity committee provides a gathering place that supports the development and application of an array of knowledge, dispositions, and skill sets that include interdisciplinary collaboration, policy analysis, and an assets-based perspective across facets of diversity. Discussions of pressing topics that concern faculty, staff, and student development (professional and personal) contribute to the input the Diversity Committee provides to the Dean of the COE.

The charge of the DC had been to center diversity in the COE and apprise the dean of any issues related to diversity that were impeding the progress of the college. The DC also focused on preparing faculty to help students meet the needs of all learners as described by NCATE Standard 4 (McHatton, Shircliffe, & Cobb-Roberts, 2011). This was a particularly important focus given that the majority of students in the COE who are teacher education majors tended to be White and female. During the spring 2010 term, 75% of undergraduates in the college were White and 78% female, while 73% of its graduate students were White and 76% female (University of South Florida [USF], 2010).

While past efforts of the DC have been documented in journal articles (McHatton, Keller, Shircliffe, & Zalaquett, 2009; McHatton et al., 2011), attention to race, racism, and antiracism in those efforts has been thin. For example, while the 2011 publication on diversity in the COE referenced a 2008 forum titled "Racism: Whiteness in the Classroom, Understanding Who We Are," the article did not address race, racism, or antiracism in the analysis of faculty or student experiences. As co-chairs who engage frameworks guided by critical social theory, our work with the DC provides a counternarrative to the dominant narrative that diversity education in the preparation of educators looms largely devoid of criticality, structural analysis, and cross-racial alliances. As co-chairs of the DC, we were entrusted to provide some guidance and support for the faculty, staff, and students through monthly meetings, annual events, and collaborative research opportunities.

While we had participated as members or co-chairs of this committee over the past three to ten years, 2012 marked the first time that we had collaborated as co-chairs. Our initiation into the role of co-chairs followed our collaboration as presenters and program committee members of the 2012 Critical Race Studies in Education Conference and submission on a co-authored article on our critical race theory (CRT) praxis in higher education as a collaborative journey. In this chapter, we address the void of discussing race, racism, and antiracism in the COE and bring a CRT analysis to the efforts and outcomes of the diversity committee with regard to infusing critical media literacy into the curriculum for and by those preparing aspiring educators, administrators, counselors, and other professionals who will likely serve at all levels of education.

CRITICAL RACE MEDIA LITERACY

Critical race theory, originally articulated by civil rights attorney and professor Derrick Bell in the early 1970s, uses counternarratives to expose the permanence of race in American society and challenge race neutral frameworks. Other critical race scholars in law directed a critical lens at issues of race, which led to the development of CRT and helped to challenge a legal tradition that was steeped in a discourse of individual rights (Crenshaw, Gotanda, Peller, & Thomas, 1995). Meanwhile, as Closson (2010) noted, "race held a 'material dimension' in people's lives" (p. 264). Further, the extension of CRT into the field of education was accompanied by some practical parameters for its use (Ladson-Billings, 1998; Ladson-Billings & Tate, 1995). The critical incidents we described herein are discussed through the following tenets of CRT: race and racism, contestation of dominant ideologies, social justice theory and practice, experiential knowledge, and historical context (Villalpando, 2004). These tenets support our analysis of the themes identified in the data (emails, polls, discussion, written reflections, media) generated by this qualitative case study.

The literature on diversity, race, racism, and antiracism efforts can be understood as a body of research contributing to critical race literacy (Yosso, 2002). We extend critical race literacy by fostering the critical examination of media as a type of text to be critiqued. Despite the multiple meanings we may glean from texts, they are not neutral (Kellner & Share, 2007). The research base that supports our conceptualization and application of critical race media literacy includes studies on racial alliances, racial microaggressions, racial battle fatigue, and White privilege in higher education (e.g., Brayboy, 2003; Gildersleeve, Croom, & Vasquez, 2011; Solórzano, Ceja, & Yosso, 2000; Solórzano & Villalpando, 1998; Yosso, Smith, Ceja, & Solórzano, 2009). Additionally, we draw media from popular culture and

American culture, which provide a societal curriculum that engages students beyond the classroom (Cortes, 1979).

THE FACULTY MEETING: FRAMING CONTEXT
FOR THE FACULTY

Our introduction of critical race media literacy to the faculty of the COE came during the first faculty meeting in the 2012 academic year. At that meeting we introduced the theme of critical media literacy and engaged faculty in activities to foreshadow future events, as well as the focus on issues of race and racism. We framed media as a powerful tool to be used toward antioppressive education by faculty and graduate students while teaching.

We showed a broadcast of local news involving an elementary school teacher who posted a derogatory comment about a Black student in her second grade class onto her Facebook page. She referred to the child as the "evolutionary link" between man and apes. Other Facebook friends and colleagues at the same school seemed humored, except for one who intervened to disrupt the discussion. The video clip also included a recorded segment of a press conference in which the student's mother recommended that further inquiry be directed at how teachers bully students. After viewing this video clip, we directed the faculty to discuss whether they would include such content in their classes with aspiring educators and administrators, and if yes, how they would do so. After having some of the small groups report out to the entire group we then provided five topics (privacy, consequences for teacher, racism, student well-being, and media representation) that we saw as relevant to the story and likely to generate productive dialogue leading to the development of cultural competence. We asked that a member representing each group respond to a poll by texting which topic of the five was most present in their discussion. The results of the poll for the 16 respondents (group representatives) were as follows: privacy 6%, consequences for teacher 44%, racism 13%, student well-being 25%, and media representation 13%.

It was unclear from the poll whether the discussions about student well-being centered on their own students (who are primarily White) or the student in the video (a Black, male child). Given that few discussions focused on issues of privacy (i.e., the teacher posting the student's initials to help colleagues guess the student being disparaged), it is likely that the focus on student well-being centered on their students in the COE rather than the student in the video, who was publicly humiliated using social media. Faculty primarily focused on the consequences for the White teacher in the video (who resembles those typically enrolled in the COE) rather than the student of color (as evidenced by the poll results) or minimized the topic of racism in the media clip while during the group discussions. Additionally, after the meeting, faculty sent emails to at least one of us, which developed into chains of discussion. These electronic discussions among a few faculty members further highlighted how the concern of the mother about teachers bullying students was sidelined by the focus on the dominant discourse on bullying between students. It was not surprising to us that faculty minimized focus on the comment about teachers since many of us in education have a professional identity developed through teaching/leading and are foremost positioned to serve aspiring teachers/administrators. Even when we interjected with an email to the entire faculty with the question: *As bullying is being discussed—is anyone addressing (as the mother mentioned in the video shared by the diversity committee) teacher (but not just teachers) bullying (or badgering)?* Only two people responded and only to a select few colleagues rather than to the entire faculty. One person said "good point" and "worth investigating," while another requested a YouTube video of a kindergarten teacher who made all her students tell one child why they did not like him. This colleague also mentioned the idea of including films in the curriculum to bring attention to oppressed groups.

While it was heartening to learn that media were being used (YouTube, film) in connection to narratives and social oppression by at least one person in the college, it was disheartening that there few examples and race was absent in these discussions even though it was so prominent in the local news. By neglecting to address the concerns of the mother with regard to the White teacher's mistreatment of her Black son and sharing his identifying information publicly, the issue of institutional racism was also neglected. The mother's narrative of her Black male child, a second grader, being bullied by his teacher provided a counternarrative to the racist narratives that criminalize Black males in media, and more specifically in popular culture (Hutchison, 1996; Jackson, 2006; Prier, 2012; Tucker, 2007). We were left to wonder why faculty did not discursively embrace the mother's counternarrative and concern for her son. We were reminded of Duncan's (2002) research on Black males that describes a social narrative that suggests they are beyond love. Critical media literacy supports further questioning of media, for instance regarding the subtleties used by journalists and newscasters to lead audiences to care about some (racialized) people and not others.

The focus on critical media literacy through a lens of critical race theory helped us bring attention to the role of media in suppressing some narratives while privileging others, and inciting some audiences to action on some topics but not others. For instance, the newscaster introducing the story in the video clip framed the story as one about being careful about what you post. This initial framing centered being careful (not to get in trouble) over being caring. In this case, the newscaster commented that typically the warning is for students to be careful about what they post to social media outlets, even though the pending-story was about the teacher. Thus, the newscaster framed the story in terms of teachers being careful so as not to harm themselves. Additionally, much of the coverage of the story focused on the question about what would happen to the teacher. Yet when the camera feed from the field was aired, it displayed a field reporter with a few students and adults holding protest signs in front of a school. The privileged perspective concerned the consequences for teachers rather than the motivations of the protesters who gathered in front of the school. Last, the media clip ended with the field reporter commenting on whether or not any action would be taken against the teacher's license. Bookended and muted between the concerns for the teacher (her licensure) was the story of what the teacher did, the protest calling for the teacher to receive a harsher penalty given the seriousness of the incident, and the mother's plea for further investigation into teacher bullying. The story's beginning and ending with the question of consequences for the teacher was a topic that seemed to resonate with our faculty. While we framed our presentation within the theme of critical media literacy, the media clip framed for the faculty a view that was seemingly neutral. A tenet of critical race theory and principle of critical media literacy is that narratives are not neutral (Closson, 2010; Share & Thoman, 2007). Instead, CRT rejects race neutrality and privileges the experiences of people of color. Those who are critically literate with regard to media are prepared to challenge textual constructions of reality that privilege or suppress views for specific purposes (CAMH Centre for Prevention Science, 2008). We posit that CRT and critical media literacy, resulting in critical race media literacy, can be a powerful analytical tool in the struggle for curriculum and instruction in preparation or professional development that promotes antioppressive education.

THE RETREAT

At the diversity retreat, we centered critical media literacy in the discussion of race, racism, and antiracism among faculty and graduate assistants. We were interested in understanding which lessons generated from racialized material (e.g., videos of students enacting Blackface) were allowed to prevail. We featured a video clip at the diversity retreat that had already generated discussion among faculty in administrative roles that referenced the concept of *teachable moments*. A critical race analysis of the events and outcomes raises questions about how the retreat to *teachable moments* shields White privilege and opens and/or closes counterspaces (Ballard & Cintrón, 2010) and counterstories (Young & Brooks, 2011). According to White and Maycock (2012), "a teachable moment is a highly subjective-reflective learning occurrence that happens during a pedagogical process or learning event...[that] can only be experienced spontaneously" (pp. 323–324). Their definition contrasts the conventional definition of teachable moments as an occurrence that is grounded upon rationally predetermined cause-and-effect pedagogy. Typically, a teachable moment is understood as an opportunity for teaching/learning that arrives unexpectedly.

Rather than ask what educators define as teachable moments and how they respond (e.g., Hyun & Marshall, 2003; Rea, 2003), we assert that more attention to the subjective nature of learning and teaching is needed when occurrences can be perceived by learners as harmful, neglectful, or oppressive. Rather than retreat to framing such moments as teachable, we might ask what is being taught and learned that makes the occurrence less than pleasant or beneficial for some students than others. In other words, we suggest that an emphasis on moments as "teachable" can circumvent or subvert extended conversations on how such moments can be perceived or experienced by students as harmful. Our approach was to emphasize a moment for learning about Blackface through media and examine it as part of a larger social and historical phenomenon. Such cultural narratives may be unpleasant to revisit or encounter as a performance of racism, especially when one sees such performances as entertaining rather than educating through disparaging and stereotyping.

CRITICAL RACE MEDIA LITERACY: RACIAL DISCRIMINATION IN THE CLASSROOM

At the COE diversity committee retreat, we introduced segments of a class video that was taped by an instructor. The video depicted a group of White students presenting a course project that included a videotaped skit titled "Racial Discrimination in the Classroom," where they were to read an article and present key points from the article to the class. They created and taped a video clip of a skit as part of the project. In the clip, a White female with long blond hair in Blackface portrayed a student of color. Class erupted in laughter when she entered the scene dressed in baggy pants, tilted baseball cap, and being loud. When the student impersonating the teacher called her Sheneneh (pronounced Sha-nay-nay) and asked why she was late for class, the laughter was even louder.

When the video was over, a student from the classroom audience asked: "Why did you pick the name Sheneneh?" One of the two White male students who had taken center stage in explaining the assignment while the White female students stood behind them, immediately put the White female student playing the lead on the spot by claiming, "She chose the name." The White female student who played the character shrugged: "Comic relief. I don't know." We found the portrayal and their responses highly problematic. The students chose to portray the Black student by re-inforcing several stereotypes and trying to make light of a very serious issue at the expense of some of their classmates (i.e., allies for racial justice). The students' portrayal of the Black student was an appropriation of ste-reotypical images of Black women (e.g., arriving late to class, using only slang) and enactment of White privilege. Their movie and responses to questions displayed a lack of understanding of how daily insults and jokes can result in stress that can be detrimental to the well-being of students of color, also known as racial battle fatigue (Smith, Hung, & Franklin, 2011). Furthermore, their decision to perform in Blackface also showed a lack of historical knowledge and the problematic nature of using Blackface to portray African Americans.

At the conclusion of the video, discussion in one group of faculty and graduate students at the retreat began with rationales that suggested the students might be beginners in college and thus unaware of the problem-atic nature of their video and portrayal. Once it was established that the stu-dents were advanced in their undergraduate studies, the group questioned the role of the professor and the quality of her/his work and insinuated that this might be an isolated incident rather than a pervasive phenom-enon among students. There was a tendency to understand and protect the White students (i.e., excuse their insensitivity). The faculty in this particu-lar group also began giving examples of their work that related to issues other than race. We noticed their tendency to avoid discussion of how we are all implicated in the construction and reproduction of stereotypical and racialized portrayals of educational experiences among students of color.

During the faculty retreat we used the racial microaggressions framework as a way for faculty and graduate students to develop cultural competence in their practice. Sue, Capodilupo, Torino, Bucceri, Holder, and Esquilin (2007) describe racial microaggressions as "[b]rief and commonplace daily verbal, behavioral, and environmental indignities, whether intentional or unintentional, that communicate hostile, derogatory, or negative racial slights and insults to the target person or group" (2007, p. 273). Sue et al. (2007) further define racial microaggressions as "explicit racial derogation characterized by a verbal or nonverbal attack meant to hurt the intended victim by name-calling, avoidant behaviors, or purposeful discriminatory actions" (p. 274).

In the video of the group presentation, we noticed how a female student of color sitting in the front row of the classroom had lowered her head on the desk while the students fielded questions from classmates. During the large group discussion none of the participants mentioned this student, nor did they express concern for her on the large post-it notes or refer to her in small group discussions to the degree that is was prominent enough a contribution to be captured by the note-taker (sitting between two groups).

Instead of considering the myriad experiences she or other students of color or antiracist allies might have when viewing this material in class, faculty diverted the conversation. Therefore they were complicit in promoting the master narrative of the racialized representation in the form of Blackface and only expressing concern about the White students.

Once again, as with the video clip of the teacher using Facebook to disparage her student, the concern for the level of knowledge or lack thereof of the White students was the privileged discourse rather than concern for the student(s) of color who might have encountered being treated like the fictionalized Black student in the video or allies against racism with any racial group affiliation. We found it troubling that there was laughter in the classroom as the fictionalized student's name rolled during credits and our audience of educators expressed little if any concern for those disturbed by the video. The possibility that the young Black woman in the video may have been experiencing racial battle fatigue was neglected as topic of discussion, as were the perspectives of mother in the news video and her son's. We posit that discussions that avoid the experience of racial minority students in majority settings encountering racial derogation (verbal or nonverbal) fit within the scope of the definition of racial microaggressions as avoidant behavior (Sue et al., 2007). While it is not up to White individuals to decide if performances such as Blackface are offensive or derogatory (Sue et al., 2007), which can be argued indefinitely as a felt personal perspective, it is up to educators to understand how White privilege operates to systematically sustain power and privilege in education. It would behoove faculty in higher education to develop critical (race) media literacy among their students given that access to media and expectations for its use in the curriculum is increasing at all levels of schooling.

OUTCOMES AND RECOMMENDATIONS

As culturally responsive educators who engage critical pedagogy and theories of race as liberatory praxis (Ladson-Billings, 1995), we decided to extend our pedagogy and curriculum into the broader context of the college and engage in productive dialogues that center diversity in general and race and racism in particular. Instead of merely reporting, we involved faculty in professional development activities by introducing critical media literacy and debriefing in small group discussions. Involving and asking the entire college faculty to discuss race openly was an area that had not been traversed in previous years, which meant that there was the potential of resistance. We were hopeful that the inclusion of critical (race) media literacy would ignite a more critical discussion of the use of media in our classrooms where students are preparing to become educators, administrators, counselors, and school psychologists. The work of the diversity committee has yielded some positive outcomes.

One outcome of our work was an increase in faculty and student exposure to the diversity committee and the reassurance that there was a space for faculty to solicit support in their development or continued efforts to provide culturally relevant pedagogy and curriculum. For instance, we were approached with a request to support a Fulbright Scholar's effort to showcase a one-woman play, *Crushhopper*, on racial identity development. The request was for the diversity committee to endorse the event and assist with advertisement. This request urged us to reflect on the meaning and rationale behind it. We believed the request emanated from a position of comfort as our colleague had attended the faculty meeting where the critical media literacy framework was introduced and likely felt the committee would be willing to support the event.

Another outcome of our work has been the inclusion of the diversity committee meetings on the agenda of some department meetings. For instance, we as co-chairs were housed in two different departments. Our department chairs had consistently included us on the agenda to provide updates on the activities of the diversity committee, thus providing an opportunity to share the work of the committee and increasing awareness about the diversity committee. These updates provided another platform for us to share information, receive feedback, and critically evaluate our successes and challenges as we attempted to shape, define, and support diversity efforts in the college at multiple levels. Furthermore, the focus on race, racism, and racial microaggressions through a critical (race) media lens generated an invitation from a colleague to co-author a book chapter on strategies for teacher educators to address the intersections of popular culture, diversity, and critical media literacy (e.g., Agosto, Karanxha, Cobb-Roberts, & Williams, 2014).

While these outcomes were moments to be celebrated, they were not necessarily reflective of the kinds of change that will lead to lasting and sustaining impact in the curriculum of our programs or the culture of our institution. These efforts were seedlings of work that we expect to continue collaboratively with a growing coalition of those interested in analyzing media for use in the curriculum and generating antioppressive media reflecting cultural competence in the context of higher education. The recommendations implied in our concluding remarks are to build coalitions (co-chairs), set the tone (provide critical perspectives), expect resistance (retreat to teachable moments rather than remain engaged in the critical moments), and persist in disseminating critical medial literacy through various events to reach students, faculty, staff, and administrators. The inclusion of theoretical tools such as critical race theory and critical media literacy supports a critical approach to culturally relevant pedagogy and multicultural education that may be in use but devoid of critical perspectives that engage issues of power, privilege, and domination.

REFERENCES

Agosto, V., Karanxha, Z., Cobb-Roberts, D., & Williams, E. (2014). Critical media literacy: Edutaining (popular) culture. In B. Cruz, A. Vasquez, C. Ellerbrock, & E. Howes (Eds.), *Talking diversity with teachers and teacher educators: Exercises and critical conversations across the curriculum* (pp. 53–71). New York, NY: Teachers College Press.

Ballard, H. E., & Cintrón, R. (2010). Critical race theory as an analytical tool: African American male success in doctoral education. *Journal of College Teaching and Learning, 7*(10), 11–24.

Brayboy, B. (2003). The implementation of diversity in predominantly White colleges and universities. *Journal of Black Studies, 34*(1), 72–86.

CAMH Centre for Prevention Science. (2008). The fourth R: Relationship based violence prevention. Retrieved from http://youthrelationships.org/about_fourth_r.html

Closson, R. (2010). Critical race theory and adult education. *Adult Education Quarterly, 60,* 261–283.

Cortes, C. E. (1979). The societal curriculum and the school curriculum: Allies or antagonists? *Educational Leadership, 36*(7), 475–479.

Crenshaw, K., Gotanda, N., Peller, G., & Thomas, K. (Eds.). (1995). *Critical race theory: The key writings that formed the movement.* New York, NY: Free Press.

Cross, T., Bazron, B., Dennis, K., & Isaacs, M. (1989). *Towards a culturally competent system of care* (Vol. 1). Washington, DC: Georgetown University Child Development Center.

Duncan, G. (2002). Beyond love: A critical race ethnography of the schooling of adolescent Black males. *Equity & Excellence in Education, 35*(2), 131–143.

Flanagan, J. C. (1954). The critical incident technique. *Psychological Bulletin, 51*(4), 327–358.

Gildersleeve, R. E., Croom, N. N., & Vasquez, P. (2011). "Am I going crazy?!:" A critical race analysis of doctoral education. *Equity & Excellence in Education, 44*(1), 93–114.

Havighurst, R. J. (1953). *Human development and education.* New York, NY: McKay.

Hutchison, E. O. (1996). *The assassination of the Black male image* (2nd ed.). New York, NY: Simon & Schuster.

Hyun, E., & Marshall, J. D. (2003). Teachable-moment-oriented curriculum practice in early childhood education. *Journal of Curriculum Studies, 35*(1), 111–127.

Jackson, R. (2006). *Scripting the Black masculine body: Identity, discourse, and racial politics in popular media.* Albany, NY: State University of New York.

Kellner, D., & Share, J. (2007). Critical media literacy is not an option. *Learning Inquiry, 1,* 59–69.

Ladson-Billings, G. (1995). But that's just good teaching! The case for culturally relevant pedagogy. *Theory into practice, 34*(3), 159–165.

Ladson-Billings, G. (1998). Just what is critical race theory and what's it doing in a nice field like education? *Qualitative Studies in Education, 11,* 7–24.

Ladson-Billings, G., & Tate, W. F. (1995). Toward a critical race theory of education. *Teachers College Record,* 97, 47–68.

McHatton, P. A, Keller, H., Shircliffe, B., & Zalaquett, C. (2009). Examining efforts to infuse diversity within one college of education. *Journal of Diversity in Higher Education, 2*(3), 127–135.

McHatton, P. A., Shircliffe, B. J., & Cobb-Roberts, D. (2011). Promoting diversity through multilevel activism: An organizational approach. *Educational Considerations, 38*(2), 7–12.

Prier, D. (2012). *Culturally relevant teaching: Hip-hop pedagogy in urban schools.* New York, NY: Peter Lang.

Rea, D. (2003). *Sustaining teachable moments on the complex edge of chaos.* Chicago, IL: American Educational Research Association Conference.

Share, J., & Thoman, E. (2007). *Teaching Democracy: A media literacy approach.* Los Angeles, CA: The National Center for the Preservation of Democracy.

Smith, W. A., Hung, M., & Franklin, J. D. (2011). Racial battle fatigue and the miseducation of black men: Racial microaggressions, societal problems, & environmental stress. *The Journal of Negro Education, 80*(1), 63–83.

Solórzano, D., & Villalpando, O. (1998). Critical race theory, marginality, and the experience of minority students in higher education. In C. Torres & T. Mitchell (Eds.), *Emerging issues in the sociology of education: Comparative perspectives* (pp. 211–224). Albany, NY: State University of New York Press.

Solórzano, D., Ceja, M., & Yosso, T. J. (2000). Critical race theory, racial microaggressions, and campus racial climate: The experiences of African American college students. *The Journal of Negro Education, 69*(1/2), 60–73.

Sue, D. W., Capodilupo, C. M., Torino, G. C. Bucceri, J. M., Holder, A. M. B., & Esquilin, M. (2007). Racial microaggressions in everyday life: Implications for clinical practice. *American Psychologist, 62*(4), 271–286.

Tucker, L. (2007). *Lockstep and dance: Images of Black men in popular culture.* Jackson: University of Mississippi.

University of South Florida (USF). (2010). "Student head count." Tampa, FL. Retrieved from http://usfweb3.usf.edu/infocenter/?silverheader=0&report_category=STU&report_type=SMAJS&reportid=84516

Van Soest, D., & Garcia, B. (2000). Facilitating learning on diversity: Challenges to the professor. *Journal of Ethnic & Cultural Diversity in Social Work, 9*(1/2), 21–39.

Villalpando, O. (2004). Practical considerations of critical race theory for Latino/a college students. *New Directions for Student Services, 105,* 41–50.

White, S. R., & Maycock, G. A. (2012). College teaching and synchronicity: Exploring the other side of teachable moments. *Community College Journal of Research and Practice, 36*(5), 321–329.

Yosso, T. J. (2002). Critical race media literacy: Challenging deficit discourse about Chicanas/os. *Journal of Popular Film and Television, 30*(1), 52–62.

Yosso, T. J., Smith, W. A., Ceja, M., & Solórzano, D. G. (2009). Critical race theory, racial microaggressions, and campus racial climate for Latina/o undergraduates. *Harvard Educational Review, 79*(4), 659–691.

Young, M. D., & Brooks, J. (2011). Supporting graduate students of color in educational administration preparation programs: Faculty perspectives on best practices, possibilities, and problems. *Educational Administration Quarterly*, *44*(3), 391–423.

CHAPTER 8

FIRST-GENERATION, PRETENURE FACULTY OF COLOR

Navigating the Language of Academia

Anjalé Welton, Montrischa Williams, Herb Caldwell, and Melissa Martinez

Academe, especially predominately White institutions (PWI), still has not made the necessary commitments to foster persons of color into the professorial pipeline, as the recruitment and retention of faculty of color in the United States remains a challenge (Diggs, Garrison-Wade, Estrada, & Galindo, 2009; Thompson, 2008). When faculty of color (FOC) secure an academic position, we are intersectionally marginalized, often experiencing multiple forms of oppression (social class background, gender, and sexuality) in addition to our race (Delgado Bernal & Villalpando, 2002; Diggs et al., 2009; Turner, 2002). Research extensive universities primarily value a Eurocentric knowledge base as "quality," legitimized research, and this dominant ideology can academically isolate FOC who research their

Envisioning Critical Race Praxis in Higher Education Through Counter-Storytelling, pages 121–146
Copyright © 2016 by Information Age Publishing
121

own communities in order to counter institutional, structural, and personal experiences with oppression (Delgado Bernal & Villapando, 2002).

Regrettably, the academic isolation FOC experience is also demographically evident. According to the most recently reported 2010 NCES data, 79% of faculty at all institutional types were White, whereas only 7% were Black, 6% Asian Pacific Islander, 4% Hispanic, and 1% American Indian/Alaska Native (U.S. Department of Education, 2011). This academic isolation also extends to rank and discipline. FOC are severely underrepresented in the associate and full professor ranks, more represented in educational and social sciences, and are rarely found in STEM departments at PWIs (King & Watts, 2004).

Additionally, FOC may face tokenism and hypervisibility as one of the few or only persons of color in our academic departments (McDonald & Wingfield, 2008; Turner, Gonzalez, & Wood 2008), cultural taxation or questioning of our teaching and scholarly credibility (Aldridge, 2001; Gregory, 2001; Stanley, 2006; Thomas & Hollenshead, 2001; Turner, Myers, & Creswell, 1999), and extra diversity-related service duties that are assigned because we *are* faculty of color. The latter does not necessarily "count" and deters from what is considered most important to evaluation for tenure—research. While existing research catalogues the barriers, less is known of the manner in which FOC *effectively* navigate the professoriate. Furthermore, most studies examine FOC issues at all ranks and do not solely focus on assistant professors who must prove themselves to the academy by achieving tenure.

Therefore, the purpose of our larger study was to further understand the views and experiences of tenure-track assistant professors of color (n=46) working within public and private four-year universities, in various disciplines and regions across the United States specifically. Also, as a point of clarification, we often use the first person pronoun such as "our," "we," or "us" in this chapter when referencing the experiences of faculty of color (FOC) because all the authors in this chapter identify as a person of color and are situated at some point along the pipeline to the professoriate—one author is a doctoral student, one is a recent PhD recipient in her first full-time research position, and the other two authors are pretenure FOC.

For this chapter we focus on a subsample of thirteen participants from the larger sample who specifically identified as first-generation college graduates. According to research, when compared to students with parents who have earned degrees, students whose parents have not earned a bachelor's degree (i.e., first-generation college graduate) lag behind their peers in achievement and express dissatisfaction in their overall college experience because higher education institutions still provide insufficient resources to support the needs of this subgroup (Jenkins, Miyazaki, & Janosik, 2009). However, despite what the research says about the disparate experiences of first-generation college graduates, we heard a *counterstory* in the narratives of our subsample of pretenure FOC, who, by the mere fact that they went on to graduate school, obtained a doctorate, and became professors, defy typical research narratives about first-generation college-going students. In addition to their racialized struggles, this subsample of FOC identified social class-based barriers related to their first-generation status that were not as prevalent in the narratives of FOC who did not identify as first-generation status.

In addition to being the first in their family to graduate college, nearly half of the subsample also self-identified as a first-generation immigrant. In this chapter, we define first-generation immigrants as "persons born and socialized in another country who immigrate as adults, although the term technically includes the foreign born regardless of their age of arrival" (Rumbaut, 2004, p. 1165). This variation among participants can add to the complexity of the lived experience of foreign-born, first-generation college graduate assistant professors of color.

Participants' struggles, as one of the first in many ways, served as an impetus to further advance in the educational pipeline to graduate school and the eventual ascension to a tenure-track faculty position. We argue that as the *first,* the pretenure FOC had to acquire a unique set of skills to navigate educational settings (in both their K–12 and postsecondary experiences) that were historically not designed with their success in mind. As such, we use Tara Yosso's (2005) concept *navigational capital* to understand how the unique experiences and struggles this subsample of FOC faced as one of the first are actually positive sources of cultural capital for traversing the tenure-track process. The navigational skills these pretenure FOC acquired over time eventually serve as an asset for them in their tenure-track faculty position, as they continue to develop a sophisticated means to deconstruct and decode the complex norms, systems, institutional practices—that is, the "language" of academia.

THEORETICAL FRAMEWORK: NAVIGATIONAL CAPITAL

Yosso (2005) coined the theoretical concept community cultural wealth, using critical race theory to challenge the assumption that people of color are deficient in social and cultural capital. A deficit narrative primarily depicts persons of color in the educational pipeline as "at-risk", in need of intervention, or a problem to be fixed, and rarely considers the extra set of strengths and skills that persons of color must possess to navigate fervently racist and classist educational structures, and unfortunately this rhetoric is used to inform policies, programs, and practices. According to Yosso (2005), this deficit narrative blames students of color and their families for challenges in academic performance and is based on the following stereotypes: "(a) students enter school without the normative cultural knowledge and skills; and (b) parents neither value nor support their child's education" (p. 75).

Bourdieu and Passerson's (1977) assertion of how cultural capital is attained is most widely used in sociology of education research. Higher education institutions, especially PWIs, preference the capital of the White middle class, and groups who do not fall within this normative category are viewed as deficient, lacking the skills necessary to be successful in the academy. Scholars who use critical race epistemology would argue that Bourdieu's definition of cultural capital primarily centers on White privilege, or the unearned/accumulated privileges that those in dominant groups have acquired (Delgado Bernal & Villalpando, 2002; Yosso, 2005). When we, as scholars of color, produce research that is based on our own communities and this scholarship is then compared to research that is more legitimized by PWIs, our way of seeing, being, and knowing is considered insufficient, lacking scholarly merit, and "inherently biased" (Delgado Bernal & Villalpando, 2002, p. 177; Johnsrud & Sadao, 1998; Stanley, 2006). Delgado Bernal and Villalpando (2002) classify the way in which faculty of color's scholarship is delegitimized as "academic apartheid":

> A Eurocentric epistemological perspective can subtly—and not so subtly—ignore and discredit the ways of knowing and understanding the world that faculty of color often bring to academia. Indeed, this Eurocentric epistemological perspective creates racialized double standards that contribute to an apartheid of knowledge separating from mainstream scholarship the type of research and teaching that faculty of color often produce (Villalpando & Delgado Bernal, 2002). This apartheid of knowledge goes beyond the high value society places on the positivist tradition of the "hard sciences" and the low regard for the social sciences; it ignores and discredits the epistemologies of faculty of color. (p. 171)

However, whether or not the academy would admit it, higher education institutions readily benefit from the cultural capital FOC *do* possess—our cultural identities and racialized experiences. Even though the service part of the trifecta of achieving tenure (the others being teaching and research) counts very little, FOC are called upon more so than our White peers to do service activities related to issues of race, diversity, and social justice. However, as FOC we have first-hand experience with issues that impact our communities. This expert knowledge/cultural capital derived from our racial identities is actually an asset to higher education institutions that seek to bolster awareness about diversity and race-related initiatives (Delgado Bernal & Villalpando, 2002; Johnsrud & Sadao, 1998). Consequently, serving on race-related committees is one form of activism for FOC as we use these service obligations to hold institutions accountable for issues of racism, equity, and access (Baez, 2000). Yosso (2005) claims that Bourdieu and scholars alike present a very narrow narrative of persons of color, one that is deficit oriented, and the complex set of assets persons of color use to "survive and resist macro and micro-forms of oppression" must be considered (p. 77).

Yosso's theory of community cultural wealth proposes that people of color possess at least six forms of capital: aspirational, social, familial, navigational, linguistic, and resistant capital. Aspirational capital represents the dreams and goals we set out to achieve in spite of perceived barriers. Linguistic capital refers to the intellectual and social assets we possess based on the language and communication skills we use in our own communities. Our linguistic capital can also be linked to our bicultural skills (see Jonhsrud & Sadao, 1998). FOC must develop a set of bicultural skills that enable them to negotiate the academy's dominant culture without capitulating our cultural values and norms (Johnsrud & Sadao, 1998). Biculturalism is defined as circumventing or switching communication styles between "two cultural milieus" in the academy (Johnsrud & Sadao, 1998, p. 320). One milieu represents our personal cultural heritage and the other is the dominant White male-centric norms of the academy.

Familial capital originates from the support and nurturing that is developed from our strong family and community ties. Unfortunately, the tenure-track process preferences individualism and competition, but as FOC we commonly value strong family ties or *familismo*, which translates to our use of *personalismo*, a communication style that emphasizes collectivism, strong personal relationships, and collaboration in order to navigate the tenure-track process (De Luca & Escoto, 2012). Social capital is networks and community ties that help persons of color navigate institutions. Resistant capital involves skills that persons of color use to challenge and resist a racist society. For example, Segura's (2003) study on Chicana faculty found that participants chose a career as an academic in order to challenge the hegemonic narratives presented about Chicanas in their respective disciplines, to accurately represent the needs of the communities in which they culturally identify, to serve as role models for historically marginalized groups, and counter the racially gendered restraints placed upon their communities. Ultimately, the Chicana faculty saw their place and scholarship in the academy as a form of activism (Segura, 2003).

While these aforementioned five forms of capital are critical for the findings in this chapter, we highlight how FOC, who are the first, use a multitude of cultural assets as *navigational capital*, one of the six forms of capital in Yosso's framework, to navigate the tenure-track process. According to Yosso, navigational capital is the sophisticated way in which persons of color draw upon the other five forms of capital to maneuver institutions that historically devalued FOCs' scholarship or denied us access to higher education institutions entirely. Because persons of color have a lifetime of experience circumventing and resisting institutional barriers, especially racism, they acquire social and cultural strategies from their own communities to navigate higher education institutions.

Defining First Generation Status

Obtaining a doctoral degree and ascending to a tenure-track position for anyone is a feat in itself. While a significant amount of research considers how race and gender impact faculty of color in the academy, limited research examines how social class (family background) as well as citizenship status are identity markers that indeed affect the educational pathway and the pursuit of tenure. Consequently, in addition to being a person of color, we found that our subsample's "status" as *first generation*— whether they were a first generation college graduate, immigrant, or both—was significant to their educational pathway, especially their decision to pursue a doctorate and ultimately enter the professoriate.

Pursuing a bachelor's degree can be a complex task filled with academic, social, and cultural transitions. These transitions may produce a unique experience and set of challenges for first-generation students who may not have equitable access to information and resources pertinent to the journey. This inequity of access does not mean a lack of ability or drive; nor should it imply the student is without life and cultural experiences that forge a viable skill set. The skills to achieve should be valued as they translate well to succeeding in the professoriate.

According to the Higher Education ACT of 1965, those whose parents or primary caregivers have not earned a bachelor's degree are considered first-generation college students. This is the working definition used by federally funded TRiO college prep and academic support programs, which target low income and first generation college-going students. This act is significant as it recognizes that first generation college students are among the most underserved and underrepresented. Because these students' experiences differ significantly when compared to traditional students, strategies and resources have been put into place to move toward equity of opportunity for first-generation college students to succeed. Lack of parental education does not equate to lack of support; rather, as first-generation students' parents have little to no direct experience in accessing and matriculating through college, students are not able to obtain particular types of information crucial to graduation.

The literature suggests there is a significant difference in how college is experienced when comparing first-generation college-going students to traditional students, or those whose parents have earned a bachelor's degree (Pike & Kuh, 2005). Traditional students are more likely to enjoy the college experience and thereby return for the second year of study compared to first-generation college students (Leone & Tien, 2009). Also, first-generation college students are more likely to take extended time in earning their bachelor's degree (Jenkins et al., 2009). Furthermore, first-generation college students are more likely to be from a lower socioeconomic background than traditional students and therefore experience financial pressure in the pursuit of their college degree. Finally, research has shown that first-generation college-going students typically do not have access to guidance, information, and support to effectively navigate the application process for college compared to their traditional peers (Roderick, Nagaoka, Coca, Moeller, Roddie, & Gilliam, 2008). It is this sort of denial of information that can hinder the first-generation college student's educational journey.

Six participants in the subsample featured in this chapter not only experienced the extra challenges that come with being the first person in their families to pursue and receive a college degree, but also bear the additional scrutiny that unfortunately comes with being a professor who is considered foreign born or holds an international status. Rumbaut (2004) shared:

> Differences in nativity (of self and parents) and in age and life stage at arrival [in the United States] ... are known to affect significantly the modes of acculturation of adults and children in immigrant families, especially with regard to language and accent, educational attainment and patterns of social mobility, outlooks and frames of reference, ethnic identity and even their propensity to sustain transnational attachments over time. (p. 1164)

Faculty who are first-generation immigrants endure a number of challenges in United States higher education institutions, and some of the major concerns that foreign-born faculty face are issues related to cultural differences, coping with loneliness, and the "red tape" involved with obtaining a visa to work in the United States. If the university does not provide the adequate support and resources, the visa application process in itself can also be time consuming and stressful for many faculty members, cutting into the time needed to devote to research and teaching (Collins, 2008). Another source of stress for these faculty members is attributed to cultural differences, as their "world-views (particularly regarding materialism), familial relationships, religious beliefs, expectations and social and cultural conventions" are often challenged both inside and outside the classroom (Collins, 2008, p. 183). Finally, foreign-born professors typically see language as the main challenge for them in the classroom and feel frustration with not being able to express themselves as they intend. These cultural differences can potentially lead to misunderstandings between faculty and students, and faculty members may have difficulty coping. Although, according to Collins' (2008) research, some foreign-born faculty do find groups to support their needs, these support systems are often not very active or well publicized. Thus, this is important to consider among participants who were foreign-born and now first-generation immigrants in the United States.

The brief overview of the literature demonstrates that first-generation (both college graduates and immigrants) FOC have a distinctive educational pathway. Despite the barriers presented in the research, many who identify as first generation, including those participating in this study, have successfully overcome barriers to become the first in their family to graduate college. The question now becomes, how does this experience either hinder or propel FOC to succeed in becoming tenure-track faculty in the same system that was seemingly unprepared for their existence as a student? Pretenure FOC who are among the first may now face many of the same challenges as a working professional as they did as an undergraduate and graduate student.

RESEARCH METHODS

The research presented in this chapter is part of a larger nationwide qualitative study on the pretenure experiences of FOC, conducted by a team of researchers at various universities in the United States. Specifically, this qualitative study investigates how tenure-track assistant professors of color working at four-year public and private universities in the United States successfully navigate academia. Individual, semi-structured interviews (Rubin & Rubin, 2005) were conducted with assistant professors who teach in various disciplines and self-identify as being of Black/African American, Latina/o, Asian/Pacific Islander, and/or Native American descent. The researchers utilized their scholarly networks to recruit participants for the study. Participants were recruited by email, phone call, and in person. Thereafter, using the snowball technique (Patton, 1990), consenting participants referred the research team members to other potential participants. The interview protocol consisted of 12 key questions and 11 probing questions. The participants were asked to share their personal and educational background, views and experiences as an assistant professor of color, as well as successes and challenges in navigating the academy.

Participants

A total of 46 participants are included in the larger qualitative study. Of the 46 professors that were interviewed, 13 indicated that they were the first in their family to graduate college, and among them six were also first-generation immigrants. The 13 participants highlighted in this chapter self-identified as follows: three Asian females, four Black females, two Black males, and four Latinas. Of the 13 participants, 11 are female and 2 are male. The professors work in a variety of fields, including apparel merchandizing and product development, communication disorders, Black studies/counseling psychology, anthropology, music, educational leadership, finance, journalism, human resource education, higher education/student affairs, and curriculum and instruction. Participants work in tenure-track positions at universities in the South or Midwest (See Table 8.1).

Data Collection and Analysis

Interviews were audio recorded, transcribed, and checked for accuracy. Thereafter, each research team member was assigned four to five interviews to analyze individually, utilizing Hyper-Research. Hyper-Research is well-known research software for qualitative and quantitative analysis of textual, audio, and video materials (Hesse-Biber, Dupuis, & Kinder, 1991).

TABLE 8.1 Participant Demographics

Pseudonym	Gender	Race/Ethnicity	Age	Department	Institution Type
Jamie	Female	African American	31	Higher Education	Midwest
Angelica*	Female	Black	39	Apparel Merchandizing & Product Development	Midwest
Maggie	Female	African American	N/A	Communication Disorders	South
Grace	Female	African American	30	Black Studies/Counseling & Psychology	Midwest
Bianca	Female	Chicana, Tejana, Mexican American	41	Anthropology	South
Monica*	Female	Latina	39	Music	South
Paula	Female	Latina	36	Anthropology	South
Thelma	Female	Latina	58	Education Leadership	South
Wendy*	Female	Asian	33	Finance	South
Beckey*	Female	Asian	31	Journalism	South
Cassandra*	Female	Asian	40s	Human Resource Education	Midwest
Mark	Male	African American	39	Higher Education/ Student Affairs	South
Paulo*	Male	Black/African	41	Curriculum and Instruction	Midwest

Note: N = 13
* Indicates first generation immigrant

Each researcher utilized an inductive analysis where emerging "patterns, categories, and themes" were identified (Creswell, 2012, p. 175) based on the individual research team member's understandings of the data, the research literature, and the critical race theory methodological framework (Solórzano & Yosso, 2002). The research team members then met to review, discuss, and compare their initial codes and themes. In this process, overarching themes and subthemes were identified to depict the subsequent counterstories.

Positionality: Telling Our Own Counterstories

As scholars and producers of knowledge, our research is driven by our positionality, which is essentially grounded in our personal history of life experiences (Chiseri-Strater, 1996). Thus, it is important to reveal the researcher's position in this research to not only understand how the study was developed, but to understand the researchers' counterstories as well. Three of the four authors are first-generation college graduates. Their narratives provide a critical lens to better understand the experiences of first generation college-going faculty of color navigating academia.

Anjalé (AJ) Welton

I am a single Black female, first-generation college graduate who grew up in a working-class, single-parent home—my mother dually played the role of father. I was raised by both family and community members and I have always used community support to navigate educational settings. Thus, I consider this sense of community a major part of my Black identity. However, the academy appears to be a competitive and individualistic environment, and unfortunately the community assets I have used in the past to navigate educational settings are typically not legitimized in the academy. I continue to struggle to find a way to authentically integrate community engagement in my scholarship and not just research that is distantly positioned from the ivory tower and selfishly meets the criteria for me to gain tenure.

Montrischa M. Williams

Being an African American, first-generation, low-income woman, transitioning into a predominantly White and Asian institution was difficult. The institutional challenges I faced as an underrepresented student on campus were more than I could endure. I utilized my social supports and academic triumph to rise above the hardships that often impeded my educational progress. It is because of my navigational capital that I was able to make it through my collegiate experience and graduate program.

Herb Caldwell

As a teen I was aware that no one in my immediate family had graduated college, so my competitive nature compelled me to be the first. Lack of finances, resources, my Blackness, and the isolation due to ignorance in how to *do* college were all identifiable to me as barriers to college success. Yet the achievement of educational goals can be attributed to a faith-based tenacity instilled by my parents. Even as I near the completion of a doctorate with the potential to join the academy, it is this achievement tenacity that both propels and gives me confidence that I can succeed at any level regardless of personal, professional, societal, cultural, or institutional barriers.

Melissa A. Martinez

I am a Latina, specifically of Mexican American decent, from the South Texas border. While I am not a first-generation college graduate, my parents did not assist me extensively with accessing and matriculating through college. Their emotional guidance and support as well as financial resources were critical, but attending a PWI straight out of high school was a culture shock since I grew up in a predominantly Latino region. This experience, coupled with my having been a bilingual teacher and counselor in public schools, inform my understandings of inequities, oppression, and politics within the academy. Moreover, my decision to continue my studies and be the first in my immediate family to pursue both a master's and doctoral degree made me more cognizant of the types of challenges a first-generation college-going student faces.

CHALLENGING DOMINANT NARRATIVES
WITH COUNTER-STORIES

We chose to highlight this subsample of pretenure FOC because as first-generation college graduates, as well as those who had the intersecting identity of being a first-generation immigrant, we recognized certain resourceful ways in which the faculty navigated the academy that were distinctively different from participants who were not first generation. We feature the following FOC counterstories: familial support and strong value of education, strong informal mentoring networks, and using identity struggles as a source of activism to strengthen a social justice-oriented research agenda. Finally, we assert that these experiences were indeed assets that aided them in understanding early on how to navigate the academy (i.e., navigational capital), which from a critical race theory perspective is a form of praxis.

Pedagogies of Childhood: "My parents didn't go to college... they were pro education"

There is notable progress in educational research and practice as it is steadily shifting from a deficit depiction of Black, Latino, and working-class families (i.e., they don't value education) (Valencia & Solórzano, 1997) to one that recognizes the existing cultural knowledge and practices, or *funds of knowledge*, that our families possess make significant contributions to our educational trajectories. Thus, we, as persons of color, engage in a community approach to learning, and this same approach can be a valuable form of social capital in a formal educational setting as it is recommended teachers incorporate the *funds of knowledge* from students' homes into classroom instructional practices (Moll, Amanti, Neff, & González, 1992; Moll & Greeberg, 1990). According to Rio-Aguilar and Kiyama (2012) (also see Kiyama, 2010), the same funds of knowledge approach that is recommended for teacher pedagogy and practices can also be used by higher education institutions, given as persons of color we use the cultural knowledge from our families and communities to help prepare for college, build college aspirations, enroll, and persist. All the participants in our subsample of first-generation FOC identified family supports as a key source of motivation for pursuing a college degree and then graduate school. These familial supports sustained our participants even when there were limited formal supports within their educational settings that encouraged them to make academia their career. It was the informal supports, the social and cultural capital of their families, that served as an impetus for their educational drive.

The educational backgrounds of our participants' families ranged from a sixth grade education to some college. Even though our participants' families' educational levels varied, all felt a sense of duty to pursue educational opportunities that were available to them but may have been inaccessible or denied to their parents' generation. For example, Cassandra's parents and her siblings were not able to pursue higher education because of a history of political upheaval in her native country:

> It's all for a reason because there are not a lot of universities when my parents were growing up... only one or two universities in the whole entire China. So with other people they graduate high school and they teach high school; it doesn't require any type of certificate and those are just recent in terms of higher education, just recently, say thirty years. You know the higher education was just recovered in 1979; that's the first after the Communist Party took over in 1929, and it's the first group of students who were able to go to college since 1979. Yes. So some of my sisters weren't able because when they were the age of going to college, college was not available and they were all over the countryside and that's when the Cultural Revolution in China was in

1966–76, a whole ten years there was no way to get a higher education... the entire generation was lost.

Cassandra's opportunity to go to college was somewhat fortuitous. Regrettably, her parents and most of her siblings were not able to pursue higher education, but the end of the revolution in her native country, China, fortunately coincided for her when she was of age to attend college. Cassandra took her country's national exam to go to college, which was "pretty tough" and she was prideful because "it's only three percent of the overall high school graduates who get a chance to go to college." Cassandra then paved the way for her youngest sister to attend college.

Even though most of the participants' parents grew up poor or working class, their parents demonstrated pride and persistence in their work that could be adopted as *funds of knowledge* for the type of diligence that is necessary to persist as faculty on the tenure track. Bianca's parents had no more than a sixth grade education, but she learned from the perseverance of their hard work:

My dad was the son of a Mexican American from Brownsville... they [mother and father] are these cross border families... my dad on a better-off ranch, my mom on a pretty poor farm. They got to the sixth grade level—seventh grade I think my mom. My dad got to sixth grade on the Mexican side and then came here. My dad passed away when we were young; he worked as a cab driver and my mom has worked as a cafeteria worker for many years, so we're the first generation college.

The hard work that her parents demonstrated was then passed down to the resolve and educational success of Bianca and all her siblings who were immensely successful, all receiving undergraduate and graduate degrees from highly selective universities:

First generation immigrants or generation of Americans there on the border; it's kind of complicated. So now my older sister is the first in the family to go to college and then she has a—she got a Bachelor's and my twin sister and I went to undergraduate and my sister has a law degree and I have a PhD.

FOC received a lifetime of messages that their economically disadvantaged childhood was of little "worth" or that being first generation was a significant setback. However, FOCs' conversations with us as researchers gave them the opportunity to revel in their achievement thus far and reflect on how their childhood experiences connected to their present successes. Fittingly, the FOC identified specific ways in which their childhood was by no means "deficient" but was actually "rich" with lessons that at the time seemed simple but were in retrospect quite significant to their ability to be quickly savvy about the rules of the tenure-track process, even when those rules were ambiguous. Because FOCs' parents had to navigate life circumstances where opportunities were hidden or denied, they used their parents' struggles as a model for how to navigate the enigmatic tenure-track process. Here Mark presents his own counterstory to the all-consuming deprivation narrative of the plight of a first-generation college graduate:

> My parents didn't go to college. I always talk about the strengths of being a first gen student and one of them was, I didn't come from a family that was education ignorant, they were very education savvy. My grandfather worked for the Encyclopedia Britannica, so we had encyclopedias at my house since birth. The kids encyclopedia, the teen encyclopedia, and the big one. And so my parents are very pro education, and always have been, always were...just cause their life circumstance they couldn't go...but very smart people. One of the advantages I think about that, I didn't realize it until I was getting ready to graduate from Southern State University. So I kind of bought into this deficit idea "I'm first gen, I'm struggling"...You weren't poor, you weren't first gen until you went to college, before that you were normal...now you're poor, now you're oppressed...well no, people have more things and my parents were like we thought we gave you good direction, on what to do...I'm going to stop saying these things like it's something to be ashamed of. I'm actually quite proud of that fact that my parents were pro education and so forth. One of the things I realized as a student, my parents said to me you have your scholarship, do your things, do the best you can. We're supporting you.

Upon reflection, Paulo also realized how the pedagogies of his childhood home were by no means "lacking" but indeed transformative, "enriching" and very much connected to his research agenda on how Black parents support their children's education. Paulo's parents as a form of resistance to government-sponsored hegemonic schooling—which was rooted in his native country's history of colonialism, racism, and violence—provided him with supplemental instruction at home.

> I mean at a great level my parents wanted me to get educated; they did everything. I wrote in my thesis where I acknowledge my parents and I say my dad would buy oranges and he taught me how to count using oranges because schools were so bad, you know. So my parents did and they didn't have even high school diplomas themselves, but they wanted me to have success as far as education was concerned, but I'm the first generation and the only one of my siblings who has a college diploma and the other three do not, so. We are the first generation.

Angelica similarly remembers the pedagogies of her childhood. Her grandmother and great grandmother told stories of the backbreaking work that they endured during the wrath of Jim Crow and demanded that it be a testament to the educational and professional opportunities Angelica now has and must fight for:

> I tell my brother this all the time it's the women in my family, it's not that I pick up the phone and talk to them on a daily basis or anything like that, but I remember my grandmother getting off the big truck that had tons of Black people on the back of it after working in the fields from sun up to sun down. My great grandmother still living on the plantation land and pretty much still there until going to the nursing home until she died. . . . I'm just like you have no excuse in life to not at least attempt something. You've been given opportunities that for generations we've never had. So we have no excuse, when you tell me I can't do something, oh I can't? Well maybe I can't do it the way that you tell me I can't do it, but I'll find a way that I can.

Despite the participants' familial educational backgrounds, both family support and struggles in accessing education served as motivating factors that played a role in the participants' academic success.

Informal Mentoring: "She had really high expectations of me, so I decided, 'Okay, I'll be someone like her.'"

Since faculty of color are still grossly underrepresented in tenure-track positions, mentoring is extremely important to ensure that we do indeed make tenure (Tillman, 2001). University-sponsored systematic and formal mentoring programs are considered most effective (Welton, Mansfield, & Lee, 2014). According to Tillman (2001), for FOC a quality mentoring relationship must consider the following: (1) FOC must be purposefully paired with mentors who are dedicated to helping us achieve tenure, (2) the mentoring partnership should be monitored and evaluated to ensure that it is the right fit and a productive pairing, and finally (3) the formal program should consider career and psychosocial functions—sense of competence, identity, work effectiveness, socialization, acceptance, and confirmation (Tillman, 2001). Though formal mentoring programs are vital, Stanley (2006) suggests that a one-size-fits-all approach to mentoring will not work for FOC at PWIs because we do not see many faculty like "us" in the academy. Thus, it is recommended FOC have access to a hybrid of informal and formal mentoring so that we receive mentoring that is customized to the unique needs of our intersecting identities. However, the FOC in our subsample received more informal mentoring and very few shared examples, given it was limited, of formal mentoring programs/opportunities at their institutions. Two FOC received mentoring from graduate fellowship programs that they independently applied for—the Ford and the Mellon Mays Fellowship.

As first-generation college graduates, the pretenure FOC were often left out of vital academic networks. FOC indeed countered the master narrative that they lacked professional assertiveness: Being given limited access to formal mentoring led them to strategically seek out lifelong mentors. These mentors were essential to providing pretenure FOC a strong set of scholarly skills so that they could be noticeably productive scholars in their respective departments. Social networks or ties in the form of mentoring were exceedingly important to understanding the rules of graduate school, applying, interviewing, and negotiating the faculty job search process, as well as knowing what activities facilitate a productive scholarly record versus what detracts from getting tenure. While in some ways acquiring a mentor was strategic, many described the importance of fortuitous mentoring connections. All FOC shared stories of a faculty mentor who was pivotal to introducing the possibility of pursuing graduate school. Also, most FOC, upon entering graduate school, never had the expectation that they were going to become professors after finishing their doctorate. However, it was an informal mentor who reassured them that they had ascertained the skills necessary to secure a tenure-track faculty position. Beckey was moved by a professor who finally showed interest in her scholarship and took the time to help her understand theoretical concepts she found challenging to comprehend. This mentor made her realize the meaningful impact a professor could have on students:

> She was just one of the professors that everybody loves. She's very nice, young, energetic, and I think she encouraged me a lot as well because I worked as her assistant for one semester and I taught several of her classes and that encouraged me a lot. And from my perspective, that's the first time I thought that I needed a teacher to teach me something or give me some guidance, . . . And she had really high expectations of me, so I decided, "Okay, I'll be someone like her."

At times it is important to have faculty mentors from your own self-identified cultural background. A same-race mentor can assist FOC in traversing the racial politics of academe in general and achieving tenure (Tillman, 2001). Also, a same-race mentor can demonstrate to FOC that someone "like them" can "make it" at a PWI. Jamie found it easier to talk with her same-raced mentor about the racial microaggressions that were imposed on her by her students. She felt it took extra effort to discuss the racism she experienced with her White colleagues because additional explanation was required for them to understand what she was going through. However, talking with her African American female colleagues about a student's racist comment did not require additional editorializing:

> She's a Black woman and guess what, I'm going to assume that she knows if something comes up. Like I told her about the whole "ghetto professor" com-

ment, and she was like able to process through that with me because I told my White colleagues in our specific curriculum area about that because we talk about all the students and I had to explain to them how historically and socially the term "ghetto" has been socially constructed to mean, Black, female, and poor.... Whereas I don't have to explain that to her.... Not that my formal mentor or my other mentor said anything more; you know they might have, but it just felt like a different interaction that I didn't have to explain all of the intricacies of what these things meant.

While same-race mentors share our cultural backgrounds and similar racialized experiences, the participants recognized a broad network was required and that sometimes White mentors can be equally supportive. Participants strategically used their own cultural ties to network. However, FOC recognized that certain dominant codes need to be deciphered if they are going to find a way to maneuver the academy and assert the type of scholarship that matters most to them. In addition to same-race mentors, White faculty mentors would help them access the unwritten rules of the academy. Jamie not only sought out her same-race peers for mentorship, but she also simply asked her White male colleagues "if anybody has any good advice on negotiating that would be helpful, and actually two men, two White guys, actually responded and sent me like all kinds of crazy stuff, like articles on negotiating." Mark was fortunate that he was connected early on in his graduate studies to African American male life-long faculty mentors who are legendary in the field of education. Mark still collaborates with these same-race mentors on major research projects and publications, and his mentors have also connected him to fellowship opportunities that provide him extra buy-out time from teaching so he can focus on writing and publishing. Even still, Mark tells his own mentees to develop a "constellation" of resources and that having White faculty mentors is equally important:

> On the other hand, students of color need to understand that mentoring does not solely exist in the realm of people like you. You can totally have meaningful and important relationships with people that are White, I mean.... So if I just said I need a Black man to work with, that would not have been to my benefit. I need a Black man and I need some White women and some White men. I need everybody. The concept we use in mentoring literature is *constellation mentoring*, the idea of bringing together different folks. Maybe it's part of me being a military kid, but I understood this very well, so I don't feel like anybody's thinking, "Mark is just draining me he has so many needs." No, I go to one guy for this and I go to this guy for this, and a number of folks across this campus I would go to for stuff and they hooked me up.

Identity as a Source of Agency: "Academia has put up some walls... my goal is to dispel some of those myths."

FOC held onto memories of their struggles as first-generation college graduates, as did those who identified as first generation immigrants; they used their "otherness" as a vehicle for struggle, resistance, legitimacy, assertion of agency, and a space for their own intellectual productivity in their departments (Segura, 2003). Participants told detailed stories of their families' educational and personal experiences, institutional marginalization, and oppression. These experiences with oppression motivated FOC to use their scholarship as an agent of social justice.

Participants remembered what it was like as the first in their family to venture to college and how confused they were by the labyrinth of the university—how to form good study habits, to whom and where to go for academic supports, and how to decipher the course content and lectures that unfortunately seemed to be mechanical, esoteric, and not student friendly. To counter academic structures and practices that impact the retention of first generation students like them, a few FOC engaged in scholarship, teaching, and service activities that would give those who share similar identities greater access to the ivory tower and its knowledge—a space where we are still limited in numbers and impeded access. For example, Angelica intentionally removes academic jargon, or academese, from much of her scholarship in order to share her research with those who have been historically denied access to higher education institutions:

> My greatest challenges, in some areas we would call it selling out.... I still want to maintain my integrity, I have this challenge of how academic to become. Academia has put up walls and made it look so much more difficult through the language that we use to make sure that no one else would want to try and get it, my goal is to dispel some of those myths. So I try to make my language very plain, even though they may be academic and using the jargon... but I'm going to say it as plainly as I can say it, and I know some people interpret me as not being as educated as they are, but I chose to speak a plain language because I want it to be something that no matter who is listening to me, whether you have a 5th grade education or a PhD everyone can understand what I'm saying... and what we end up doing is isolating the individual and making them feel like they can't do it, and I think that I'm here because I'm the accidental PhD student, accidental doctor to show that it is doable for the vast majority of us.

Mark also made sure that his very presence in the academy was in itself an agentic act by demonstrating to other students of color in the community that it is possible for someone like them to gain access to a PWI as a college student, graduate student, and maybe even one day as faculty.

> I want to see students of color inspired and motivated by the fact that you can go to school here and not be a 4.0 student and come back here as faculty, but it can be excessive at times, and that can be the tipping point when is it too much, and you have colleagues who meaningfully tell you say no to doing everything. Well that doesn't work for people of color because we come from collective communities. So, if I tell a Black or Brown person or someone from my neighborhood that I can't be there ... c'mon man what's up with that, you work at [Southern State University] now, you can't talk to the kids in the neighborhood, and I'm like I never want to be that person. And so I go to elementary schools every year for their college week. Seven in the morning I get up at the butt crack of day and drive the [south side] to talk to the kids and I say, "You know what, college is a possibility and let me tell you why, I lived right there, that's where I grew up," and I point out the window ... and the kids are like wow, this is not somebody who went to college from somewhere else, this is somebody from up the street.

FOC who were first-generation immigrants acknowledged that they not only had to decode the language of the academy but they also had to, according to Paulo, work "three times" as hard to decode the language of a "foreign land" because "you don't know how, as a first-generation person, and I don't speak English as a first language." Wendy readily acknowledged she had more identity markers to contend with, especially considering, "you have to get good teaching evaluations and that's challenging for me because I felt like, as a female professor, petite, foreign, you're at a disadvantage." For Wendy, the publishing part of teaching, research, and service is easiest to grasp because she can write in isolation, whereas teaching and service require social interactions. Sadly, because of cultural differences/ racism, social engagements were antagonizing for her. Wendy stated, "So what's challenging again for me as I guess a professor of color is the language barrier, cultural barrier, how to socialize and get popular" and she observed that professors without the cultural/racial barriers, especially White male faculty, did not put forth as much effort with their teaching, but they still were popular with students and received high marks on their teaching evaluations. Monica, on the other hand, had to exhibit extra exertion to counter the discrimination she experienced as a foreign-born professor. Even when Monica's abilities were questioned because of her speaking accent, all doubts would be eliminated when she captivated people with her scholarly talent.:

> I would say in retrospect, perhaps during my graduate studies, I would say, I was ostracized, as were all of us international students ... I don't know if it was a bad thing or if it affected me negatively, except that I sometimes, I

wondered, is this person inviting me to play because I am really a good pianist or are they inviting me cause they want to have some entertainment, at the expense of my accent. But I quickly put those things away, because I knew I was a good pianist for example in terms of that. It's, I try not to think, but I know academically in my own research, I am going to talk about that, because I am getting to the topic of music—the type of music we cultivate in academia.

Navigational Capital: "Tap into people who have gone before me . . . and take initiative on my own."

Despite the numerous barriers along the pipeline to academia, FOC realized they accumulated significant social and cultural capital along the way that would ease navigating the tenure-track process. A combination of family/community supports, resiliency in spite of a history of racial and class based oppression, and significant support from informal mentoring networks served as an array of capital that, in the end, helped FOC configure how to navigate institutions that were not designed with them in mind. Because FOC had few resources throughout their educational pathways that would provide a step-by-step road map to accessing college, graduate school, and the professoriate, they had to rely on their own wherewithal to comprehend the language of academia.

As Mark explains, he eventually realized how this skill-set of grasping as he called the "unexplored" was actually a skill that could be applied to navigate the unwritten norms of graduate and now faculty life, and this unique navigational capital may be a skill that some of his peers from White and affluent backgrounds may not possess:

> And every step of the way for me educationally has been sort of unexplored territory, but part of the thing about being first gen but also a military kid is that you know as a military kid you're always new, always moving someplace, so what you learn is how systems work, you learn how to observe organizations, so I can probably go to an orientation that I don't know anything about...and be really quick about, this guy is doing good stuff so I need to find out what he's doing and I've always been good at this sort of thing. Part of the power is knowing what you don't know, not assuming you know things, because I don't know what the hell is going on here so I need somebody to help me through this process. Whereas, I had colleagues who I think often thought they knew what was going on, and later found out, yeah, that wasn't right. And that was one of the things that I thought was a huge advantage for me.

FOC often times felt left out of important information networks throughout their educational trajectory; they assumed that with every new situation they were relatively unknowing and for this reason used whatever resources that were at their disposal to figure out any new organizational and institutional space. With every new experience, FOC intensely asked questions and used peers for support. Brenda always "felt like I had to take initiative on my own" when preparing for exams in her graduate program and preparing for the job market, as well as teaching graduate level courses. In order to learn systems and rules of academia, Brenda "had to tap into my friends, people that had gone before me. I couldn't have done it without people that helped me. The generosity of former students and colleagues was amazing." Brenda recognized a key asset she possesses is that she "could take initiative":

> That's one of the things I feel like helped me get the job, and I figured out how to do it. The juggling of all the classes and logistics—I really don't think there is a set guide, and you can't know how to really do that without jumping in.

Similarly, Angelica identified the process as "kinda the trial by fire just like the dissertation process," thus revealing the hit-or-miss nature of navigating the academy. However, she acknowledged that she at least has "the tools" to help her along the tenure process and has a support group she established along with another colleague who assisted her in the writing process. The trial by fire technique used to navigate the tenure-track process is a tool the participants in this study acquired along the way, considering as a first-generation college student, they did not have pre-existing knowledge on how to navigate higher education institutions (undergraduate, graduate school, professoriate). For these reasons, the trial by fire method is a legitimate navigational tool.

DISCUSSION AND RECOMMENDATIONS

FOC continually experience a "chilly climate" when navigating the tenure-track process. This study sought to understand the experiences of first-generation FOC in postsecondary institutions. From the counterstories presented, we learned that FOC often utilized navigational capital, specifically drawing on familial educational background, mentorship, and identity as tools to survive in hegemonic postsecondary institutions, where their representation as faculty is minimal. The experiences of FOC in this study are similar to current research that reveals overall FOC in postsecondary institutions frequently experience negative occurrences such as marginalization, isolation, heavy service loads, lack of mentoring from their home department, as well as overt and covert racism, discrimination, and high levels of stress, and for women, sexism (Alfred, 2001; Back, 2004; Blackwell, 1989; Johnsrud & Sadao, 1998; Turner, 2002). Additionally, FOCs' academic knowledge and ability to conduct research is often challenged (Aldridge 2001; Gregory 2001; Thomas & Hollenshead, 2001; Turner et al., 1999). These incidences inevitably make the tenure process more challenging for FOC, and ultimately, compromises their dossier when the time comes for them to come up for promotion, tenure, and review (Solórzano, 1998).

To this end, we call on leaders of higher education institutions to think about and change their institutional culture but also develop practices or programs that provide FOC a more welcoming environment and inclusive experience. Leaders can play a role in enhancing FOCs' experiences earlier on in the pipeline by assisting in the implementation of programs such as the Summer Research Opportunities Program (SROP),[1] which was established by member universities belonging to the Committee on Institutional Cooperation (CIC),[2] or the Ronald B. McNair Post baccalaureate Achievement Program,[3] established by the U.S. Department of Education. Both programs were specifically created to increase the number of underrepresented students engaging in graduate programs and research. Additionally, the Barbara L. Jackson Scholars Program, sponsored by the University Council for Educational Administration (UCEA), was established to assist FOC transitioning into tenure-track positions by providing social support, professional development opportunities as well as mentorship. These aforementioned programs are prime examples of how leaders can implement supports and resources that facilitate the transition from graduate school into the academy, ultimately enhancing FOCs' experience in institutions of higher education. Yet these programs are isolated, not systemic supports, and focus more on increasing the pipeline of FOC. Unfortunately, the number of programmatic examples do not address the racism, both structural and attitudinal forms, deeply rooted in higher education institutions and academic departments. PWIs have considerable work to do towards improving the culture and climate for FOC. There needs to be more apparent strategic efforts to systemically eradicate racism at PWIs.

The counterstories in this study are important because they contribute to the growing body of literature that documents the experiences of FOC in the academy. Without the documentation of what goes on behind closed doors, leaders in higher education are not held accountable for their institutional culture and cannot take the necessary steps to establish inclusive environments, where all faculty, regardless of their background, are welcomed. Efforts to increase the number of FOC in higher education are a challenge, and establishing an environment where FOC are not subjected to instances of racism, sexism, heterosexism, and further marginalization and isolation is just as difficult. However, this does not excuse leaders of higher education from making a concerted effort to change their institutional culture. It is the simple strength of continuing to, as what one participant from this study stated, "[call] the institution out" and utilizing counterstories as ways to demonstrate what social and institutional supports are necessary to ensure pretenure FOC are successful. This study is one of many that contribute to the general goal toward various ways we can enhance the experiences of FOC navigating the tenure-track process.

Lastly, this work is instrumental in highlighting and validating the experiences of FOC and how they make light of institutional barriers that impede their tenure-track process by showing how FOC employ their navigational capital as a form of praxis to facilitate progression through the tenure track journey. For every hurdle jumped and obstacle stumbled upon, the counterstories presented reveal that FOC beat the odds by utilizing navigational capital as praxis to transform challenges into opportunities. It is through the counterstories presented in this chapter that we can firmly understand that navigational capital is a traditional form of praxis for FOC who are seeking to cross the tenure(d) finish line.

NOTES

1. SROP was designed to "increase the number of underrepresented students who pursue graduate study and research careers" (Committee on Institutional Cooperation, 2013) and essentially is a gateway to the professoriate (Davis, 2008), specifically tapping into undergraduate students.
2. Research universities that are part of CIC include the following: The University of Chicago, The University of Illinois, Indiana University, The University of Iowa, The University of Michigan, Michigan State University, University of Minnesota, Northwestern University, Ohio State University, Pennsylvania State University, Purdue University, the University of Wisconsin–Madison and finally, the University of Nebraska–Lincoln.
3. The federally funded Ronald B. McNair Post-baccalaureate Achievement Program (U.S. Department of Education, 2013) was established to increase the number of low-income, first-generation, underrepresented students entering doctoral programs through research and professional development opportunities.

REFERENCES

Aldridge, D. P. (2001). Redefining and refining scholarship for the academy: Standing on the shoulders of our elders and giving credence to African-American voice and agency. In L. Jones (Ed.), *Retaining African Americans in higher education: Challenging paradigms for retaining students, faculty & administrators* (pp. 193–205). Sterling, VA: Stylus.

Alfred, M. (2001). Reconceptualizing marginality from the margins: Perspectives of African American tenured female faculty at a white research university. *The Western Journal of Black Studies, 25,* 1–11.

Back, L. (2004). *Ivory towers? The academy and racism.* In I. Law, D. Phillips, & L. Turney (Eds.), *Institutional racism in higher education* (pp. 1–6). Sterling, VA: Trentham Books.

Baez, B. (2000). Race-related service and faculty of color: Conceptualizing critical agency in academe. *Higher Education, 39*(3), 363–391.

Blackwell, J. E. (1989). Mentoring: An action strategy for increasing minority faculty. *Academe, 75*(5), 8–14.

Bourdieu, P., & Passeron, J. (1977). *Reproduction in education, society and culture.* London, England: Sage.

Chiseri-Strater, E. (1996). Turning in upon ourselves: Positionality, subjectivity, and reflexivity in case study and ethnographic research. *Ethics and representation in qualitative studies of literacy,* 115–133.

Collins, J. (2008). Coming to America: Challenges for faculty coming to United States' universities. *Journal of Geography in Higher Education, 32*(2), 179–188.

Committee on Institutional Cooperation. (2013). Summer Research Opportunities Program. Retrieved from http://www.cic.net/students/srop/home.

Creswell, J. W. (2012). *Qualitative inquiry and research design: Choosing among five approaches.* Thousand Oaks, CA: Sage.

Davis, D. J. (2008). Mentorship and the socialization of underrepresented minorities into the professoriate: Examining varied influences. *Mentoring & Tutoring: Partnership in Learning, 16*(3), 278–293.

De Luca, S. M., & Escoto, E. R. (2012). The recruitment and support of Latino faculty for tenure and promotion. *Journal of Hispanic Higher Education, 11*(1), 29–40.

Delgado Bernal, D., & Villalpando, O. (2002). An apartheid of knowledge. *Equity and Excellence in Education, 35*(2), 169–180.

Diggs, G. A., Garrison-Wade, D. F., Estrada, D., & Galindo, R. (2009). Smiling faces and colored spaces: The experiences of faculty of color pursuing tenure in the academy. *The Urban Review, 41*(4), 312–333.

Gregory, S. T. (2001). Black faculty women in academy: History, status, and future. *The Journal of Negro Education, 70*(3), 124–138.

Hesse-Biber, S., Dupuis, P., & Kinder, T. S. (1991). HyperRESEARCH: A computer program for the analysis of qualitative data with an emphasis on hypothesis testing and multimedia analysis. *Qualitative Sociology, 14*(4), 289–306.

Jenkins, A., Miyazaki, Y., Janosik, S. (2009). Predictors that distinguish first-generation college students from non-first generation college students. *Journal of Multicultural, Gender & Minority Studies, 3*(1).

Johnsrud, L. K., & Sadao, K. C. (1998). The common experience of "otherness": Ethnic and racial minority faculty. *The Review of Higher Education, 21*(4), 315–342.

King, K. L., & Watts, I. E. (2004). Assertiveness or the drive to succeed? Surviving at a predominately White university. In D. Cleveland (Ed.), *A long way to go: Conversations about race by African American faculty and graduate students* (pp. 110–119). New York, NY: Peter Lang.

Kiyama, J. M. (2010). College aspirations and limitations: The role of educational ideologies and funds of knowledge in Mexican American families. *American Educational Research Journal, 47*(2), 330–356.

Leone, M., & Tien, R. (2009). Push vs. pull: Factors influence student retention. *American Journal of Economic & Business Administration, 1*(2), 122–132.

Mansfield, K. C., Welton, A., Lee, P., & Young, M. D. (2010). The lived experiences of female educational leadership students. *Journal of Educational Administration, 48*(6), 727–740.

McDonald, K. B., & Wingfield, A. M. H. (2008). Visibility blues: The paradox of institutional racism. *Sociological Spectrum, 29*(1), 28–50.

Moll, L. C., Amanti, C., Neff, D., & González, N. (1992). Funds of knowledge for teaching: Using a qualitative approach to connect homes and classrooms. *Theory into Practice, 31*(2), 132–141.

Moll, L. C., & Greenberg, J. (1990). Creating zones of possibilities: Combining social contexts for instruction. In L. C. Moll (Ed.), *Vygotsky and education* (pp. 319–348). Cambridge, UK: Cambridge University Press.

Patton, M. Q. (1980). *Qualitative evaluation methods.* Beverly Hills, CA: Sage.

Pike, G. R., & Kuh, G. D. (2005). First-and second-generation college students: A comparison of their engagement and intellectual development. *The Journal of Higher Education, 76*(3), 276–300.

Rios-Aguilar, C., & Kiyama, J. M. (2012). Funds of knowledge: An approach to studying Latina(o) students' transition to college. *Journal of Latinos and Education, 11*(1), 2–16.

Roderick, M. R., Nagaoka, J., Coca, V., Moeller, E., Roddie, K., & Gilliam, J. (2008). *From high school to the future: Potholes on the road to college.* Consortium on Chicago School Research at University of Chicago. Retrieved from https://consortium.uchicago.edu/sites/default/files/publications/CCSR_Potholes_Report.pdf

Rubin, H. J., & Rubin, I. S. (2005). *Qualitative interviewing: The art of hearing data* (2nd ed.). Thousand Oaks, CA: Sage.

Rumbaut, R. G. (2004). Ages, life stages, and generational cohorts: Decomposing the immigrant first and second generations in the United States1. *International Migration Review, 38*(3), 1160–1205.

Segura, D. A. (2003). Navigating between two worlds the labyrinth of Chicana intellectual production in the academy. *Journal of Black Studies, 34*(1), 28–51.

Solórzano, D. G. (1998). Critical race theory, racial and gender microaggressions, and the experiences of Chicana and Chicano scholars. *International Journal of Qualitative Studies in Education, 11*, 121–136.

Solórzano, D. G., & Yosso, T. J. (2002). Critical race methodology: Counter-storytelling as an analytical framework for education research. *Qualitative inquiry, 8*(1), 23–44.

Stanley, C. A. (2006). Coloring the academic landscape: Faculty of color breaking the silence in predominantly White colleges and universities. *American Educational Research Journal, 43*(4), 701–736.

Thompson, C. Q. (2008). Recruitment, retention, and mentoring faculty of color: The chronicle continues. *New Directions for Higher Education, 143*, 47–54.

Thomas, G. D., & Hollenshead, C. (2001). Resisting the margins: The coping strategies of Black women and other women of color faculty members at a research university. *Journal of Negro Education, 70*(3), 166–175.

Tillman, L. C. 2001. Mentoring African American faculty in predominantly White institutions. *Research in Higher Education, 42*(3), 295–325.

Turner, C. S. V. (2002). Women of color in academe: Living with multiple marginality. *Journal of Higher Education, 73*(1), 74–93.

Turner, C. S. V., Myers, S. L., Jr., & Creswell, J. W. (1999). Exploring underrepresentation: The case of faculty of color in the midwest. *Journal of Higher Education, 70*(1), 27–59.

Turner, C. S. V., González, J. C., & Wood, J. L. (2008). Faculty of color in academe: What 20 years of literature tells us. *Journal of Diversity in Higher Education, 1*(3), 139–168.

U.S. Department of Education (2011). *National Center for Education Statistics. Digest of Education Statistics, 2010* (NCES 2011-015) Retrieved from https://nces.ed.gov/pubs2011/2011015.pdf

U.S. Department of Education. (2013). Ronald B. McNair Postbaccalaureate Achievement Program. Retrieved from http://www2.ed.gov/programs/triomcnair/index.html

Valencia, R. & Solórzano, D. (1997). Contemporary deficit thinking. In R. Valencia (Ed.), The evolution of deficit thinking in educational thought and practice (pp. 160–210). New York, NY: Falmer Press.

Villalpando, O., & Delgado Bernal, D. (2002). A critical race theory analysis of barriers that impede the success of faculty of color. In W. Smith, P. Altback, & K. Lomotey (Eds.), *The racial crisis in American higher education* (pp. 243–269). Albany: State University of New York Press.

Yosso, T. J. (2005). Whose culture has capital? A critical race theory discussion of community cultural wealth. *Race, Ethnicity and Education, 8*(1), 69–91.

CHAPTER 9

LIBERATORY GRADUATE EDUCATION

(Re)Building the Ivory Tower Through Critical Race Pedagogical Praxis

Jessica C. Harris

This chapter presents a counterstory that illustrates how pedagogy, including teaching practices and hidden curriculum in higher education, reproduces structures of racial and gender inequity for women graduate students of color. The narrative offered below exposes and deconstructs these structures and presents educators with tools that allow for a reconstruction of a more inclusive and liberatory approach to graduate education for women of color specifically, and minoritized students more broadly. To do so, this chapter argues for the enactment of critical race pedagogy in graduate education. Critical race pedagogy offers "an analysis of racial, ethnic, and gender subordination in education that relies mostly on the perceptions, experiences, and counterhegemonic practices of educators of color" (Lynn, 1999, p. 615). Educators are crucial in the realization and implementation of critical race pedagogy as a tool to analyze and deconstruct racism and its

Envisioning Critical Race Praxis in Higher Education Through Counter-Storytelling, pages 147–164
Copyright © 2016 by Information Age Publishing
147

interlocking systems of oppression in education (Lynn, 1999). This liberatory pedagogical style stems from both critical pedagogy and critical race theory (CRT). Implications found within this chapter are multifaceted and target both individual and organizational levels.

* * *

"SCHOLAR SISTERS" RECONNECT

Exiting the conference hotel I stepped into the warm air and paused for a moment soaking up the bright sun. It was the first time in 48 hours I had been outside. Conferences seem to do that to me, keep me holed up from the rest of the world. I turned right out of the hotel lobby's rotating door and began to walk past the few individuals who were, like me, braving the early morning. While the sun certainly put vigor in my step, it was my destination that I was looking forward to most. I was never much of a morning person, but Patricia had a presentation to give at 10:45 a.m., hence the 8:00 a.m. meeting at a local café.

It had been about four months since I had seen Patricia, or Pats, as I lovingly came to refer to her. We were both enrolled in, and had recently graduated from, the higher education doctoral program at Mountain University (MU) (pseudonym). As women of color traversing the doctoral process, we immediately gravitated toward one another due to our shared social identities. Pats and I collected our data at the same time, entered the daunting writing process side by side, and defended our dissertations two weeks apart from one another the summer of 2013. As if on cue, we both accepted jobs as tenure-track faculty members in higher education programs on the very same day. However, diverging from our apparent inseparability, we took positions at institutions on separate sides of the country—Pats on the east coast, and I, on the west coast. Throughout the doctoral process, Pats became like a sister to me, always offering me support with her "you got this" motto and ability to make the most stressful situations dissipate. Today would be no exception. I fully intended to soak in every ounce of wisdom and comfort Pats had for me as a new assistant professor.

As I drew nearer to the restaurant, my heart skipped with anticipation. I marveled at how excited I was to see the other half of the "scholar sisters," as we often referred to ourselves. As I opened the door to the restaurant I scanned the eight tables in the small front room. It was easy to see that I was the first to arrive. Upon noticing the "Please Seat Yourself" sign, I strolled over to a table with two seats located near a window that allowed the sun to stream in. Just as I finished scooting my chair up to the table, a small bell signaled the opening of the restaurant door. I looked up to see Pats, in a stylish white suit, strut into the restaurant's small foyer. I watched as Pats scanned the room and spotted me. She threw up her hands as if in celebration and screamed "Serene!" Usually, I would be thoroughly embarrassed by Pats' overly dramatic exclamation, but I was just as excited to see her as it seemed she was to see me. I stood up with a large grin on my face and mimicked her movements, yelling "Pats!" a bit quieter so that only half the restaurant turned to stare. Pats strolled over to me with her hands still out and embraced me in a tight hug. "You have no idea how much I have been looking forward to sitting down with you!" Pats stated. I responded to her with a large grin.

Taking our cues from each other, we sat down opposite one another and pulled our menus out from the holder on the edge of the table. We had gone out to eat together enough times to know we must first order and then catch up, otherwise we would never place our order and eat. After the wait staff left, we hastily put our menus back in the holder and looked at one another. Pats was the first to break the silence. "Serene, what is going on? Tell me every ounce. I know we have caught up here and there, but I feel like you have not been telling me *everything* that is *really* going on. Are you taking time for yourself? You know that is important. What about research and students? Are you enjoying the city? Have you even had time to explore?"

STRUCTURES OF DISILLUSIONMENT

Not quite sure where to start with Pats' multiple questions, I tackled the one that would lead me into getting advice on what I really wanted to chat with her about. "Well," I began, but decided to stay silent for another moment to formulate my thoughts. "Well," I started again, "I've been thinking about this a lot lately, analyzing it," I cleared my throat, "but I've just been struggling a bit in my faculty position. I know it's only been six months, but I feel like MU, our doctoral education, spoiled me a bit. It made me forget about the inequity, microaggressions, and macroaggressions I continually encountered in educational environments, and more specifically, the classroom. When I took this faculty position I thought my experiences, as well as my graduate students', would be just like those I had at MU. However, when I started to settle into faculty life I realized that the majority of educational institutions, including my current one, do not function with the holistic student in mind as MU's program did."

The mission of the program was to prepare students from diverse backgrounds to enter into positions that allowed them to create positive change in education and society. This mission became actualized within the pedagogy of the program. Existing course titles, such as Learning in Organizations, began to shift in both title (Diversity in Organizations) and content.

The diversity and higher learning track, meant for students interested in "enhancing diversity, access, and equity in organizations" (Danowitz & Tuitt, 2011, p. 48), quickly replaced the teaching and learning concentration within the program.

The delivery of this inclusive curriculum was innovative. Within the classroom, professors replaced the "banking system" of education with bell hooks' notion of engaged pedagogy (Danowitz & Tuitt, 2011). Personal experiences, reflections, and examining one's positionality within the system of privilege were regular and developmental aspects of a single class period. This coupling of pedagogy and curriculum "laid the groundwork in the classroom and in professional settings for male students to begin to engage with gender equity issues and for white students to reduce their privileging in language" (Danowitz & Tuitt, 2011, p. 47). In order to make *all* students feel comfortable and enhance development, professors shared their own identities and experiences in class sessions.

Reflecting on the foundation and purpose of MU's program made retelling my struggle all the more perplexing. "Pats," I started, "I'm confined by the walls of my institutions, by my program. During our doctoral program we were taught how to make positive change in education and now here I am telling you I just can't see myself doing it."

Pats responded with obvious concern, "Serene, tell me a bit more about what exactly is going on in your program that has left you so disillusioned?"

I looked down at my breakfast sandwich that had been placed in front of me while Pats waited patiently to hear the thoughts running through my head. I slowly started to explain, "Okay, so I mentioned that MU prepared us to create positive change within the classroom using innovative and inclusive pedagogical practices. However, I feel like my new colleagues, as well as the policies and procedures of my current program, obstruct the small strides toward educational emancipation I attempt to nurture within the classroom for women graduate students of color I work with." I paused, not quite sure if I should go on, nor what I would say if I did.

Pats read my hesitancy and followed up, "I think I see where your frustration is coming from. You expected to not only create an inclusive classroom that fosters liberatory education, but also to be supported in building that environment. However, you have come up against a very different scenario—one where you are met with resistance on several levels, which hinders your chance at creating this inclusion. Am I right?"

"Yes," I started again slowly. "Let me give you a bit more context. I have found myself mentoring several master's- and doctoral-level women of color in the program. The other day one of them told me a story of how from kindergarten to her master's degree she had never seen herself reflected in the canon, nor the classroom. She had never had a woman professor of color, nor did she find herself reading literature by individuals with this same identity. This student expressed frustration with the fact that all of her current professors were White men and that the majority of her cohort were also White men or White women. Because she is of a different race and gender than the majority of individuals in the program, she let me know that she feels like an anomaly in the classroom." I took a pause, remembering the pain I saw in this student's face as she explained even further her experiences within the program. "I suppose I feel a bit helpless because I can't teach all of the classes that make up the program. While I can do my part in my one class, it's still not enough. I can't single handedly restructure the not-so-hidden racist and sexist aspects of the curriculum and program to reflect the voices of women of color and other marginalized students, especially when I continue to meet resistance from the department on several issues that are not on their agenda, such as gender, race, and inclusive pedagogy. For instance, last week the department chair scolded me for allowing a woman doctoral student to bring her six-year-old child to class because her babysitter cancelled at the last minute. The only other option was for her to miss class, which seemed like a punishment for having a child. I wonder if this would have been a problem had a White man brought a child to class. This is just one example of how racist and sexist structures impede the ability and willingness to recognize and support realities outside of Whiteness and maleness in the academy. A month ago, I asked for travel funds from my department to attend the first annual Critical Thought in Education (CRE) conference. I received word yesterday that my application for funds was denied because it was not a 'well-known' conference. Unfortunately, many of the 'well-known' conferences reinforce the hidden curriculum within the academy. CRE would have given me critical tools to deconstruct racist and sexist curriculum and structures. Unfortunately, the denial of funds further upholds the status quo. What's even more confusing is that I don't understand why it is so hard to infuse this into the curriculum and create this positive change I was hoping to foster. I'm at a complete loss."

Pats was visibly reflective at this point. She reached over to gently place her hand on mine. She spoke cautiously, "I *do* understand what you are saying Serene. I, too, have been coming up against structures that do not permit me to foster inclusivity and transformative learning in the classroom. As soon as I noticed the problem I began looking for a possible solution, and I think I found one." Pats took her hand off mine to lift her suit sleeve, glancing at her watch as it emerged from the white fabric. "Sorry, just checking that we have time. We have plenty," she explained. "Would you like to hear a little more about what I have found?"

Catching my eager glance, Pats drew in a deep breath and continued, "I've been doing some research and it's helping me understand why it is so difficult to expose and deconstruct these dominant structures. I know you are aware of inclusive pedagogical styles because of MU, but have you heard of critical race pedagogy?"

Thoroughly intrigued, I shook my head to answer "No."

CRITICAL PEDAGOGY MEETS CRITICAL RACE THEORY

Pats began, "Critical race pedagogy focuses on race as well as other inter-locking systems of oppression to expose and deconstruct power dynamics in the classroom and work toward a more liberatory education for students of color (Jennings & Lynn, 2005; Lynn, 1999). This movement within education stems from both critical pedagogy and CRT. Critical pedagogy was first introduced to the world in the mid 1900s and stemmed from ideology formulated by critical theorist belonging to the Frankfurt School, such as Theodor Adorno, Walter Benjamin, and Max Horkheimer (Giroux, 1997). Critical theorists, such as the aforementioned, attempted to critique the social world so that structural domination was exposed, and emancipation from oppression was made possible (Levinson, 2011). In applying critical theory to education, Paulo Freire first introduced the concept of Critical Pedagogy to the world in his 1970 book *Pedagogy of the Oppressed.* Freire (1970/2000) believed that education could be utilized as both an oppressive and liberatory tool. To be used toward liberation, pedagogy must focus on developing a critical consciousness in students who are oppressed, as well as in teachers (who often do the oppressing), so that all may examine and deconstruct the inequitable structures that surround them. This creates praxis, or the synthesis of reflection and action to transform society, and by way, education (Freire, 1970/2000)."

Pats continued, "Since 1970, critical pedagogy has gained respect and praise in the field of education but has also garnered critiques for its inability to address the realities and needs of marginalized identities. To address these critiques, 'educational researchers of color have looked outside of their field of study for a theoretical construct that would provide a critical analysis of race within the context of pedagogy' (Jennings & Lynn, 2005, pp. 24–25). Many have found their answer in CRT, a critical tool of analysis that was born out of civil rights leaders' awareness 'that dominant conceptions of race, racism, and equality were increasingly incapable of providing any meaningful quantum of racial justice' (Matsuda, Lawrence, Delgado, & Crenshaw, 1993, p. 3). CRT emerged from legal scholars' growing awareness that advances made during the civil rights movement had stalled in the 1970s (Delgado & Stefancic, 2001). However, more recently it has become a useful tool through which various academic disciplines, namely education, can examine how privilege and oppression shape racial identities and experiences across contexts and spaces. CRT in education facilitates a critical examination of systemic racism throughout the United States educational pipeline, including higher education (Ladson-Billings & Tate, 1995). With the coupling of these two theories, critical pedagogy and CRT, critical race pedagogy emerged. Critical race pedagogy offers 'an analysis of racial, ethnic, and gender subordination in education that relies mostly on the perceptions, experiences, and counterhegemonic practices of educators of color' (Lynn, 1999, p. 615). Utilizing key tenets of CRT as a foundation, critical race pedagogy focuses on the negotiation of power, calls for a critique of self, and asserts the need for counter-hegemony within educational spaces (Jennings & Lynn, 2005; Lynn, 1999)."

Pats paused to take a breather and check in on me, "Are you with me so far?" I blinked, lost in her methodical speech. Pulling myself out of her eloquent explanation, I drifted lightly back into reality. "This all sounds great Patricia, and you've clearly researched what this is all about, but how can this help me so that I may transform not only my classroom, but also the program, into a more inclusive space for students?"

CRITICAL RACE PEDAGOGY: WHAT IS IT ALL ABOUT?

"Well," Pats began again, "first I must mention that encompassed within critical race pedagogy is the understanding that race is just one of many social identities that intersects and influences students' experiences within the classroom (Delgado & Stefancic, 2001; Lynn, 1999). When you mentioned that you have grown disillusioned by your own experience as a woman of color, as well as your women students of color's experiences, I knew I wanted to share my thoughts on critical race pedagogy with you. This pedagogical method accounts not only for race, but also for gender, class, religion, and so much more. It allows us, as professors, to validate and make visible all students, regardless of background, in order to foster learning and academic success."

Seeing the growing confusion on my face, Pats started again, "Okay, let me move to an example of how the first characteristic of critical race pedagogy might be utilized. This first concept, which aligns with a key tenet of CRT, can help us understand more in depth the structures in place that uphold the normality of racism in the classroom. Critical race pedagogy realizes that racism is endemic to society, and therefore, racism is deeply embedded in U.S. educational structures (Delgado & Stefancic, 2001; Jennings & Lynn, 2005; Lynn, 1999). The endemic nature of race means that racism is ordinary, commonplace, and normalized within society (Delgado & Stefancic, 2001). As a microcosm of this society, racism is commonplace within higher education, making it difficult to address and redress. A prime example is the racism implicit in hidden curriculum, which may plague women graduate students of color's experiences in the classroom."

After a quick break to take a sip of water, Pats continued, "Margolis and Romero (1998) interviewed women of color graduate students in sociology programs to gain a better understanding of their experiences with hidden curriculum and its role in reproducing gender and racial inequities. The authors found that hidden curriculum appears in two forms, weak and strong (Margolis & Romero, 1998). The weak form aligns with the socialization process in that it functions to (re)produce (White or Whiteness in) professionals. The strong form of hidden curriculum is more blatant in its reproduction of social inequities and encompasses several themes that are relevant to their pedagogical experiences in the classroom, including stereotyping, the exclusion and ostracism of students who want to focus on race and/or gender issues, a lack of women of color in the canon, and the absence of women of color in the program faculty and students (Margolis & Romero, 1998). Here we see how hidden curriculum, which maintains the status quo and the normality of racism, is deeply embedded in educational policies, procedures, and structures (Hanks, 2011) making it hard to expose, let alone deconstruct. This is particularly concerning as the hidden nature of this curriculum makes it hard to name, expose, and deconstruct. Therefore, the racism and sexism within the curriculum and graduate education are often unconsciously reproduced by educators and unknowingly consumed by students. Unfortunately, racist structures, such as hidden curricula, become emotionally and spiritually taxing for students whether they are consciously or unconsciously encountered (Lynn, 1999)."

"Well," I said thoughtfully, "that certainly relates back to what some of my students have been experiencing. Their feelings of marginalization and mattering within the classroom are certainly due to this endemic racism you've just explained. It's so pervasive and suffocating; perhaps, that is also why I grow so frustrated. It's all around me…us, and I'm not quite sure where and how to start battling it." I let out a small sigh of frustration, took a sip of coffee, then clarified, "From what you just said, Pats, it seems like critical race pedagogy will help us expose this implicit racism that is couched within White students' and White faculty's treatment of women graduate students of color. But will it also give me a place to begin the deconstruction of the structures of racism and dominant ideology we have now exposed?"

"That's a great question!" Pats exclaimed with what looked to be a smirk on her lips. "The answer brings me to my next point. Critical race pedagogy claims that this pervasive racism gives rise to a 'culture of power' (Delpit, 1995) in the classroom. A culture of power confers privileges to the dominant culture while subordinating all of those who do not have power, like marginalized students. We see this culture of power at play in the socialization process for graduate women of color. Dunn, Rouse, and Seff (1994) describe doctoral socialization as 'the process by which individuals acquire the attitudes, beliefs, values and skills needed to participate effectively in organized social life' (as cited in Tierney, 1997, p. 4). Successful socialization into a terminal degree program is a determining factor in how far a doctoral student may progress in her studies. Unfortunately, the difficulty in adapting to institutional socialization is reflected in the startling 50% attrition rate for doctoral students, a number that is found to be even higher among racial minority students (Nettles & Millett, 2006). Delpit's (1995) understanding of a culture of power may help explain these alarming statistics. Within a culture of power there are rules that are created by those in power, in this case White males (Delpit, 1995). Those who are not in the dominant culture are best served when they are aware of the rules, even if they cannot control them. Therefore, with a lack of understanding for these rules and thus a lack of power, it may be of no surprise that women of color may feel displaced by the socialization process within the academy (Gardner, 2008).

Pedagogy, a key component in the socialization process (Weidman & Stein, 2003), does not escape this culture of power, as it is constructed by and for the majority who control the academy. As I explained above, this dominant ideology constructs hidden curriculum, which pervades the classroom, and subsequently, the experiences of women graduate students of color. So Serene, the endemic nature of racism helps to construct and maintain the hidden curriculum in the academy, which confers privilege to the dominant majority and helps give rise to a culture of power. What we must realize is that the dominant group is in control of what makes curriculum valuable, making it hard to push back against this majoritarian stance if your values do not align."

Pats was ready to go on, but I interrupted her, needing a moment to process. "So we see that the endemic nature of race produces hidden curriculum. White individuals create this curriculum to uphold Whiteness, which is a form of racialized privilege that upholds the status quo and is only granted to those who can perform Whiteness (Harris, 1993), right?" Pats slowly nodded her affirmation. I started again, "Okay, so can you speak more to this culture of power? How does it operate within the academy? And Pats, how in the world can we deconstruct it? Or can we?"

"We can," Pats cleared her throat. "To understand further how this culture of power works, let's delve deeper into the hidden curriculum, and more specifically the omission of women of color's voices within class discussions. When the dominant majority controls the classroom, both teachers and students, the class is constructed around that culture. Therefore, as one of your students mentioned, these women of color are taught by White men, about White men, while sitting in a class with White men (and women). Their omission from the cannon and course materials as well as class discussions is normalized by the endemic nature of racism. The pervasiveness of this

Whiteness secures the status quo within the academy. On the rare occasion that race does become the topic of conversation in the classroom, White students become disinterested and removed from the topic (Souto-Manning & Ray, 2007). Often, this silence from White students surrounding race forces women of color to become native informants (hooks, 1994; Souto-Manning & Ray, 2007). Moreover, when these students do feel comfortable enough to speak on the topic of race in an all-White classroom, they feel that their voice is not heard, relegating them to an invisible status in the room. Souto-Manning and Ray (2007) asserted that this 'literal silence around race in the classroom reflected the institutional silence surrounding these issues in the academy at large' (p. 285). The devaluing of one's presence and voice within the classroom environment stifles the collective learning community (hooks, 1994). These negations silence women graduate students of color in the classroom while simultaneously conferring more power and privilege to Whiteness, or the culture of power."

"Patricia," I interrupted again, this time rather forcefully, "I just feel so helpless. These students are coming to me, asking me what to do, willing me to help. My doctoral education taught me how to infuse inclusive pedagogy into my own courses, but I never knew I would be battling against an entire program's curriculum that, as we have clearly just explored, is deeply entrenched in racist structures, cultures of power if you will, that do not allow for the deconstruction of this racism and sexism..." I trailed off. My defeat was palpable.

Pats must have been sensing my growing frustration as she spoke, because she came right back at me with an answer, "Serene, we do indeed hold power. It may not seem like a lot, but I assure you that it is. Critical race pedagogy addresses the power that we, as scholars of color, possess. It advocates for researchers, scholars, and faculty to participate in reflexivity (Jennings & Lynn, 2005). Reflection, coupled with action, creates praxis so that a critical awareness of oppression is gained and individuals, such as us, are more readily able to create liberation through education (Freire, 2000). This exploration of self, 'helps define Critical Race Pedagogy as a valuable tool in understanding our own worldview while simultaneously helping to better illuminate the world of those we study' (Jennings & Lynn, 2005, p. 27) and those we work with. This reflexivity is pertinent to all educators, regardless of identity. Reflexivity is critical to understanding our positionality and power in shaping education, and more specifically classroom experiences for students with marginalized identities. Serene, if we practice reflexivity we can recognize our own positions of power so that they may push against the hegemony created in the classroom by a culture of power. This challenge to dominant ideology will help to disrupt the status quo, allowing us to inspire a truly liberatory education for all students. Critical race pedagogy argues for teaching *and* learning that is liberatory and thus will inform equity and social justice not just in education, but also in society at large (Freire, 2000; Jennings & Lynn, 2005)."

I did not have to say anything for Pats to know I was still a bit frustrated with what was being said. While I understood that critical race pedagogy worked toward emancipatory education, what she explained left me feeling disillusioned and a bit lost. If these structures were so engrained in society and higher education, what would be the chances that I, a woman of color within a White academy, would be able to deconstruct them? Pats clearly saw my frustration and attempted to offer me further assurance with her words.

CRITICAL RACE PEDAGOGY IN ACTION: TOWARDS PRAXIS

Pats continued, "From here, I think it beneficial to remind ourselves why we would enact this type of inclusive pedagogy in the classroom. Critical race pedagogy helps us achieve a liberatory education for all students, as well as ourselves, other faculty, and by the way, society. According to Jennings and Lynn (2005), 'The primary characteristic of a liberatory pedagogy is its goal of advocating for justice and equity in both schooling and education as a necessity if there is to be justice and equity in the broader society' (p. 28). One of the most beautiful things about this approach to pedagogy is its emphasis on intersectionality. While there is a great focus on race, this approach to teaching would not exist if we did not recognize individuals multiple identities. While we have been talking about women of color, race, and gender, critical race pedagogy also addresses religion, ethnicity, age, class, and so many other identities that are alive in the classroom but are often invisible."

"You're right, Pats," I responded. "Sometimes I, myself, struggle with bringing in identities that I do not understand or identify with. It would be interesting to see how critical race pedagogy could address this struggle I often encounter."

"Yes!" Pats exclaimed. "This brings me to the reflexivity that we must undertake in order to help create a community of colleagues and students that can partake in emancipatory education." Pats paused to take a sip of coffee and then continued, "Serene, just now you were frustrated because you felt powerless against the dominant structures that constrain you and several of your women graduate students of color. I want you to think about your position within the culture of power in relation to your students: Do you think you hold more power or less power?"

"Well, I suppose I hold more power than my students, but I'm not sure what the quantification of power will do to end oppression," I replied. Pats offered a rebuttal, "I am in no way saying you need to quantify your power.

It's more about recognizing your power, where you stand, and where you can position yourself as a leader to create change with this positionality. As a scholar, a leader, and teacher you are positioned in ways that other individuals of color are not—although I must point out that as a woman of color, your examination of privilege will be quite different from those in the majority. Regardless, this reflexivity must happen in order for you, and others, to position yourself in the most advantageous ways to create change."

I had a sudden thought and interrupted Pats recommendations, "I'm seeing what you are saying. Light bulbs are going off for me." I paused to gather my thoughts, "So even if I meet resistance from those in power of the culture of the academy, I still have some, though it may be little, power to change these structures?" The question was more to myself, which Pats understood as she allowed me to continue my thought process uninterrupted. "I was recently given the task to review the mission of the program. I would almost guarantee I was given this job because it seems minute, not worth anyone's time. But as was done at MU, I see that so much of a program's curriculum and teaching stems from the mission. I'm going to see how we can infuse inclusivity into the mission of our program, whether that be through the wording of the actual statement or making an argument for a wider, more deconstructive take on the mission..." I trailed off, waiting to hear Pats' thoughts.

"Great," she nodded, "I too have been thinking about where I stand in the academy. I think all too often 'critical scholars of color are co-opted by the majority community so as to be complicit in their own marginalization and the marginalization of others' (Jennings & Lynn, 2005, p. 27). Reflexivity will allow me to reflect on my relationships and positions with others, namely colleagues and students, so that I do not become an architect of my own and others oppression. It is also imperative that those in the majority practice reflexivity as well. This entails White professors reflecting on their own role in the dominant narrative and working towards emancipation from these patterns. We must first recognize our positions within the hegemonic academy in order to deconstruct it."

"Okay," I said while giving my empty plate to the wait staff. "So I understand that while I may not be a part of the culture of power that constructs the norms of the academy, I have some power to deconstruct these norms. However, I am still wondering what exactly this means for me. I come back to my original question; armed with critical race pedagogy, how can I make positive change within education and within the classroom?"

"Great question, Serene, and I hope I have as equally a great answer for you," Pats responded with a grin. "We must expose and deconstruct the culture of power that is prevalent in the academy and seeps into every facet of the classroom. Jennings and Lynn (1999) explained 'This conception of power in the classroom is largely grounded in an understanding

of whiteness that makes explicit the privilege of being white in America'
(p. 27). Therefore, to deconstruct this power we must deconstruct Whiteness by introducing all other voices who have been silenced by this privilege
back into the classroom."

"Okay, that makes complete sense. But it does not seem like it is as easy
as you say it is. If it were, wouldn't it be done already?" I asked. "It's not easy,
Serene," Pats answered, "but with the help of critical race pedagogy we can
not only deconstruct this dominant ideology but also construct an inclusive
classroom environment that allows for the rearticulation and affirmation
of all students' voices. First and foremost, we must make sure that the classroom makeup in itself is not homogenous. Historically, and currently, the
majority of graduate degrees have been conferred to White males. Subsequently, the majority of professors are also White men. This homogenous
classroom makeup ensures the status quo by allowing those who participate
in education to also be the ones who construct education. Therefore, we
must examine and change admissions standards so that there are no access barriers to students from marginalized identities. For instance, some
students may see application fees as a financial barrier. Therefore, educational leaders should ensure that fee waivers are advertised and offered to
students who need them. Interview weekends may also be another barrier
to students from minority backgrounds applying and enrolling in graduate
programs. Potential students may have to work or care for families, and
they may not have the finances to visit an institution for a weekend. Offering phone interviews, encouraging current students to host prospective
students, and allowing families to attend these weekends are crucial tasks
that may ensure a diverse student makeup within graduate classrooms."

I thought about what Pats had just posited, remembering my own search
process. I murmured, "I've always been aware of the requirement of standardized test scores, more specifically the GRE, as being an impediment
to some students applying to graduate programs. It's not a cheap test and
it certainly privileges those who have access to tutors, time, and materials.
However, I had never thought of these other barriers you just mentioned. I
agree that a diverse makeup is critical in building the inclusive classroom.
I can't even begin to count how many times Black women students have
told me that having more Black students would improve their graduate
student experience (Johnson-Bailey, Valentine, Cervero, & Bowles, 2008).
Removing these barriers to the graduate school application, admission, and
enrollment process seems like a great first step to creating an inclusive environment. But surely it's not as easy as that, Pats?"

"No, it's not," Pats shook her head but maintained her grin. "If we have
a diverse makeup of students in the classroom, it is still not enough to disrupt the culture of power the dominant group holds and constructs. We
must also implement ways in which these students can be seen and heard.

As your students expressed, students with marginalized identities often feel silenced and invisible within the classroom. This could be because they are 'the only one' but the fact that they are not reflected within the curriculum is another contributing factor to this marginalization." I looked at Pats quizzically, willing her to go on. Gracefully, she continued, "For instance, if you are teaching a History of Higher Education course, what perspective do you think you will teach this from?" I was not sure if the question was rhetorical, but I posited an answer anyway, "Well, I suppose my perspective. I would teach more of what I was interested in, what I was comfortable with."

"Right," Pats responded, "So this is where reflexivity comes in. How do we infuse your interests, informed by your identity, with students' interests and identities? All too often the professor controls what is read, and all too often these readings reflect the positionality of the professor. I remember taking a Diversity in Higher Education course, taught by a White woman, and all we read were articles by White men and women, on, what seemed, White men and women. This is problematic because unless all your students are White, marginalized student's interests, identities, and voices are not reflected in the readings, and subsequently, the course. As leaders, we must be intentional in the canon we assign in our courses."

"Well," I started, "I suppose I have not thought of it that way. I assumed I was doing pretty well, assigning readings by Black men and women, looking at an array of topics. I suppose I have been negating some of the identities I myself may marginalize, such as age and religion—and even races that I do not often give attention to, such as Native American students. This certainly gives me something to think about."

"And Serene," Pats added, "It's also about how we deliver this curriculum that is crucial to making students visible, and subsequently, academically successful. We must take into account students learning styles. Dominant ideology normalizes the banking system of knowledge (Freire, 2000) within the academy. This means that lectures and facts and figures are utilized to deliver knowledge to all students. However, this is not the way all students prefer to learn. For instance, many Native American cultures hold knowledge, power, and culture in a dialogical relationship, where culture informs one's knowledge, which supplies power (Brayboy, 2005). This powerful education may involve learning about one's culture through dance, art, and other media. Unfortunately, the culture of power pushes against this understanding, forcing dominant norms on these students, subsequently stripping them of their own knowledge and power. As educators, we must understand what our students need in the classroom in order for them to be heard and seen, let alone learn. This is also true outside of the classroom. For instance, assigning students papers that must be written in American Psychological Association style may stifle a student's creative process. They may prefer to work on assignments that involve photography, oral presentations, and/or poetry. While it may be easier for us to sit down and grade 20 papers of the same form and length, this may not be the most effective way to use our power as educators. Instead, by offering students an array of media and methods to not only disseminate, but also convey knowledge, we are encompassing several learning styles, creating space for multiple perspectives, and ensuring the academic success of a diversity of students."

Before I even had time to open my mouth, Pats continued, "Now Serene, I know you're still wondering 'Is that it? Is this all we can do?' Well, to answer your question, no. I have saved what may just be the most important factor for the end. While we examine our power within the institution and how we might use it to end systemic oppression, we must also examine the power dynamics within the classroom. How do we, or do we, assert ourselves and use our power conferred to us as 'teachers' to enact inclusivity? We, as educators, must engage in a dialogical and personal process with our students, which may allow for women of color's voices to be heard, allowing them to feel visible and valuable within the classroom (Tuitt, 2010). This entails acquiring skills that help facilitate inclusive and safe dialogues to take place in the classroom. This also necessitates the understanding that professors, you and I, are not the only 'teacher' in the classroom. We must encourage and embrace the experiential knowledge and wisdom that *all* students have to offer. This community of learners will not work if power is conferred to one, or a few individuals. All students must feel empowered in order to co-construct knowledge."

Pats drew in a breath with a bit of hesitancy. She stayed silent as she cocked her head to one side, waiting for my reaction. I was not quite sure what to tell her. I felt like I had just been on a rollercoaster ride inside this tiny café. At first I was at a loss for what to do, and then felt even more disenchanted when Pats explained to me the culture of power that upholds racist classroom structures. However, upon her explanation of praxis and critical race pedagogy, I felt a tinge of hope, something I had not felt since leaving MU. Pats glanced at her watch quickly so I would not notice. I, however, picked up on this quick movement. "It's okay," I assured her, "I know you have a presentation to get to. I'm just sorry our time was spent talking about me and my problems."

"What?" Pats exclaimed while throwing up her hands, "You must be kidding me. This is not just *your* problem, nor does it only affect you. Other professors and students are encountering this same exact issue. I'm just happy I was here to dialogue with you." I smirked at her word choice; Pats was ever the educator. Knowing she had somewhere to be, but that she would sit in that café with me all day if I did not tell her to go, I decidedly pushed my chair away from the table and stood up in one swift movement. Pats took my cue, stood up, and snatched up the bill that must have been placed on our table at some point during the conversation. "This one's on me!" Pats declared.

I started to protest but she waved me away. "No, no, no," she exclaimed, "What you don't know, Serene, is that you just helped me immensely with the presentation I am about to give." Pats flashed her coy smile once again and I could not help but smile back at her. "What does that mean?" I asked. Pats quickly responded, "My presentation is on using inclusive pedagogy in the classroom, namely critical race pedagogy." She gave a chuckle. "Now I certainly did not intend to give you my full presentation, but it just seemed so pertinent... I'm sorry. Don't be upset," she pleaded.

At her apologetic request I burst out laughing. While I could never imagine being mad at Pats, it was even more absurd to be upset with her for sharing this invaluable knowledge with me. Pats relaxed a bit as I pulled her into a tight embrace to quell her mounting bewilderment. "Girl, everything you said has helped me immensely," I drew in a quick breath, "I just know that I have my work cut out for me!" "Yes, we both do," replied Pats. "But you must know that this work does not just fall to us. It calls on all future and current educators, the individuals who are in some position of power. And we must remember that we can, and should, utilize one another."

As she finished paying at the register in the front of the café I continued to smile. I was not sure if it was the quality time I had spent with my friend, the critical conversation, or my renewed hope in emancipatory education that pleased me. Perhaps it was all three. When she placed her wallet back into her purse, I grabbed her hand, gave it a squeeze, and led her out of the restaurant into the mid-morning sun.

This is where we left one another. Pats was heading back to the conference and I was meeting a group of colleagues for yet another round of coffee. In the past few months, I walked away from meetings at my new institution disappointed. But on the walk over to the restaurant I was determined to reflect on my positionality within my program and the strides I may be able to make in this one meeting. I shook off these thoughts for a moment so I could say goodbye to Pats and wish her good luck with her presentation. We embraced one last time and then she held me out at arm's length. "You got this, Serene," she asserted. I grabbed her shoulders back so that we mimicked one another's stance and said, "You got this, Pats." This was something we said to one another whenever we spoke. What exactly "we got" had changed over time, but our assurance and support of one another, implicit in the statement, was what mattered the most. We dropped our embrace, aware that time would not stand still for us, gave each other one last smirk, and turned to go our separate ways.

As I began to walk, my mind started to churn, "Positionality... positionality... how am I positioned to create positive educational and pedagogical change..."

* * *

CONCLUDING THOUGHTS

In order to mitigate the negative interactions that many women graduate students of color encounter in the classroom, we must examine pedagogical practices. Pedagogy, which includes teaching styles and curriculum development, is a crucial piece in the puzzle of success for these students. Infusing critical race pedagogy into graduate programs allows for a rearticulation of knowledge for women students of color, which actualizes and affirms their experiences and identities both inside and outside of the classroom. Critical race pedagogy provides faculty and educators with the tools to expose and deconstruct the normative values of the academy as well as work toward a more inclusive environment that supports success for marginalized students. Therefore, it is pertinent that faculty and educators gain a better understanding of critical race pedagogy and how it can be operationalized within educational settings in order to affirm students' multiple identities and deconstruct inequities that dominant pedagogical practices uphold. Critical race pedagogy is important in higher education because it "has the potential to unify existing critical explications of educational phenomena in education and to provide more theoretical grounding and direction for educators who are concerned with issues of racial, ethnic, and gender inequality in the U.S. educational system" (Lynn, 1999, p. 622). When enacted, critical race pedagogy allows for a truly liberatory education for not only students, but also faculty and staff and, in the end, society.

REFERENCES

Brayboy, B. M. J. (2005). Toward a tribal critical race theory in education. *The Urban Review, 37*(5), 425–446.

Danowitz, M. A., & Tuitt, F. (2011). Enacting inclusivity through engaged pedagogy: A higher education perspective. *Equity & Excellence in Education, 44*(1), 40–56.

Delgado, R., & Stefancic, J. (2001). *Critical race theory: An introduction.* New York, NY: NYU Press.

Delpit, L. (1995). *Other people's children: Cultural conflict in the classroom.* New York, NY: New Press.

Dunn, D., Rouse, L., & Seff, M. A. (1994). New faculty socialization in the academic workplace. In J. C. Smart (Ed.), *Higher education: Theory and research, vol. 10* (pp. 374–416). New York, NY: Agathon.

Freire, P. (2000). *Pedagogy of the oppressed.* New York, NY: Continuum. (Original work published 1970)

Gardner, S. K. (2008). Fitting the mold of graduate school: A qualitative study of socialization in doctoral education. *Innovative Higher Education, 33*(2), 125–138.

Giroux, H. (1997). *Pedagogy and the politics of hope: Theory, culture, and schooling.* Boulder, CO: Westview Press.

Hanks, C. (2011). The double-edge of reason: Jürgen Habermas and the Frankfurt School. In B. A. U. Levinson, J. P. K. Gross, C. Hanks, J. H. Dadds, K. D. Kumasi, J. Link, & D. Metro-Roland (Eds.), *Beyond critique: Exploring critical social theories and education* (pp. 80–112). Boulder, CO: Paradigm Publishers.

Harris, C. (1993). Whiteness as property. *Harvard Law Review, 106*(8), 1709–1791.

hooks, b. (1994). *Teaching to transgress: Education as the practice of freedom.* New York, NY: Taylor and Francis.

Jennings, M., & Lynn, M. (2005). The house that race built: Critical pedagogy, African-American education, and the re-conceptualization of a critical race pedagogy. *Educational Foundations,* Summer-Fall, *19*(3–4), 15–32.

Johnson-Bailey, J., Valentine, T. S., Cervero, R. M., & Bowles, T. A. (2008). Lean on me: The support experiences of Black graduate students. *The Journal of Negro Education, 77*(4), 365–381.

Ladson-Billings, G., & Tate, W. (1995). Toward a critical race theory of education. *Teachers College Record, 97*(1), 47–68.

Levinson, B. A. U. (2011). Introduction: Exploring critical social theories in education. In B. A. U. Levinson, J. P. K. Gross, C. Hanks, J. H. Dadds, K. D. Kumasi, J. Link, & D. Metro-Roland (Eds.), *Beyond critique: Exploring critical social theories and education* (pp. 1–24). Boulder, CO: Paradigm Publishers.

Lynn, M. (1999). Toward a critical race pedagogy: A research note. *Urban Education, 33*(5), 606–626.

Margolis, E., & Romero, M. (1998). The department is very male, very White, very old, and very conservative: The functioning of the hidden curriculum in graduate sociology departments. *Harvard Educational Review, 68*(1), 1–32.

Matsuda, M. J., Lawrence, C. R., Delgado, R., & Crenshaw, K. W. (1993). Introduction. In M. J. Matsuda, C. R. Lawrence III, R. Delgado, & K. Crenshaw (Eds.), *Words that wound: Critical race theory, assaultive speech, and the first amendment* (pp. 1–16). Boulder, CO: Westview Press.

Nettles, M. T., & Millett, C. M. (2006). *Socialization. Three magic letters: Getting to Ph.D.* Baltimore, MD: Johns Hopkins University Press.

Souto-Manning, M., & Ray, N. (2007). Beyond survival in the ivory tower: Black and brown women's living narratives. *Equity and Excellence in Education, 40*(4), 280–290.

Tierney, W. G. (1997). Organizational socialization in higher education. *The Journal of Higher Education, 68*(1), 1–16.

Tuitt, F. (2010). Enhancing visibility in graduate education: Black women's perceptions of inclusive pedagogical practices. *International Journal of Teaching and Learning in Higher Education, 22*(3), 246–257.

Weidman, J. C., & Stein E. L. (2003). Socialization of doctoral students to academic norms. *Research in Higher Education, 44*(6), 641–656.

ABOUT THE CONTRIBUTORS

Dr. Vonzell Agosto is an associate professor of curriculum studies in the department of educational leadership and policy studies at the University of South Florida. Her research agenda engages theories of social oppression in connection to curriculum and leadership. Namely, she explores curriculum in the contexts of teaching, leading, and learning and attends to the preparation of educators, administrators, and youth—their experiences within and influence on educational contexts to be (more or less) oppressive especially in regard to culture, race, gender, and dis/ability. Dr. Agosto has presented her research at major conferences including the American Education Research Association, Association for Association the Study of Higher Education, National Association of Multicultural Education for Teacher Educators, Bergamo, and the University Council of Education Administrators. Her publications include handbook chapters and journal articles in *Race Ethnicity & Education, Teachers College Record, Journal of Negro Education, Journal of School Leadership,* and the *Journal of Research on Leadership Education.*

P. Herbert Caldwell has a background in enrollment management with a passion to support students from admittance to degree completion. Herb has over 17 years of experience at various institutions including work with precollege, adult, and online students. He currently serves as assistant dean in the School for Professional Studies at Saint Louis University. He is completing the PhD in educational policy studies at the University of Illinois at Urbana–Champaign where his research interests are centered on student identity and overcoming barriers to degree completion.

Envisioning Critical Race Praxis in Higher Education Through Counter-Storytelling, pages 165–171
Copyright © 2016 by Information Age Publishing
165

Dr. Deirdre Cobb-Roberts is an associate professor in the department of educational and psychological studies at the University of South Florida and a former McKnight Junior Faculty Fellow. Her research agenda encompasses historical and contemporary examinations of responses to diversity in American higher education. Her primary line of inquiry is teacher preparation with an emphasis on resistance to cultural diversity, and the role of social justice in culturally responsive and responsible pedagogy. She has presented her research at major conferences including the American Educational Research Association, American Educational Studies Association, History of Education Society, and the Critical Race Studies in Education Association Conference. Dr. Cobb-Roberts has co-edited a book and published in journals such as *the History of Education Quarterly, American Educational Research Journal, Journal of Teacher Education, International Journal of Educational Policy, Research and Practice, Educational Considerations,* and the *Negro Educational Review.*

Dianne Delima is a doctoral student in higher and postsecondary education at Teachers College, Columbia University. She is a graduate research assistant for the Metropolitan Colleges Institute for Teaching Improvement. She is also a member of the Defining Good Teaching research team, led by Dr. Anna Neumann, which is investigating the pedagogies of liberal education. Dianne's research interests focus on teaching and learning in higher education institutions. Particularly, Dianne is interested in the learning experiences of first-generation college-going students and a funds of knowledge approach for teaching in higher education. Dianne's research interests are informed by her prior work in elementary schools in Southern California and her work as research assistant for the Department of Mexican American Studies at the University of Arizona. Her research interests in higher education are supplemented by her prior work as a student affairs administrator at Barnard College.

Eugene Oropeza Fujimoto, PhD, is an assistant professor in educational leadership at California State University, Fullerton. His research includes critical analysis of leadership in higher education, efforts to close racial achievement gaps, and the hiring of diverse faculty. He worked for over 20 years in higher education in equity, diversity, and affirmative action, and he has taught in ethnic studies, organizational leadership, instructional leadership, and organizational theory. His recent publications include a counterstory in *Occupying the Academy: Just How Important is Diversity Work in Higher Education?* (Clark, Fasching-Varner & Brimhall-Vargas, Rowman & Littlefield, 2012); an article in the *Community College Review,* and co-authored articles in *The Urban Review* and the *Association for Mexican American Educators Journal.*

Jessica C. Harris is a visiting assistant professor of higher education administration at the University of Kansas. Her research focuses on multiracial students, critical race theory, campus climate, and qualitative approaches to research in higher education.

Ignacio Hernández, PhD, is an assistant professor in the department of educational leadership at California State University, Fresno where he teaches graduate courses in higher education, administration, and leadership. Ignacio turns to community colleges as a source of inquiry within the broad institutional landscape of higher education in the United States. His research seeks to highlight the experiences and lessons learned by Latina/o leaders in community colleges that may serve to re-imagine normative definitions of community college leadership and the social practice of leadership in higher education.

Dr. Zorka Karanxha is an associate professor of educational leadership and policy studies at University of South Florida. Her research agenda focuses on educational leadership policies that positively influence marginalized communities through continued investigation of two interwoven conceptual strands: (1) Social justice leadership praxis to reduce educational inequities and (2) Social justice leadership to reduce inequities in legal education policy and policy implementation. She has conducted research on educational leadership preparation, education law, and charter schools. Dr. Karanxha has published her work in journals such as *Educational Administration Quarterly, Race Ethnicity and Education,* and the *Journal of School Leadership.* She has co-authored a book on student teaching and the law and served as co-editor of the *Journal of Cases in Educational Leadership.*

Joyce Lui (PhD) is a research analyst at San Jose Evergreen Community College District. Her research interests include Asian American students, community college and transfer student success, as well as social justice. She has published in *Community College Journal of Research and Practice, Journal of Applied Research in the Community College,* and *Race, Ethnicity, and Education.* She earned her doctorate at Iowa State University in higher education. She received her masters from San Diego State University in post-secondary educational leadership, student affairs. Her undergraduate majors were economics and sociology at University of California, San Diego. She grew up in San Francisco with her three older sisters. Her mom was a seamstress and her dad was a custodian for a community college for many years. She and her husband enjoy great food and pop culture references in TV shows. She identifies as an immigrant from Hong Kong, Chinese-American, Asian American, woman, Womyn of Color, and so much more.

Melissa A. Martinez, PhD, is an assistant professor in the Education and Community Leadership Program at Texas State University. Her research focuses on equity and access issues along the P–16 educational pipeline for students of color, primarily college access and readiness issues, the preparation of equity-oriented educational leaders, and faculty of color. Some of her scholarship has been published in *The High School Journal, Journal of Latinos and Education, International Journal of Qualitative Studies in Education, The Urban Review,* and the *Journal of School Leadership.*

Noemy Medina, MS, is a program manager for degree completion at Utah Valley University in the office of first year experience and student retention. She has also worked as an outreach and recruitment coordinator in the Office for Student Equity and Diversity at The University of Utah and research manager at the Center for Research on Educational Access and Leadership at California State University, Fullerton. In addition to her work in student affairs, she has taught student development to first year students, ethnic studies, and co-taught a graduate course, Diversity Access, and Equity. Her most recent publication was published in the *Association of Mexican American Educators Journal:* "Alternatives to the School-to-Prison Pipeline: The Role of Educational Leaders in Developing a College-Going Culture" (2013). Her interests include historically underrepresented student populations in higher education regarding issues of access and equity, under representation of minority males in higher education, and leadership of women of color in higher education.

Brenda L. H. Marina, PhD, is an associate dean of academic affairs at Baltimore City Community College. She served as an associate professor teaching graduate courses in educational leadership and higher education administration at Georgia Southern University. She also serves as an affiliate faculty and executive board member for a women and gender studies program. Her scholarship explores women in leadership, mentoring for leadership, multicultural competence in higher education, and global education issues from a womanist perspective. Dr. Marina is a board member for the International Mentoring Association (IMA) and a peer reviewer for the *International Journal of Mentoring and Coaching in Education.* She is the editor of the *Georgia Journal for College Student Affairs,* a journal sponsored by the Georgia College Personnel Association (GCPA). Dr. Marina has published book chapters related to identity development for female students of color, religiosity and spirituality in leadership programs, and managing diversity in workplaces and society, as well as journal articles on cultural competence and the glass ceiling. She recently published a book entitled *Mentoring Away the Glass Ceiling in Academe: A Cultured Critique.* Marina is currently working on a book that articulates a vision for equitable, fair, and just spaces for women faculty of color within academe in the United States.

Kimberly Robinson, EdD, recently graduated from Georgia Southern University's doctoral program in higher education administration–educational leadership in December 2012. She is the director of Open Arms Children's Network, Inc. a nonprofit organization dedicated to serving girls and their families who have been abused or neglected and cannot make a successful adjustment in their regular homes or foster care. Her scholarship explores women in higher education and multicultural issues affecting higher education institutions. Dr. Robinson's focused research and publication agenda includes a published paper, book chapter collaboration, International Conference in Women and Gender studies, Women's Empowerment Conference, and women and multicultural issues affecting higher education institutions. Her career as an educator includes teaching undergraduate first-year experience courses at Georgia Southern University. Dr. Robinson's doctoral research explored the *Under-representation of African-American Women in Higher Education: Perceptions of Women in Leadership Positions.* Her scholarship at the doctoral level involved using theoretical constructs to guide implications on various multicultural and gender issues.

Sabrina Ross, PhD, is an associate professor of curriculum studies at Georgia Southern University. Her scholarship involves intersections of race, gender, and power within formal and informal educational contexts. She has published articles in *Educational Foundations, The Journal of African American Education, The International Journal of the Scholarship of Teaching and Learning,* and *Teaching in Higher Education.* She was co-editor (with Svi Shapiro and Kathe Latham) of *The Institution of Education* (2006) and guest-edited (with Donyell Roseboro) a special issue of *Vitae Scholasticae: The Journal of Educational Biography* (2011) examining the pedagogies of U.S. Black educators and a special issue of *The Journal of Curriculum Theorizing* (2012, with Ming Fang He) examining narrative of curriculum in the U.S. South.

Lisette E. Torres is a doctoral candidate in higher education at Iowa State University with a certificate in Social Justice. She holds a BA in religion studies and earth and environmental science from Lehigh University and a MS in zoology with a certificate in ecology from Miami University. Torres is the Assistant Director of the Cooper Foundation Center for Academic Resources and Supplemental Instruction Supervisor at Nebraska Wesleyan University where she also works with the Iowa Illinois Nebraska STEM Partnership for Innovation in Research and Education (IINSPIRE) of the Louis Stokes Alliance for Minority Participation (LSAMP). She is an interdisciplinary scholar interested in the sociocultural context of science and the intersection of race and gender in higher education in general, and science in particular. She employs critical race theory, critical discourse studies, visual methodologies, and feminist theories to interrogate race and gender construction as well as representations and rhetoric around Whiteness in higher education.

Blanca E. Vega, EdD, is a native New Yorker and the daughter of Ecuadorian immigrants. She earned a doctorate (EdD) from the higher and postsecondary education program at Teachers College, Columbia University. She recently defended her dissertation, entitled: *Beyond Incidents and Apologies: Toward a New Understanding of Campus Racial Conflict.* Between 2006 and 2014, she worked as director of the Higher Education Opportunity Program (HEOP) at Marymount Manhattan College. Blanca earned her Bachelor of Arts degree in anthropology from Brandeis University and a Master of Arts degree in higher education at New York University. Blanca's research, teaching, and administrative work centers on access to, persistence in, and completion of postsecondary education for underserved populations. Her work is informed by her interest in the role of race and racism in educational settings. Blanca has publications and has done research in the following areas: campus racial culture and critical race theory, undocumented immigrants in higher education, and performance funding in higher education.

Anjalé D. Welton, PhD, is an assistant professor in the department of education policy, organization and leadership at the University of Illinois at Urbana-Champaign. Welton's research examines how shifting social-political contexts influence how school leaders dialogue about issues of equity, especially race, in their school improvement decisions. Other research areas related to equity include college and workforce readiness and access, especially for students of color, and the role of student voice in school improvement efforts. Most recently, Welton had the privilege to work with high school students engaging in social justice education and youth participatory action research (YPAR). This partnership was honored with the AERA Leadership for Social Justice Special Interest Group 2014 "Bridge People" Award. She continues to collaborate with the high school students and their teacher on presentations and publications. Welton is published in *The High School Journal, Teachers College Record, The Urban Review, Education and Urban Society,* and *Educational Administration Quarterly,* among others.

Kendall Williams, MA, is a native of Chicago, IL, and a graduate of the University of Southern California and the Teachers College–Columbia University. She currently works in higher education in Los Angeles, CA. Her previous research and work has been surrounding higher education, critical race studies, cross-cultural exploration of the Afro-Brazilian Diaspora, and multicultural development as well as order and disorder in global affairs.

Montrischa Williams, PhD, is a qualitative researcher with expertise in college access and college readiness efforts geared towards traditionally underrepresented students, and student persistence in STEM along the educational pipeline. Currently, Dr. Williams supports the American Institutes for Research (AIR) STEM education research, and the application and effective use of Early Warning Interventions and Monitoring System (EWIMS) for leaders in high schools that seek to support student progress and success in 9th grade and beyond. In addition, she serves as a technical assistance liaison and expert for the College and Career Readiness and Success Center, where she is the lead on delivering supports for state education agencies, federal regional comprehensive centers' members, and additional stakeholders in their effort to conceptualize and implement related Common Core State Standards polices and practices. Dr. Williams holds a B.A. in political science with a minor in education from the University of California Irvine, and an EdM and PhD in educational policy studies from the University of Illinois at Urbana–Champaign. Some of her work has been published in *The High School Journal* and *The Journal of Women and Minorities in Science and Engineering.*

CPSIA information can be obtained
at www.ICGtesting.com
Printed in the USA
LVHW080406240920
666980LV00007B/1166